ENGAGE

"This 'counter-archive' is essential reading for those of us working in the university and inside institutions that help the state wage war. The students, faculty (bus drivers and librarians), cultural workers, parents, and organizers send us dispatches from their specific locations of struggle. The conversations— sometimes direct, sometimes oblique—are examples of how we talk to each other under institutional surveillance and subject to the reins of philanthropic funding. While the conversations are informed by histories of Black, Indigenous, and Afro-Indigenous struggle, they unfold in unexpected ways and in the real time of our perilous and shifting grounds. These are conversations to turn and return to."

—Tiffany Lethabo King, author of *The Black Shoals: Offshore Formations of Black and Native Studies*

Photograph by Carol Wayne White

ENGAGE

Indigenous, Black, and Afro-Indigenous Futures

Edited by
Joy James

First published 2025 by Pluto Press
New Wing, Somerset House, Strand, London WC2R 1LA
and Pluto Press, Inc.
1930 Village Center Circle, 3-834, Las Vegas, NV 89134

www.plutobooks.com

British Library Cataloguing in Publication Data
A catalogue record for this book is available from the British Library

ISBN 978 0 7453 5030 1 Paperback
ISBN 978 0 7453 5032 5 PDF
ISBN 978 0 7453 5031 8 EPUB

This book is printed on paper suitable for recycling and made from fully managed
and sustained forest sources. Logging, pulping and manufacturing processes are
expected to conform to the environmental standards of the country of origin.

Typeset by Stanford DTP Services, Northampton, England

Simultaneously printed in the United Kingdom and United States of America

Contents

III. Liberation Education

Land and Labor Acknowledgments[*]

We respectfully acknowledge that Williams College stands on the ancestral homelands of the Stockbridge-Munsee Mohicans, who are the Indigenous peoples of the region now called Williamstown. After the tremendous hardship of being forced from their homelands, the Stockbridge-Munsee Mohicans continue as a sovereign Tribal Nation in Wisconsin where they reside today.

We acknowledge that the Mystic Seaport Museum sits on the traditional lands of the Pequot and Mohegan people. The name "Mystic" is derived from the Pequot word "missi-tuk," a large river whose waters are driven into waves by the tides or wind. We pay our respects to their ancestors, their elders, both past and present, and to their future generations.

We pay honor and respect to their ancestors past and present as we commit to building a more inclusive and equitable space for all. The Pequot word "WuyeepuyÃ´q" means, "Come in a good way." Let us strive to come in a good way as stewards of this land and these waters and as good relatives to those with whom we share them.

We recognize that the institutions we occupy, where we are privileged to learn and teach, have developed in sites where Indigenous and African people have been enslaved and rendered unfree in other ways. Given the labor extraction that is foundational to such colleges and universities, we ask for and seek ways of making restitution that will constitute some forms of freedom.

[*]Compiled from several roundtables.

Introduction

ORIGINS

This anthology evolved from roundtable dialogues and conversations on social justice. One year into a Mellon grant for the humanities, we began to think about conversations that might further our understandings of ethics and communities, specifically Indigenous, Black/African American, Afro/a-Indigenous. The Williams College roundtables and presentations were taped, transcribed and edited for clarity in order to create this anthology. Williams College Just Futures[1] grantees worked with the primary entity that created the opportunity for this grant shared with Williams–Brown University's Center for the Study of Slavery and Justice (CSSJ). The grant largely focused on New England history, with the majority of content emphasizing Indigenous culture, but expanded to address the impact of enslavement of those of African descent and Afro-Indigenous communities throughout several regions. With Williams colleagues Christine DeLucia, Tom Van Winkle, and Ngoni Munemo (now Hamilton College Vice President of Academic Affairs and Dean of Faculty), our collaborative work studied and supported alliances with Indigenous, Afro-Indigenous and Black/African American communities. Focusing on education and the humanities, we discussed justice for historically disenfranchised, colonized and enslaved peoples. During the colonial and ante-bellum eras, New England enslaving ships regularly docked in New York City harbors to sell human cargo. Enslavers began accumulating ill-gotten gain by trafficking Indigenous peoples from their homelands into the Caribbean where they would largely be worked to death. Following the mass killings of Indigenous communities, traffickers began to seek and capture Africans for labor which led to mass deaths in the Atlantic and on the continent during European colonization.

Grappling with that history of conquest, we discussed the concept developed by Mystic Seaport Museum director Akeia de Barros Gomes: "Entwined." Exploring "Entwined," the first roundtable focused on spirituality, with Gomes. Our hopes in focusing on the (inter)connections of Indigenous, African, and Afro-Indigenous communities proved somewhat unrealistic and did not reflect the separation and alienation between the three groups: Indigenous, African, Afro-Indigenous. Alliances exist among these communities and nations; yet, often alienation, and limited analyses left "Afro-Indigenous" as an afterthought and disconnections based on racial identity and culture.

One book cannot adequately describe the centuries of injustices and violence waged against Indigenous and African peoples on this continent or point to convergences in solidarity as a stable occurrence for nations of peoples subjugated as captives and decimated by genocide. However, we attempted to engage with our commonalities and our dedication to justice and critical thinking and education. Co-PI Christine DeLucia and I discussed the need for a more expansive "Land Acknowledgment," one that reflected the communities central to this project. DeLucia wrote the Land and Labor Acknowledgment for this text. *ENGAGE* offers an "acknowledgment" that seeks restorations and reparations for land theft, loss of kin, and enslavement on several continents. The Acknowledgment does not structure a common template for Indigenous, African, and Afro-Indigenous peoples. It does note that an adequate response to capture and subjugation requires the return of land and compensation (restitution/reparations) for those who faced genocidal violence and theft of land, language, culture, removal or disappearance of children; and communal rights to agency, sovereignty, and bodily, intellectual, and emotionally integrity.

ENGAGE offers discussions and debates about and from communities. As we learn and teach within classrooms, community centers, and playgrounds, in rural, suburban, and urban communities. Given democracy's limitations and historic betrayals, we need varied tools to spark conversations that interrogate repression and offer strategies for a future that rejects the violent and genocidal past.

Diverse politics appear in this anthology. We worked to expand the conversations beyond academic discourse, and to invite community-based intellectuals and actors to dialogue with academia.[2] We attempt to archive narratives and analyses that align with liberation pedagogies. We note the spirits of the oceans whose waters reflect capture, flight and burial grounds, of refugees and captivities from the past to the present day. The Atlantic Ocean's beauty and powers function as the corridor for the terrifying Middle Passage where countless African and Indigenous peoples were dragged into slavery and premature violent death.[3] The gray, dead stillness and the educational exploration shape this attempt to explore and better comprehend freedom struggles and analyses that counter colonizing violence.[4]

Beaded images on poster attributed to Keisha Erwin Wapahkesis, https://fiveoaksmuseum.org/ua-wapahkesis/

BOOK STRUCTURE

ENGAGE is a "talking book." It reflects convergence and divergence in conversations and dialogues focused on our varied cultures before and after chattel slavery, genocide, linguistic erasure, boarding schools, child theft, and violent disappearances.

Part I consists of four chapters based on public-facing roundtables hosted by Williams Just Futures in spring 2022, presented from February to May. Most speakers in Part I are academic intellectuals, and many served as members of the Williams Just Futures Advisory Committee. Chapter 1, "Spiritualities," the first of our virtual roundtables for spring 2022, focuses on academics, community educators, and a doctoral student: Director of the Mystic Seaport Museum Akeia de Barros Gomes, UMass Amherst professor Whitney Battle-Baptiste, Brown University Indigenous community-alliance/ educator Leah Hopkins, and Princeton Seminary doctoral student Rebecca Wilcox. Williams College historian Christine DeLucia serves as moderator. Chapter 2, "Security," took place the following month with Williams professor of geosciences Brittany Meché; Columbia University Director of the Resilient Coastal Communities Center Paul Gallay; Tufts University professor Mary McNeil; and Williams professor of geosciences José Constantine. Director of Williams-Mystic Tom Van Winkle moderates this session.

With a focus on how to protect water and the environment, political scientist Ngoni Munemo, former Associate Dean for Institutional Diversity at Williams, now Vice Provost for Academic Affairs and Dean of Faculty at Hamilton College, moderates Chapter 3, "Sovereignties." Discussants include Indigenous educator-teacher Brad Lopes, Williams-Mystic professor Katy Robinson Hall, and Chair of the Riverkeeper Board of Directors Ernest Tollerson. Chapter 4, "Freedom," offers a roundtable discussion with Anthony Bogues, Director of Brown University's Center for the Study of Slavery and Justice; then-UMass Amherst Dean Barbara Krauthammer (now Dean at Emory University); UCLA professor of Indigenous Studies Kyle Mays; Vassar College Africana Studies professor Jasmine Seydullah; and ENGAGE editor Joy James.

Part II, Chapter 4, "Study and Struggle" – its title is borrowed from the Mississippi non-profit which provides books to the incarcerated[5] – consists of three roundtables on community organizing and political theory. In Chapter 5, "Abolition, Care, and Indigenous Liberation," Indigenous scholars Dian Million and Stephanie Lumsden dialogue with this editor about love for communities, and security strategies to contain state violence. Margaux Kristjansson coordinated and moderated this dialogue.

In Chapter 6, "An Ontology of Betrayal," the acknowledgment of "I don't know" is repeated. Participants were Williams Just Futures Visiting Faculty Selemawit Terrefe (Tulane University professor of English), UC Irvine professor Frank Wilderson, III (co-theorist of Afropessimism), moderator Taija Mars-McDougall, and this editor. Academics also discussed the then-pending execution of Kevin Johnson in a Missouri prison[6] (Johnson was executed on November 29, 2022).

Chapter 7, "Family, Freedom, and Security," February 8, 2023, was shaped by leaders in social justice struggles. Joyce McMillan, the founder of J-MAC for Families, calls for the abolition of the foster care system as a carceral site that disproportionately destabilizes poor families. Samaria Rice, the mother of 12-year-old Tamir Rice executed by Ohio police in 2014, critiques her attendance at President Joe Biden's 2023 State of the Union. Amanda Wallace, a former social worker who refused to remove children from families that provided care for minors, shares her critique of child removal within a political economy of state budgets with federal funding. Dawn Wooten, the "ICE Whistleblower," describes the structural violence within Immigration, Customs, and Enforcement (ICE) camps that threaten, abuse, and medically cripple birthing people seeking to have and raise children.

Part III, "Liberation Education," includes a roundtable and professors who in their youths had participated in Black liberation organizations. In Chapter 8, Christine DeLucia moderates the Indigenous Pedagogies roundtable with: Chadwick Allen, professor of English and American Indian Studies at the University of Washington; Sandra Barton, author and Training and Improvement Coordinator for the Stockbridge-Munsee Community; Américo Mendoza-Mori, lecturer in Latinx Studies at Harvard University; endawnis Spears, museum coordinator who works at the Brown University Native American and Indigenous Studies Initiative; Tesia Zientek, Director of the Potawatomi Nation's Department of Education.

The final section on liberation and pedagogies focuses on professors who were student activists in the Civil Rights and Black Power movements.[7] They dialogued with students in a 2023 "Black Panther Intellectualism" seminar. Chapter 9 focuses on Rowan University professor and Harlem Panther veteran K. Kim Holder. Chapter 10, Rosemari Mealy, a former member of the Philadelphia BPP, and retired professor from the City University of New York, discusses her research and publication on the historic 1960 meeting of Fidel Castro and Malcolm X at Harlem's Hotel Theresa. In Chapter 11, former Bay Area Panther, English Professor Emeritus of San Diego City College, Roberta Alexander dialogues with her son Paul Khalid Alexander, also an English professor at San Diego City College, about intergenerational organizing and multilingual texts in education and community care. The Conclusion, by Christine DeLucia, addresses academic contributions and contradictions, and emphasizes the need to correct historical and contemporary harms against Indigenous, Black/Afro-American, and Afro-Indigenous peoples and communities.

– Joy James, August 2024

SOURCE NOTES

1. "Mellon 'Just Futures' Project at Williams College." *Just Futures*. Accessed August 11, 2023. www.williams.edu/justfutures/ As part of this grant, American Studies seminar students interviewed Williams College alumni engaged in ethical support for diverse communities.

2. Brown University's Center for the Study of Slavery and Justice, the primary and lead recipient, describes the endeavor:

   > The collaborative project, titled "Reimagining New England Histories: Historical Injustice, Sovereignty and Freedom," will create new work and study opportunities at all three institutions, particularly for scholars, curators and students from underrepresented groups. It will result in a new Mystic Seaport Museum exhibition on race, subjugation and power, and a "decolonial archive" spotlighting a diverse collection of stories from several New England communities.
   >
   > The grant was awarded by The Andrew W. Mellon Foundation as part of its Just Futures Initiative, which in summer 2020 invited 38 colleges and universities to submit project proposals that would address the "long-existing fault lines" of racism, inequality and injustice that challenge ideas of democracy and civil society.

   See "$4.9 million grant project to interrogate legacy of colonialism, subjugation in New England," *News from Brown*. www.brown.edu/news/2021-02-02/justfutures

3. See "The Middle Passage." *Digital History*, University of Houston. Accessed July 19, 2023. www.digitalhistory.uh.edu/disp_textbook.cfm?smtid=2&psid=446

4. Resources that address the historical and contemporary gravity of violence against Indigenous, African/Black and Afro-Indigenous peoples, and communal resistance to said violence include: Douglass, Frederick. "'What, to the Slave, Is the Fourth of July?' (1852)." *BlackPast*, August 24, 2020. www.blackpast.org/african-american-history/speeches-african-american-history/1852-frederick-douglass-what-slave-fourth-july/; Carmichael, Stokely. "Black Power." *Voices of Democracy*, December 14, 2021. https://voicesofdemocracy.umd.edu/carmichael-black-power-speech-text/; Peltier, Leonard. "Statement from Leonard Peltier." *Liberation News*, February 8, 2023. www.liberationnews.org/statement-from-leonard-peltier/; Laura G. Fleszar, MPH. "Trends in State-Level Maternal Mortality by Racial and Ethnic Group in the United States." *JAMA*, July 3, 2023. https://jamanetwork.com/journals/jama/article-abstract/2806661?resultClick=1; Rickert, Levi. "Voices of the MMIP Crisis Testify at Not Invisible Act Hearing." *Native*

News Online, June 12, 2023. https://nativenewsonline.net/opinion/voices-of-mmip-crisis-are-heard-at-not-invisible-act-field-hearing; Thompson, Darren. "July 4 March Raises Awareness for Native Americans Targeted by South Dakota's Criminal Justice System." *Native News Online*, July 5, 2023. https://nativenewsonline.net/currents/july-4-march-raises-awareness-for-native-americans-targeted-by-south-dakota-s-criminal-justice-system; Burton, Orisanmi. "New Docs Link CIA to Medical Torture of Indigenous Children and Black Prisoners." *Truthout*, June 22, 2023. https://truthout.org/articles/new-docs-link-cia-to-medical-torture-of-indigenous-children-and-black-prisoners/

5. Its website describes the non-profit thus: "'Study and Struggle' is a collective concentrated in Mississippi that organizes toward abolition through political education, mutual aid, and community-building across prison walls. We believe that study and struggle are necessary, complementary parts of any revolutionary movement, and that dismantling the Prison Industrial Complex (PIC) requires centering criminalized people." See www.studyandstruggle.com/

6. Kalonji Changa and Joy James. "Kevin Johnson Speaks from Death Row about His Impending Execution This Month." *Truthout*, December 14, 2022. https://truthout.org/articles/kevin-johnson-speaks-from-death-row-about-his-impending-execution-this-month/?utm_campaign=Truthout+Share+Buttons&s=09

7. See Zinn Education Project. "March 8, 1971: FBI's COINTELPRO Exposed." *Zinn Education Project*, March 9, 2022. www.zinnedproject.org/news/tdih/cointelpro-exposed/; Foster, Hannah. "COINTELPRO [Counterintelligence Program] (1956–1976)" *BlackPast*, February 6, 2020. www.blackpast.org/african-american-history/cointelpro-1956-1976/; Wolfe-Rocca, Ursula. "COINTELPRO: Teaching the FBI's War on the Black Freedom Movement." *Rethinking Schools*, June 5, 2020. https://rethinkingschools.org/articles/cointelpro-teaching-the-fbi-s-war-on-the-black-freedom-movement/

I

Entwined?

1

Spiritualities

Akeia de Barros Gomes, Whitney Battle-Baptiste, Leah Hopkins, Rebecca Wilcox, and moderator Christine DeLucia

February 28, 2022

Akeia de Barros Gomes

I want to provide some background on my perspectives when I engage in and work with communities regarding spirituality. Last week, I was asked to speak in Wethersfield on Black mariners. I think people were pleasantly surprised when I talked about African spirituality regarding water and how that may have been a factor in the Black maritime experience. As a scholar, my own path and respect for the way that spirituality is integral in every aspect of the lives I work with and write about began to make more sense to me as I learned from Indigenous communities here in the northeast, and then traveled and learned in Rastafarian communities, and then in Benin.

As a professional, I've been fortunate enough to befriend, work with, and learn from individuals such as Tall Oak Weeden of the Mashpee Wampanoag Tribe, Kendall "Seigo" Petersen, a Rastafarian community leader in the Virgin Islands, and Bernard Ajibodo, a priest in Benin, who all showed me the ways in which the kind of work all of us are doing is inherently spiritual, if we choose to acknowledge the work as such. This is why I've always found it difficult to theorize or rationalize spiritual beliefs, myths, rituals, and practices through a Western lens, even as an anthropologist. Most often you just can't. The example I like to give to demonstrate that is the Zangbeto, a ritual in Benin.[1] Watching that ritual, there is no way to explain what is happening through a Western lens, through Western science or concepts of time. You can look at it on *YouTube* if you'd like to experience it from far away yourself.[2]

I often think that my inability to rationalize or use theory to explain things like this is probably why I didn't last in academia. I refused to do it, which hurt my chances of publishing quite a bit. Last year for the American Anthropological Association meeting, I gathered scholars and hosted a panel titled "The Anthropologist as 'Other'" to challenge our own discipline's lip service to cultural relativism, while it still by and large relies upon colonial practice and cultural imperialism. The question we were all ultimately posing was, what do you do with your spirituality if you're both a scholar and an Other? Typically, in order to get published or employed, we must, in the words of Frantz Fanon, "put on a Western mask," suspend our own belief system, and accept Western modes of thought, time, and cosmology.[3]

As an example of that, after I did extensive work in the Rastafarian community in the Virgin Islands, I decided that anything I published would present the belief system, the culture, as a valid mode of thought. And time and time again, when I submitted the work for publication, the response would be, "This isn't anthropology. Where's the theory? What are you trying to say here?" It took me ten years. I ultimately got it published in an academic journal that focuses on consciousness and thought.[4] But for ten years I could not get it published.

I once had a Taíno friend explain to me, through his own family history, why he believes Afro-Indigenous culture emerged and why it was just common sense. He imagines that when his Nigerian ancestors came to the shores of Boriken in chains, the first thing they saw that brought them any comfort were the petroglyphs of the divinity Yemaya that West Africans would've immediately recognized, as their divinity goes by many names – Mami Wata is one of them. And they knew they had encountered brethren and sistren. I think of this story often in my work as I try to imagine the scale of destruction colonialism inflicted on this global spiritual connection and cosmology, alongside the painful contradiction that colonialism was also the means through which my friends imagined an encounter took place.

Similarly, my work with Rastafarian communities highlighted a similar narrative when I first engaged with the community and discussed how my scholarship highlights the Hindu spiritual roots of Rasta belief in practice. Although this was not a concept they had ever heard in this particular community, one of them immediately said, "You are right, even though you don't know why, you're right. Well yes, Hindus are from the Cradle too," meaning Ethiopia, Egypt, and Sudan. "Some of us went west and some went east. It was destiny that we came back together in the Caribbean and reminded ourselves of who we are."

To end my section, I'm going to read a very long quote from that same article that took me ten years to publish, because I think it's an example of the power that comes when we stop theorizing spirituality and begin acknowledging cycles, timelessness, and rebirth. And I like to think of it as an example of something my friend Tall Oak told me the first time we met at the end of a very long conversation regarding spirituality, where he said, "The Creator gave every tribe one piece of the puzzle, but just one piece. We won't really understand until we all come together." And so, when documenting this as a scholar, and personally, I view the information contained within this quote as both inherently valid and at the same time only one piece of an overall puzzle.

Excuse the length because it's very much an epic narrative that really begins at the beginning, but it's also told with the understanding that there really is no beginning and that we are all one. We come from the same Creator, though we give the Creator different names. When listening, try to suspend how you conceptualize timescale, geography, and race, and the concrete ways in which we define dates in history, because this quote very much comes from a spiritual explanation, beyond individual experience.

We are the children of Haile Selassie. We are the children of Rastafari. That's our strength since the beginning of time. Let me tell you something. Before we civilized the Ganges and called ourselves Krishna, and before we civilized the Yangtze and called ourselves Buddha, which is the same Judah or Yehuda, the Creator; before these things, we civilized the Nile River, we smoked the chalice with the herb; that is the oldest culture. Everything else is a necessity. This is a spiritual luxury. You know the Dogon, they call them "pygmies"? They have one of the oldest cultures and they smoked the herb before anybody. You see, all of the empires were created by We. You go to Asia, you go to the Amazon River, and we civilized it. That's why you find pyramids all over the equator, because we Nubian Cushite Ethiopian Black men civilized it, and charted it, and documented it.

If we could cross the sea of dryness, then we could cross the Atlantic Ocean. And we mounted 200 ships and made a journey across and came to the mouth of a great river. We saw the fresh water flowing into the sea and we followed it. We built cities of water, and the pyramids on the mountainside. We moved mountains. We actually moved mountains and built them higher. We took the swamps and made highways of gardens. We never left the equator. We knew that leaving the Garden of Eden through the ring of fire was hardship. We had to hunt our own food, we had to hunt for shelter, and we had to hunt for clothing, but we stayed on the equator because we know it was provided for us. We know that the whole equator is the Garden of Eden. The reason we did that? Rasta ain't nothing new.

We exceed in such intelligence. We learned what the white man has learned the hard way; that technology should only be used for the care-taker of the Earth. If it's used for the pleasure of man, it will destroy us. The wise man is the man who stays in the jungle and smokes the herb. That was Noah, who knew the Flood was going to come. When the Dogon took the white man into the cave and showed the design of the universe, the white man found no smoke, so it wasn't done by fire, it was done by spirit. And then that white man took the design of the universe and matched it with what he knew from his telescope, and his universe came up short. So, he has technology, but still couldn't see what my ancestors saw.

We want to study the constellations, but they say we are devil worship-ers. They tell us a man talked to a burning bush, but when my ancestors talked to plants and trees and animals, they called us pagan. But all the knowledge comes from my ancestors. We don't know why we think like this, Haile Selassie, from the time we heard the name, we knew this was right. And the Bible says, when the new name comes, mother will turn against him, and father will turn against him, and village will turn against him. I don't see nobody turning against you for Jesus. I don't see nobody turning against you for Buddha or Krishna's name. But because we carry the name of the ancient king, Rastafari, for that we're condemned. In the heart of Babylon, all men come to drink from the cup of abomination, but we don't come to follow the ways of Babylon. We come to follow the ways of our ancestors. It's in our DNA.[5]

Whitney Battle-Baptiste

I wanted to talk about my experience trying to separate my personal life from my professional life. The spiritual practices that were a part of my childhood which would, actually, not only inform but become the work that I do. I'm a trained archaeologist, and I started out in history. I started out looking for those stories that were absent, and a part of that absence is due to my understanding of the kind of lineage that I was denied understand-ing, but also racialization and our nation's emphasis on the fact that you are either Black or Indigenous.

I'm the great-great-granddaughter of someone who was born into slavery, yet I'm the great-granddaughter of a woman who was raised by parents who told her to hide who she was because she was an Eastern Band Cherokee.

These are the ones who stayed in North Carolina and did not travel along to other places where the Cherokee reside today. And the idea of being hidden in plain sight is that my great-grandmother became mulatto, and then she became Black, and I realized that those are defined through colonial eyes, the eyes of the census taker, because that is the power of how race is defined; how anthropologists love to talk about race doesn't exist, but we understand that there are serious consequences to the ways in which people are defined.

There's so much of what I don't know about my great-grandmother, so much she never talked about. She was discouraged from talking about her Indigeneity. And I am a granddaughter of the Great Migration, so my grandmother went from North Carolina and settled in the Bronx, New York; and therefore, I am the daughter of a mother who grew up in the South Bronx, and I am of the generation that shaped a whole culture we call hip hop today. I grew up in an African traditional religious community. I grew up from a young child not Catholic, not Christian, not Muslim, but from a group of folks who stemmed from Black nationalism in New York City, and so we consider ourselves Yoruba-Lucumí. My mother was initiated, I am initiated, and my children are all initiated. We have three generations of these practices.

There's this idea of Egún, which is the idea of our ancestors. When we eat, Egún eats. When we have problems and we have troubles, we go to our ancestors because we understand that they are a part of our living lives today. As an archaeologist touching material things, I don't have a problem with talking about the things that I hear, the things that I feel, the things that I know, and being told that that wasn't archaeological – if I didn't consult my ancestors, I don't think I would've made it in this field. And I pushed and I pushed, and somehow, I'm still around.

For me, trying to separate what my good friend Courtney Morris calls "Egún work," or what my friend Christina Sharpe calls "wake work" is impossible. It is the work that helps me to become whole again, and to not separate myself by the colonized ideals of what race is or what archeology is, or the fact that archeology is only about the artifact. The artifact is the beginning of the conversation, about how a community interacts with that piece of material. How this idea of the tangible is an extension of that Egún work. It's an extension of who we are as people, and as growing up with a household that had altars and symbols of the Orisha that we consult on a daily basis, a practice that allowed me to understand the power of material. I understood the power of materialism and that objects are not often just objects. When things are buried, sometimes they should stay buried because they were buried and put there for a reason. As an archeologist, that's a little bit of a controversial way to think about archeology. But if we also know that archeology and the digging up of the Earth is not sustainable, and if we believe that we have enough on the shelves that a) needs to be returned to where their homes are; and, b) we have enough to study for the next century, then we don't necessarily have to continue to dig. And that idea of the connection between material and people and spiritualism and all of that for me is something that I eventually began to understand, that I did not have to separate. I did not have to compartmentalize. I could talk about the kinds of feelings that I had as I was walking on certain spaces and certain terrains.

Because if I define myself by the geography of the mothers who came before me, I need to understand how my understanding of the world fits into the geographies of the past, of folks I will never know, or folks that even if I learned their names, I don't necessarily know exactly what their lives were like. But for me, it is about that connection with the human, the human being, and the idea that the past, as Saidiya Hartman would say, "is not quite past." There are residuals that we're living with. I am still searching for my great-grandmother's family and trying to understand what it was to be an Eastern Band Cherokee, blended and integrated into a town in North Carolina, and then trying to figure out why it's so hard to find my people. Why is it so hard to connect the dots?

We need to understand the collective, and we need to understand how we are entwined. As we share and as we incorporate our spirituality, our practices, our beliefs, and the things that we call intuition, we must understand that it's probably your ancestors giving you some direction. As you open your ears and eyes to spiritual practice, you come to the idea that it is the process of understanding the connections between all peoples, and especially peoples that occupied these lands way before colonization hit. Spirituality allows us to understand the connections of people torn from their homes and then put in a collective – people who weren't stripped of their beliefs or minds, but perhaps names – what is created is a part of who we are now in this moment. We understand the consequences have always been to separate [us].

The consequences have always been to say, you have to be an individual in the academy as an anthropologist, you must study the other Akeia alluded to, "What happens when you are the other?" What happens when you begin to read, as Margaret Mead would say? I just am so excited about the ability to vocalize and talk about the fact that I am no longer – I don't think I ever was – afraid to combine these worlds because they aren't separate. They are part of who I am. If I am a scholar of the past and captivity, then it would not be wise for me to ignore the connectivity and the ways in which colonization has attempted to separate us and our multiple selves.

Leah Hopkins

Let me preface my words tonight by saying that I am a relatively young person; and, in my society there are many more qualified people to speak ahead of me. There are elders, there are people with stations, people with responsibilities, [who are centered] when we talk about spirituality. So, whenever I'm given the opportunity to speak in this capacity – or sometimes I'm given the opportunity to also say a prayer on behalf of – I always like to excuse myself, especially in front of my elders, in front of those who have come before me, and in front of my ancestors. I also like to excuse myself for speaking in this new tongue that has come to this land and not speaking in our traditional words. I try to speak, as my mother would say, with the Creator alongside of me. I try to open and use our language as much as possible.

I also like to acknowledge where I am. I currently reside in my traditional homelands of the Narragansett people, but every day I am living and working and traveling and driving and dropping my son off at school in the confluence of the Narragansett, Wampanoag, and Nipmuc people. Every time I cross the bridge, every time I drive up the road to go to the grocery store, I'm thinking of the ancestors of those places because, first and foremost, I would not be here without them. I would not be here without the complexities of our ancestors, the work of our ancestors, and the sacrifice of our ancestors for well over 20,000 years.

I consider myself lucky to be part of this deep-time history here on this land. The work that I do, I approach from a community aspect, and I always tell people that I'm working with from non-Indigenous communities, first and foremost, that I want to be transparent because, at the end of the day, I have to go home to my Indigenous communities, to my Indigenous families, to my ancestors and my people, and I have to do right by them before I can fulfill a job.

Working in museums is very interesting because they are oftentimes at odds with what I grew up with in terms of community, and what is valued in terms of community. As we all know, spirituality is a deeply personal experience. I, myself, do not have a station in life where I am a medicine person, a medicine woman, a healer. These titles were not bestowed upon me. I have not been chosen by my community for that. I firmly believe that it is not my calling in life to go after that. I have other callings as a teacher, an educator, and a mother, but I understand and I respect that there are others in our tribal nation and in our societies here, collectively in New England, that they have those rights to pick the medicines, and to carry the pipes, and to heal the community and sing the songs.

My experiences with spirituality have been in a non-official but very community-oriented capacity. Every time I go out on the lands, every time I go out and I plant corn, or go fishing, or process meat, I am thinking of those beings that gave their life so that we can live. I think today we live in a very disconnected society where it's very easy to get in your car and drive to the grocery store and purchase some meat that was processed by many humans, and driven across the country, and you're not interacting with the life of that animal. You are not interacting with the humans who processed this animal. How can you feel grounded? How can you feel connected when you are not given that opportunity? I think about all of these things, every time I'm either grocery shopping or processing my own food, that there is a sacred connection.

This goes beyond just food; it goes into being able to walk and be in my homelands and actually feel my ancestors around me. For over 20,000 years, we have been living, and breathing, and eating, and feasting, and living, and having children, and getting married, and meeting people, and making friends, and dying, and being interred in this land, all over the place. The connection that I feel is very, very strong. And living in this Western, colonized mindset and society, that is really interested in compartmentalizing, and separating, and disorienting your connection to your family, to your ancestors, to creation and to community, it can absolutely be wearing.

Working in a Western institution such as a museum, even if it is a tribal museum, you're working in an institution where you are expected to look at the belongings of people in a clinical sense. For me, that's very conflicting because I can see in such personal belongings whether they were intended to be created and used in a ceremonial fashion or not; I look at those belongings and I see the relatives that made them, even if those relatives are far across the sea.

Hearkening back to what Whitney said, when I work with these materials, I have a connection. I'm inherently connected to the materials that my ancestors and surrounding ancestors have made, but I cannot approach this in a very clinical way. Similarly, anthropology and, by extension, museums have often been so extractive of people worldwide; but I can only speak to the toll exacted on Indigenous people. It's been extremely extractive, not only of materials, but of knowledge. The harm that has been caused, and the recoil that we have ... It's also interesting to be asked to talk about spirituality, because immediately your hackles go up as a Native person, and you say, well, that's none of your business. For so long things have been taken from us, they have been twisted in certain ways, whether through governmental policy, through anthropology, or anything else, and they have been used against us in certain ways.

As Akeia was saying, our traditions – thinking of your words about the burning bush especially – when we talk about that it's a deeply spiritual experience for many people. But then when we, as Indigenous people or other people, are talking about our relations, our plants that we are harvesting as our relatives, and as our older brothers and sisters, we are considered the pagans. We are considered the heathens. So, I really love the idea of approaching spiritual reclamation in a collective sense. As my elder and respected community member, Tall Oak, said to Akeia, we all have a piece of that puzzle. I have one little piece of the puzzle. My nation has a piece of the puzzle, and we have to work collectively together in order to see the bigger picture.[6]

Likewise, worldwide, we all have a piece of that puzzle. And when we can zoom out and see this entire picture, we can see that it is so much more, I think, than just us. It's our task to implement that in our work – and it takes a lot of work; it takes so much convincing to have those who are either empowered or those who are running different institutions or universities – we have to educate them on this journey. And that takes a lot of emotional labor.

Bringing people up to the point of respecting and taking seriously our spirituality is also wearing on us as professionals who have to straddle that line. These are just my personal experiences. With everything that I incorporate into my work, as stated before, I think of my ancestors. I think of my relationship with those beings around me. My little one, who's 5, asks these beautiful questions, like: "Mom, is this alive?" It's a pen and I [say] "That's not alive." And [then my little one asks:] "Mom, is this alive?" It's a leaf [so I say] "Yes, that's alive." It is inherent in our language of what is animate and what is inanimate.

In some languages you have terminology – you have two genders, male and female, in [Romance] languages [derived from] Latin. In our languages, we have two genders, and those are animate and inanimate.[7] There are different constructs and rules for what is considered animate and what is considered inanimate. The boilerplate explanation that I like to give to my little one is: Things that are animate are things that were made by the Creator, and things that are inanimate are things that were made by humans. It gets to be much more complex than that. And there are nuances, but how can you really boil that down to the brain of a five-year-old? These are just ways that I think about in my home and in my work, seeing animate objects, seeing animate belongings in a museum and looking at those objects as my relatives – it's truly meaningful, but it can also be deeply hurtful when these objects want to go home, and they can't.

Thinking about it on a much larger level, my work is goal-oriented to always returning the objects back to the people and the homes that they belong in.

Rebecca Wilcox

My contribution runs with this ongoing theme about what it is to be recovered; what is to be discovered; what is to be returned; and this idea of an inner self that has to come into fruition in order for us to know anything about what our purposes are.

I want to enter this conversation from the questions that shape my own work, as well as from this moment and this space that we're sharing, in a deep struggle to figure these things out. I want to think of a religious experience through the logics of the founder of Black religion, Charles Long. I know a lot of times there are people who say that "religion and spirituality are different" – "there's a distinction between the two." My collapsing of spirituality and religion is not due to a misunderstanding of the distinction between the organized functions of religion and the very machinations of violence that it causes, but because I want to think with Charles Long about his distinction between a religious experience and a theological one.

What Long says about theology is basically that it is too transparent to capture the experiences of Blackness. He's contextualizing this to say that a religious experience is about how we make sense of and orient ourselves in relationship to the world. That's very different from a theological understanding of trying to interpret the things that we experienced, the suffering that we may travel through, the ways of knowing the world through these theological – what he would name "Christian-type frameworks."[8] I'm specifying Christianity as a Western modality that has overdetermined the logics of spiritual practices, as well as the forces of imperial violence. In thinking of a religious experience as how we make sense of ourselves in relationship to the world, or a spiritual formation, we arrive at how we make sense of ourselves in relationship to the world. I also want to think with Long on his notion of opacity, because he says, "A religious experience is about one's self in relationship to the world," which is something that everyone who has access to an experience can account for.[9] But a Black religious experience is about opacity, and opacity is this idea of non-transparency. It's something that cannot be interpreted. It's the limits of what can be said about the experience, the limits of what we can know about one's own self. The limits of what we can know about one's past, one's future, and one's current.

In thinking about that, I want to think of opacity within the logics of what you all have shared as something that is to be searched for, something that constantly puts us in a position of longing, searching, discovering the things that have been lost under the colonial and anti-Black violence of the Western, modern, new world.

I want to think of Blackness as that position that is always in search of those things that have been lost, that is always in search of those things that are to be returned, and what the inherent inquisition of that search may mean for people who are having a hard time retrieving it.

When we're doing work around the land, when we're doing work around our own religious formations, our communities, our histories, our genealogies, and our lineages, we are thinking specifically with the concept of racial slavery, which Saidiya Hartman names not only complete loss, but one that does not have an actual return, one that is constantly stuck in this kind of ambiguity of silence.[10] One that cannot make coherent the things that have been before us, or after us; it's just this constant place of silence, this constant place of loss, and also this constant place of desire to discover all of those things that have been lost. And in thinking of that as a spiritual formation, these are religious questions that I've been thinking through.

The questions that I've been pondering are whether or not the very desire for a return or for a search to become or to belong to something is the structure of the antagonism that we experience through the modalities of violence. How to understand that is, if we are promised something and that something has been stolen or taken from us, but we use these spiritual technologies as a way to access those things that have been stolen and taken from us, does the impossibility of that return structure the antagonisms that define anti-Blackness? That's an important place to start the conversations about spirituality because we have to determine if spirituality is about a discovery, a search, or a becoming process of the self; or if spirituality has some type of teleological aim, which is to say a promise or an end of a liberatory freedom modality, that in many of our struggles, seem to be an impossibility.

Not that it is an impossibility, but it seems to be an impossibility in the midst of the struggle. I want to think of this logic of opacity that Long presents us with as one that, unlike Long would say, is a nexus of possibility, is the source for where what can't be made transparent is grounds for us to think of the futures, think of the possibilities for it. I want to think of opacity as actually the site of violence because nothing can be said of it, because of the limits of what can be said of it, and because it offers the incapacity to return or to belong into a space that doesn't actually claim a genealogy – that we can actually claim as a definite genealogy, rather. Does that search and discovery process create the grounds by which we are antagonized and struggling to have a spiritual experience? The spiritual experience is not simply a matter of one's inner self, and becoming a better person and aligning ourselves with the universal purpose.

The spiritual experience is about this idea of recovery. That is what is lost, this idea that if we can create a world that is not like the one that we have, then that can be the function and driving force of a liberatory spiritual and religious experience. These are the things I'm thinking through, and these are questions that I have. But I'm wondering if the spirit itself is supposed to move us somewhere that inevitably coincides with liberatory purposes. And if that is the case, then we have to think of spirituality.

Is spirituality about world-making? Is it about our capacity to make worlds and continue to make worlds? And can we make worlds outside of the modalities of violence that we're already experiencing? I think those are questions about how we connect this idea of the material world with a type of transcendence; a transcendence of this material world. I think I want to leave it there. I'm thinking about spirituality under the logics of what can't be said about our own spiritual formations and the logics of what it means to be in the violence that Whitney brought up earlier, and Hartman's notion of the afterlife of slavery and the violence of this afterlife of slavery, constantly forced to be opaque.

We can't say what we are. We can't say where we're going, because we don't actually have a map of how to get there or how to return there. But there is this type of opacity that comes with a spiritual formation, and that's demanded by a spiritual formation. It's a lack of transparency. We're supposed to be contingent upon faith, contingent upon a desire to move. I don't mean faith in the traditional sense. I mean faith in the sense of moving toward the unknown. This idea of silence. The not knowing of where we're going, that long places in archaic silence is something that is behind us, but also in the present, has a temporal aspect, but cannot be made clear to us. The object of faith cannot be made transparent to us.

The very act of trying to define it is where we limit the possibilities for what it can be. I'm really interested in the very act of creating a future or creating a world that we cannot predict, we cannot access. We cannot know what we cannot anticipate, rather what will come of that world; but the very act of the desire to discover and create it as a way of belonging and rather transcending the violence that we experience becomes the very antagonism of our spiritual formations. And can our spiritual formations be thought about beyond those antagonisms?

I'm thinking of not just a decolonizing. I think of a Derridean move of deconstruction. If the very act of a spiritual formation is what Derrida means by remaining in deconstruction, then what does it mean to remain in the deconstructive position as people who have spiritual commitments, rather than the constructive …? How do we create a future? How do we create a world? How do we move [forward] … rather than just realizing that none of us actually exist outside of the logics of these modalities of violence, and the possibility that whatever we create might just represent or replicate the very structures that we're trying to critique? We've seen that dilemma play itself out over and over again.

The spiritual mandate might be the deconstructive move, which is insufficient. I would agree, but the deconstructed move is to not be antagonized by the demand to solve the problem, but rather the demand to constantly remain in the struggle. The overbearing solidarity to the struggle is one that does not offer relief. I think about this through the new construction that Dr. James offers us with the Captive Maternal as the thing that has this capacity.[11] The Captive Maternal has this capacity to not only sustain a community but also go to war with the very violence that is structured around our ability to sustain our communities. And this capacity becomes in many ways like the ground for these spiritual formations. It's when we think about our own parents who have made ways out of no ways, as we've heard in many Black church cultures.

The antagonism that is inherent to the idea of making ways out of no ways is what Dr. James offers us: regardless of the path, making a way becomes a stabilizing force in some capacity, whether it's stabilizing for the community or to the very violence of the state. It's stabilizing in its machinations to not be able to transcend the very violence under which it's constructed over. I'm thinking about that capacity as the antagonism of a spiritual formation, because it's through the spiritual formation, through discovery, searching, and longing, that we actually develop the capacity to endure. Endurance becomes the capacity by which we postpone the urgency to be. I'm trying to figure out how to explain this in a way that won't sound too academic.

The project of endurance can develop the capacity to never be alive. To never be alive to the idea that a world can be just, in a very real way. That the very logics of what can be made of a world by anybody who is here, anybody who can think liberation, is always structured and informed by the very antagonisms that suppress us in our capacity to create and recreate those suppressions. While these limiting terms make us never be alive to this idea that we can create a future that wouldn't replicate it, it is possible that we can always deconstruct a now that would at least put intention, the very antagonisms, and violence that we experience.

Battle-Baptiste

I think that Rebecca has given us a lot to chew on. I think of spirituality as not necessarily a struggle, but in my own experience that spirituality, its practice, language, action, and recognition, has a connectivity that also speaks to the violence under which we live as folks spread throughout the Americas. It reminds me of the first time I went to Brazil in 2000, having grown up at arm's length of a spiritual practice that was active for folks who were practicing *Candomble*.

Of course, it's not modern Yoruba, but it's a Yoruba from way back. We're speaking Old English. It's like this moment when you're sitting there and you realize that you're not speaking Portuguese, and you're not speaking English, that the songs that you're singing are the same. There are variations, but you know the words, and you don't know how you know the words. And that idea of the energies that are within this diasporic space means that geography gets, in some ways, collapsed. And for me, it was that spiritual experience of understanding; this spirituality that I practiced brought me to a space where there is no distance.

There is a way in which this spiritual faith was held onto when folks came across the ocean. And yet at the same time, the ocean, which held those ships up to get us to the Americas, also engaged us in a different kind of spirituality. And it is very interesting talking about the animate and the inanimate and understanding that everything is living – I know that I need to do this thing by bringing these herbs and these animate objects together in order to create something to help with a sickness or to help with spiritual malaise or to make you feel closer to home. To me, that spirituality is what helps us to also adapt. Maybe that is what you're talking about in terms of the captivity and the violence that brought you over here and took you away from your home. We name people after those who have died, not because of any type of worship, but because we understand that connection; calling their name keeps them alive. But also understanding that even though you don't know names, you are giving an uplift to your ancestors through a spiritual lens that's not necessarily understood in a formal religious context.

Wilcox

That makes a lot of sense. I'm not suggesting that spirituality is the modality of the violence. I'm saying that there are limits to what can be said about that spirituality because of the dispossession that you're talking about. With that being said, spirituality becomes the thing that structures the antagonism for a buried practice. Spirituality is shaped around that reconnection – or it's shaped around that ability to allow there to be a portal between the dead and the living, to in some way galvanize the resources; it becomes the structuring antagonism for what I want to name, to be a modality of anti-Black violence that is fundamentally rooted in Black death. Spirituality functions as a modality of anti-Black violence by focusing on a concept of aliveness or re-connectivity. It is antagonized by its own impossibility.

Whether or not there can be different conditions is not necessarily my claim or my point. That's actually my critique of futures. I don't know if we can commit to creating a world that doesn't look just like this one. I don't know what to do about the future conversation. But for the sake of the world that we're in, and the struggle of what it means to be in this world, and be in solidarity with this world, the spiritual impetus has to be an unwavering solidarity to that level of suffering that seeks to reconnect with the things that in some way can be like a lifeline or a life jacket or the things that we navigate.

I'm not saying that I wouldn't agree with you about these technologies. I do think that there are technologies. I do think that they work, and I do think there is a way to, in some way, use these technologies to navigate the structures of violence that we do navigate. However, I think the problem is that there is an assumption that there is not something unique that happens in the making of slavery. I think this is where we get to turn to slave religion. There is a different type of antagonism and a different type of violence that happens – not only as you mentioned Christina Sharpe's work – in the hold of the slave ship. When it actually comes to the formation of plantations … we learned through slave religion, is that the religion is not rooted in the idea of a better world, but more so in a type of intimate necromancy.

It is like a type of intimacy with one's own death as the liberatory force: "before I'd be a slave, I'll be buried in my grave, and go home to my Lord and be free."[12] So that structure, that structuring antagonism of moving from a commitment to, what they would say, choosing the sea. It's not a matter of the choice between the sea and the land. It's not about who lifts us up so that we can go to the new world, and who jumps overboard. It's all captivity. The purpose of me invoking Dr. James's work of the Captive Maternal is because what she invites for us is what you were naming, Christina Sharpe's wake work,[13] of how that type of care work, that type of love, that type of stabilizing for this re-connectivity.

Because we're not going to let each other die, we're not going to be over-consumed by this type of necromancy that shapes these antagonisms. It becomes the thing that builds our capacity to be stabilized, and then the state will build upon that stability, as Dr. James says, "For its own coherence."[14] And that building upon the stability that we've used to stabilize each other becomes the structured antagonisms of the very violence that we're trying to escape, which builds our capacity for adaptability. It allows us to adapt to the structured antagonism. So, spirituality is not just the thing that's stabilizing us and reconnecting us, it's also the thing that is necessary for our stability, so that the state can make sure we're stabilized, so that way they can consume or build, or in some way extract consumption upon that stability. I'm just trying to rethink the logics of stability, reconnection, discovery, and searching. I'm trying to think through the longing for those things, as things that cannot be expropriated by the state. I can't figure out how to do that yet. I have to pause on the subject of futures. It seems that the ability to recreate and reconnect is something that is necessary for us to keep our communities and ourselves intact, and also to retrieve these traditions.

I don't think that's untrue. I think that these traditions have to be reclaimed because in many ways these have been the technologies that have allowed us to throw each other life jackets and lifelines. But I'm wondering: What does it mean to have a lifeline in a world that doesn't actually need you dead, but needs you alive in order for us to consume? And it's at that point that I have to think of spirituality as a structuring antagonism, as something that is necessary for the state's consumption. That's the tension that I'm sitting in.

Christine DeLucia

If I could pick up on the tensions that you're describing here – because I think everyone was speaking to tensions in different ways, especially regarding some of the keywords I have written down here about academia,

particularly: extractive, disconnective, disconnecting, alienating, compartmentalized. All of these ways in which the professional work is undermining
these other forms of relations, and the tension that each of you is navigating
in that and finding strategies or in the process of seeking them. Leah and
Akeia, I'm especially wondering if you wanted to extend some of those reflections on how you have approached belongings, restoration, repair, keeping
in mind, Leah, I think what you were saying about every day coming home
to a community, and having that as a foundational orientation, and the day
job may be creating very, very different kinds of pressures and of where to
go with that.

Hopkins

I'm happy to elaborate a little bit more. We live in this compartmentalized
space where work is not supposed to – *supposed to* – touch upon personal
life, or family life, or your spiritual aspects. For so many people, going to
an office job and going to church on Sunday are two very different things.
They are two very different events. For the most part, they do not cross
wires, unless there is a community involvement. I'm thinking of smaller,
removed communities. You have a big-city office job, and you go to church,
and those are your two compartments. And there isn't necessarily fluidity or
movement between them. I cannot do my job without the backup of my own
spirituality, many colonial traumas have removed and separated Indigenous
people and our spirituality.

   I really like the framework that the San Diego Museum of Us has created,
which is the Colonial Pathways Policy.[15] Assuming that all objects have come
into the museum through colonial pathways, through harm, through maybe
people selling objects to collectors and museums under duress. I understand
this, as my husband is an artist, and he makes beautiful art, which he sells
to museums because he likes doing it, but also because it pays the bills. That
technically is a colonial pathway, because it's supporting our system and our
structure to keep the lights on, to pay for the internet, to pay for food in
this capitalistic society, where prior to Europeans coming to our shores, we
didn't have to do those types of things. In a museum setting, I see all objects
that are coming into our spaces in some form of colonial pathway. This is
not to talk or knock down any, especially contemporary, artists who want to
have their work in museums.

   I just recognize that there are roads that lead into museums that tend to
be colonial in some particular way, and mostly stem from violence, in some
manner. A way that I personally deal with that is through my own spiritu-

ality and my own connection, whether it's to the objects, or … times when, working in different museums, I've come across objects that either don't sit right with me or have caused harm to other human beings. There are many different things, and I have had to take a step back. At the end of the day, I've had to go to my medicine person, and I've had to ask for their help: how do I process this and moving forward, what should I do in the case of these objects and handling them?

For me and for many Indigenous people, spirituality has been a coping mechanism, as we were not allowed to practice our own spirituality until 1978.[16] The trigger comes up: That's none of your business because I can't talk about it; because if I talk about it, I'm going to go to jail." For so long that [repression] has happened to our people. There's a reticence to talk about it and to discuss it in a public fashion. You keep things quiet, or else the state is going to come in and you're going to have a lot of personal problems. I once heard a college professor say that personal problems are caused by public policy. I try to remember that in a lot of my work, but [also] just in general, in my life. Spirituality is just that coping mechanism, and that healing mechanism for me. I can go back to my community and I can separate, but not compartmentalize my work and my spirituality.

Gomes

It was a cop-out earlier when I said my spiritual commitments are why I didn't make it in academia. I think I knew it wasn't the place for me. I've been told so by several people that I've worked with professionally, who felt the need to give spiritual advice in a professional setting about my path, and staying on my path, and honoring my path, and what was meant for me. It all came together once I started listening and stopped doing that separation, as Whitney referred to, in saying: "I can't say that, or I can't write about that." A few years ago, I was in Jamaica Plain, and I went to a botanica because I needed to get some herbs and some other things. I turned a corner in the aisle and saw a former student of mine, and we both just sort of stopped and looked at each other.

I think it was the same thought, "Oh, she's seeing me in here right now. How do I explain this?" It turned out it was her family business, and I was there shopping. She brought me in the back to talk to her mother and say, "This is the professor I was talking to you about." It was almost an "aha" moment. At every step of my career since about 2010, 2011; when I started listening, when I was in Benin, and I was told that my path was the water, and respecting the water, and understanding stories about the water – shortly after that, I got a job at the New Bedford Whaling Museum, and, while in that position, found a picture of my ancestor on a whaling ship. I did not know that he was a whaler. I've been told time and time again that I didn't find him – he found me. That's why I was there. That's why I found that position. I feel the same way, without going into too much detail, the work that I'm doing now, the things that I have been told to do, not distinguishing between this is my job, and this is my spiritual purpose, but my job is the same as my spiritual purpose, has been so empowering. And I don't think it's taken away from the professionalism, the research that I do, I've seen it enhance it in so many ways. Even with my work here in Newport.

I was asked over the summer to speak at an event called Religious Tolerance. They needed someone who would speak about the Black religious experience in colonial Newport. I said, "I'll only do it if I don't have to speak about conversion to Christianity." Because in the oldest house in Newport, under attic floorboards, a Nkisi bundle was discovered.[17] And, I said, "I want to talk about that. I want to talk about the limits of tolerance." I want to talk about how spirituality was something that these teenage girls that were in a 3-by-3 attic, still called upon their ancestors, they found a way somehow, to have cowrie shells, and nails, and broken glass, and bundle them to call on divinities and their ancestors, as Leah said, as a coping mechanism for comfort, maybe for retribution. But in my mind, I'm thinking part of that is also reciprocity.

This idea that you cannot take anything without giving back. And that became my problem with academics; the idea that you're supposed to report, and do fieldwork, and take, and that's where it ends. That's why working in that Rastafarian community was so integral to my growth. Working with Indigenous communities here, working in Benin and being trained in spirituality, was really the thing that I think, after all of the degrees in the academic career, I finally listened to Tall Oak and put my feet back on my path and did the things I was supposed to do as opposed to the things that I thought I was supposed to do as a professional. So much like Leah said, I don't think of the two as two different compartments. I think that one very much informs the other, and it's very circular. I wouldn't be able to do one without the other.

Battle-Baptiste

It's so integral to archeology to be taking from the land and not giving anything back. It's not something that I could do. It's this weird moment where you're putting something down, whether it's tobacco, whether it's alcohol, and then my white colleagues are looking at me and ask, "What are you doing?" And I'm responding, "Do you want to know what's going on here? Or do you just want this to not come to fruition? You all can do what you need to do, but I need to actually give something because I'm taking something away." It was important for my dissertation that I connected with descendants of Jackson's Plantation, which my family was not happy about me working on, but it's that idea of that reciprocity, and being able to write about that meant that my work was accessible to people who understood that type of spiritual connection and reciprocity.

I think that we are in a moment where you are not really thinking, you're working where you're working. I think about reciprocity as a continuation of things unseen that we don't need to explain and/or write about sometimes.

Wilcox

I agree. I'm just thinking of spirituality as capacity. What needs to be interrogated about capacity and the very practice of endurance itself that we get from these technologies that is not just about our own individual care, and our own individual transformations, but about how through these technologies of care, through these technologies of love, through these technologies of connection, we're building our own capacity to not actually shift. It's not an actual shift from the very structure that builds upon the capacity that we have. It's thinking of spirituality as a function of capacity – and not just spirituality, it's all the technologies that we use.

All the resistance that we use, in various ways, not only for our own self-transformation, but for our communities and for our own commitments to liberatory work, it's not necessarily just a critique of futures, but an interrogation of whether that future has the capacity to not look like now. That might just be a critique about how you all have been talking about compartmentalization, about how we think of time as you invoked in this space earlier through Saidiya Hartman's notion of the "afterlife of slavery."[18] It's not actually a transition from the past to the present to the future. It's about time itself being a reenactment of how the structures of violence are able to mutate, and how we are able to build our capacity through these mutations to function or have some type of livability in the heart of the violence. And I'm interested in interrogating the ways that we build the capacity to do that.

DeLucia

One quick question for Akeia. What is the name of the source of the first reading you shared?

Gomes

I went down to the Virgin Islands as an archeologist and got very interested in the community's concept of what was going on in this archeological site and why they were resistant to it. I was told one thing by the contractor, but it turned out not to be the community's ultimate concern. I went to this speech, and just was so enamored with the community that I dropped my archeology hat and put on my anthropology hat and decided to start doing fieldwork within a Rastafarian community. After a couple of years, I was finally assumed to be a trustworthy enough person that I was told that I was going to meet one friend, and it turned out, little by little, that other men were coming into the circle of conversation.

I realized, once the conversation was going, that I was actually invited into a reasoning session, but I wasn't told ahead of time. And what I thought was pretty amazing about that is usually women have their own reasoning sessions, and the men's reasoning sessions are separate, but because I was an academic and because I had the power to share the knowledge globally, they thought that it was important that they reason with me, and their words taught me how to be a reasonable person. There was a two-hour conversation where we talked about Bible verses and we talked about colonialism. Eventually, I took pieces of that conversation to publish something called "Narratives of Transfer, Dependence, and Resistance." This is the same article that it took me ten years to publish because I flipped the script.[19] I decided to use the Rastafarian perspective as a way to theorize and critique colonialism, as opposed to using colonial methods and academics to critique Rasta thought and wisdom.

That quote is actually at the end of the article where I am just documenting Rasta thoughts on US colonialism in the Virgin Islands. It was actually the end of the conversation. And I felt like it was almost the person saying: "Look, we've gone through this two-hour conversation. Let me summarize it for you." And that was the summary of everything we had discussed over those two hours.

SOURCE NOTES

1.   www.youtube.com/watch?v=jyFByfd9qoE; www.youtube.com/watch?v=PG 8ppCpl7gw; www.youtube.com/watch?v=XaXAnW_ALxc

2. Battle-Baptiste, Whitney. *Black Feminist Archaeology*. London: Routledge, 2017.

3. Bremen, SchädelMädel. "Zangbeto Voodoo Benin." YouTube, January 27, 2019. www.youtube.com/watch?v=p4B2ku08us0&feature=youtu.be

4. See also: Fanon, Frantz. *Black Skin, White Masks*. London: Paladin, 1970.

5. Benard, Akeia A. "Narratives of Transfer, Dependence, and Resistance: Rastafarian Perspectives on Colonialism in the Virgin Islands." *Anthropology of Consciousness* 30, no. 2 (2019): 117–131. https://doi.org/10.1111/anoc.12114

6. Ibid.

7. Bloesch, Sarah J., Meredith Minister, and Charles H. Long. "Perspectives for a Study of Afro-American Religion in the United States." Essay. In *The Bloomsbury Reader in Cultural Approaches to the Study of Religion*, 126–134. Bloomsbury Academic, 2018.

8. Long, Charles H. "The West African High God: History and Religious Experience." *History of Religions*, 1964, 328–342. https://doi.org/10.1086/462641

9. Hartman, Saidiya. *Lose Your Mother: A Journey along the Atlantic Slave Route*. S.l.: Macmillan, 2008.

10. James, Joy. "The Captive Maternal and Abolitionism." *TOPIA: Canadian Journal of Cultural Studies* 43 (2021): 9–23. https://doi.org/10.3138/topia-43-002

11. "Reading together the Middle Passage, the coffle, and, I argue, the birth canal, we see how each has functioned separately and collectively over time to disfigure black maternity, to turn the womb into a factory (producing Blackness as abjection much like the slave ship's hold and the prison), and turning the birth canal into another domestic Middle Passage with black mothers, after the end of legal hypodescent, still ushering their children into her condition; her non-status, her non-being-ness," from Sharpe, Christina Elizabeth. *In the Wake. On Blackness and Being*. Durham: Duke University Press, 2017.

12. "Oh Freedom!" African American Spiritual.

13. Sharpe, Christina Elizabeth. *In the Wake. On Blackness and Being*. Durham: Duke University Press, 2017.

14. James, Joy. *Resisting State Violence: Radicalism, Gender, and Race in U.S. Culture*. Minneapolis: University of Minnesota Press, 1996.

15. Colonial Pathways Policy. *San Diego Museum of Man*, June 2018. https://museum.bc.ca/wp-content/uploads/2023/02/Museum-of-Us-Colonial-Pathways-Policy-Public-Janauary-2020.pdf

16. In 1978, the American Indian Religious Freedom Act was passed. American Indian Religious Freedom Act of 1978 (AIRFA) (42 U.S.C. § 1996). Accessed July 11, 2023. https://www.law.cornell.edu/uscode/text/42/1996

17. "Nkisi are bundles of objects that are believed to hold spiritual power and reflect the beliefs of the Bakongo people of western Central Africa. Often found buried near dwelling sites of enslaved people, the objects shed light on early faith practices and cultural continuity among African people." (Nmaahc. "Enslaving Colonial North America." National Museum of African American History & Culture. Accessed July 11, 2023. www.searchablemuseum.com/enslaving-colonial-north-america).

18. Hartman, Saidiya. *Lose Your Mother: A Journey along the Atlantic Slave Route.* S.l.: MacMillian, 2008.

19. Benard, Akeia A. "Narratives of Transfer, Dependence, and Resistance: Rastafarian Perspectives on Colonialism in the Virgin Islands." *Anthropology of Consciousness* 30, no. 2 (2019): 117–131. https://doi.org/10.1111/anoc.12114

2

Security

Brittany Meché, Paul Gallay, Mary McNeil, José Constantine, and moderator Tom Van Winkle

March 15, 2022

Brittany Meché

I want to open with a newspaper article published 47 years ago to the day, on March 15, 1975, in the *Chicago Defender*, one of the most prominent and influential Black newspapers in the United States. Under the headline, "Ali Sets Example," the article reported on a pledge made by famed boxer, Muhammad Ali, to contribute a portion of the proceeds of an upcoming championship fight toward drought and famine relief efforts in West Africa.
 The article stated,

> [B]y his offer to turn over to the drought-stricken African countries part of each ticket price for the closed circuit telecast of his coming championship bout, Muhammad Ali is setting a classic example of generosity at a critical moment in Africa's history. The six-year-old drought, which parched fields where vegetation was once luxuriant, and where crops yielded an abundant harvest, became graveyards for [the] millions dead. Ali is eminently right in calling his effort, "just a grain of sand in comparison to what has to be done." It is a grain of sand that could be multiplied, a thousand-fold. If other Black athletes swimming in wealth would follow Ali's lead and contribute a share of their opulence to allay the suffering of their starving and dying brothers in Africa, the land of their forefathers, that would be laudable.[1]

Gendered exclusions notwithstanding, in its simultaneous critique of Black celebrity culture and wealth-hoarding, alongside its faith in expanding the purview of Black kinship making, the article gestures toward carving out avenues for international solidarity rather than simple charity. The article itself was part of sustained coverage by the *Chicago Defender* about the ecological calamity unfolding in the West African Sahel, which is an area of the African continent, just south of the Sahara. Between 1968 and 1985 across the African Sahel, late rains and famine induced by the vagaries of commodity markets under global racial capitalism led to the deaths of an estimated 1.2 million people, and the displacement of millions more.

The Sahel famines were covered in depth by African American periodicals. While mainstream publications, like the *New York Times*, emphasized African neediness and desperation, Black periodicals by contrast often stressed the colonial legacies and racist undercurrents of the famines, and championed African Indigenous expertise in addressing the crisis.

These efforts to forge transnational Black ecological sensibilities, attentive to the environmental calamities impacting Black people globally, built on themes from the US Civil Rights movement, including support for Black agricultural workers and calls for food sovereignty. Indeed, Civil Rights activists asserted at the time, "the Sahel has to survive, if not, neither will the poor of Mississippi or Harlem."[2] But also central to the *Chicago Defender*'s analysis of this environmental crisis was a trenching critique of US militarism.

The article further noted,

> the United Nations is not doing enough, and the White House is doing nothing worth mentioning for Africa. The administration would rather spend hundreds of millions of American dollars in Cambodia in pursuit of a cause that is militarily and politically lost, than rescue Black Africans from the jaws of death. American Blacks must begin searching their souls to see if they do not have a moral imperative to share the burden of their starving brothers in Africa.[3]

Here, the article specifically names the US war in Vietnam and its shadow theater in Cambodia, as well as the hobbling of international organizations, [such as] the United Nations [UN], as impediments to equitable responses to an unfolding catastrophe.

I use this example to flag what had become two key components of my research. First, I'm interested in exploring what kinds of global solidarity and affinity have emerged historically that can be used in the present to address the disproportionate impacts of environmental disasters for communities of African descent. Secondly, I'm committed to highlighting the importance of reckoning with architectures of global militarism and security and empire, if we are to have any hope of actually responding to the impacts of climate change.

In the present moment, the West African Sahel remains one of the regions most vulnerable to climate change. It has simultaneously served as a theater for foreign-led military interventions under the banner of security. My current book project, tentatively titled *Sustainable Empire: Nature, Knowledge and Insecurity in the Sahel*, situates the West African Sahel as a key region from which to theorize the progression of environmental knowledge-making, the development of humanitarian expertise, the consequences of global militarism, and the possibilities for different ecological futures. Beginning in the 1960s, the book argues that ecological knowledge about the Sahel informed both the conceptual and institutional bedrock for future climate change science. It also birthed nascent claims about what became known as environmental insecurity, and this is the idea that environmental change would lead to a new era of global conflict.

The book further shows how environmental insecurity discourses pave the way for the future elaboration of the global "War on Terror," in which, as I previously noted, the West African Sahel would become an important theater. The book concludes by showing how the progression of the war and terror in the Sahel worked to undermine responses to the urgencies of climate change by effectively constraining the latter within the prisons and logics and prescriptions of the former. It shows how investments in "securing" the Sahel had the opposite effect, making communities both more vulnerable to armed conflict and ecological disturbances while naturalizing both as accepted and predictable hazards of Sahelian life. Ultimately, my current research calls for greater attention to the reconstitution of imperial power in an age of climate change, and I insist that what has happened, and what continues to happen, in the West African Sahel is deeply consequential for envisioning just ecological futures.

Paul Gallay

Before I begin, I wanted to acknowledge that my home and my university are both located in Lenapehoking, the ancestral homelands of the Munsee Lenape and Wappinger peoples, most of whom have long been in the diaspora. I hope that many of you, especially those of you who are connected to Lenapehoking, will want to learn more about the Lenape diaspora and the Lenape people who remain in a small portion of their homelands in northern New Jersey to this day.

My remarks this evening are drawn from my experience in government, land conservation, and clean water activism, and from my work at the Columbia Climate School as the Director of the Resilient Coastal Communities Project, which seeks to support learning and foster effective solutions developed in partnerships with frontline communities, governments, and other stakeholders to climate-related threats. To add some context for what I want to say this evening: First, freedom from the harmful impacts of air, water, and waste pollution is essential not just to our and our family's health, but to our security as a community. Pollution undermines a community's economic security, its educational security, its vibrancy and cohesion, and so much more. Second, the fight for environmental justice is essential to the fight for security because of the enormous racial disparities that exist in people's ability to live without the burdens of pollution and with the benefits of nature and open space.

For example, Black Americans are exposed to 56 percent more pollution than they produce, and non-Hispanic white Americans are exposed to 17 percent less pollution than they produce. Non-Hispanic Black children continue to have higher blood lead levels than non-Hispanic white children with the same level of income.[4] Third, climate change makes the fight for environmental justice and security even more essential because African, Indigenous, and Afro-Indigenous communities are generally the ones most vulnerable to climate impacts like flooding and excessive heat. Efforts to fight climate change like the federal Justice 40 program, the California Climate Investments Program, and New York State's Climate Leadership and Community Protection Act, represent an opportunity to redress historical disparities in community, health, and security. Statutes such as the 2019 New Jersey Environmental Justice Law made New Jersey the first US state to prohibit new sources of pollution if they would have a disproportionate impact on overburdened communities.[5]

With all of that in mind, will we achieve environmental justice and security? And if so, when? First, something about the process. Now, Justice 40 and all those other laws that I mentioned, they're wonderful things, but despite them the road to environmental justice and security for Black, Indigenous, and people of color (BIPOC) communities remains incredibly fraught. To achieve the goals of these statutes, governments involved will need to make fundamental changes in the way they do business. I have spent 13 years in government, and so I can say that I know that firsthand.

Flood protection is a perfect example. The processes by which communities are to be protected from flooding generally fail to take local community needs and knowledge into account. Instead, the focus is most often narrowly placed on protecting property with evaluation metrics that tend to skew toward wealthier and more powerful groups, which reinforces historical inequities and injustice. Despite this, frontline and BIPOC communities are working in good faith to foster coastal resilience and good planning. Examples here in New York include the East Side Coastal Resiliency Project and Planning for the Future of the Hunts Point area and Sheridan Expressway in Hunts Point Market in the South Bronx. But the results of these and other processes are often incredibly frustrating. They begin with high expectations and promises, and end with the government not implementing the plans communities have created. I'm going to provide a newspaper article that summarizes the experience of communities, especially on the East Side Coastal Resilience Project.[6]

These sorts of outcomes are why one of my colleagues at Columbia recently wrote back to a government official who had requested us both to assist in planning a series of workshops. He said: For workshops and community outreach more broadly, an important question is whether feedback from the community can change the process and/or the products. And when this is the case, it's important to document how the process changed and was enhanced as a result of community outreach. It's in this spirit that communities are starting to call on the government to decide collaborative processes with them, to come to their table, or at least to really share power. In some cases, they're considering whether to decline participation if the government does not show how that participation will actually foster change, as one advocate put it to me this week, "We're not going to be part of some BS process that will take them away from other important work and not change outcomes."

Communities are increasingly applying the following standards for deciding whether to engage in resilience planning processes. Will I be heard and supported? Will my concerns become the government's concerns as well? Will anything change because I took the time to engage and will that change, take root, and grow over time? In other words, they're asking for the government to go beyond providing notification of planning and taking public comments, which may provide for local awareness, but gives communities no real power beyond providing responses to public comments, and start to bring the community into the actual decision-making process, which is the start of meaningful consultation and ultimately share leadership on project design with the community, which would reflect a true partnership – not just a seat at the table, but a seat at the table where the decisions are made and where they can be heard and will be listened to.

As we start to conclude these remarks, the question remains, will we create environmental justice and security? What outcomes would define that when it comes to coastal resilience? Communities want coastal resilience plans that invest in keeping them safe in their communities – in their homes, schools, and businesses – and keeping them dry and cool in those places that strengthen the fabric of communities through mutual support and effective communication and provide for other benefits, like more energy efficient homes and locally owned green businesses, not just green jobs, but green business empowerment in the community.

So, where to go from here? I think we can count on governments to increasingly make pronouncements and at least theoretical commitments that reflect an awareness of their responsibilities in the area of environmental justice and security. They will say that they want to make the journey toward inclusion, empowerment, and justice, but will they provide for that journey? Will governments not only speak about climate justice, but also do climate justice? To help them live up to their goals, we must call on the government to fully fund effective community engagement, develop trust in communities through transparency, requesting consent, fostering reciprocity, not rushing the process, and actually use what they learn in such proceedings, and make it an intrinsic part of their final project design.

Finally, our role. I want to finish these remarks about Just Futures by asking you all to consider how we can take what we're learning in these wonderful roundtables and use it to support a more just future. We need to ask ourselves what we as educators and researchers do to support groups who are on the front line of coastal resilience, groups like the New York City Environmental Justice Lines, our partners at the Resilient Coastal Communities Project, the Water Leaders Institute in Orleans, Troy Water Justice Lab across the border in New York, and Melanin Unchained a little farther to the south of Williams in Newburg. Will we help groups like these make connections, build strength, and exchange knowledge? Will we support their participation in government coastal resilience planning with our expertise where we connect them with members of our research teams, when they have research needs that they have to have, or questions they need help answering? I think this sort of deeper partnership between researchers and practitioners would be quite a wonderful thing to say that we had a hand in creating, and I hope this Just Futures Project will be the beginning of a dialogue that actually takes us there.

Mary McNeil

I always make the joke that I pursued graduate study because I'm selfish, that I wanted to have the space and the time to think through questions of history, identity, and political struggle that were deeply personal to me, the daughter of a Wampanoag woman from many places in Massachusetts and an African American man from many places in the US South. As a child, it was the stories of my parents, grandparents, and aunties that instilled in me a deep love of history and countered common historical narratives about Black and Indigenous peoples that sought to relegate us solely to the space of deficit or objection.

As an undergraduate student, I found myself drawn to courses in the humanities that centered a practice of telling history "from the ground up" and, in doing so, asserted that everyday people have played just as integral of a role in shaping American history as settlers and enslavers, politicians and corporations. It is my belief that we have a lot to learn from the "freedom dreams" of our ancestors and our elders, and that their strategies of survival and survivance can provide us with schematics for imagining what the future can and should look like. Indeed, it was this deeply rooted determination and political will that created the conditions that allowed my family to continue and for me ultimately to be born.

As a [former] doctoral candidate in American Studies, I'm interested in research, writing, and teaching that attends to histories of Black and Indigenous enslavement, dispossession, displacement, and resistance across a long span of years. More specifically, my dissertation turns to the late 1960s and the 1970s to think about Black Power and Red Power as social movements that were responding to a broader historical period in US history that has certain eerily similar parallels to our present moment. I'm particularly interested in the Black Power/Red Power era because it is the era of my parents' coming of age. I'm also drawn to the Black Power/Red Power era because it was a period of rapid spatial and racial transformation in urban centers across the United States, and particularly in New England.

At the most general level, I'm guided by the following questions: how did Black, Indigenous, and Afro-Indigenous political actors center notions of self-determination and sovereignty in their movement agendas? What political critiques of the United States as a settler colonial and anti-Black nation did they proffer? And where did these critiques intersect, enabling the space for Black and Indigenous solidarity to emerge, and where might they have created spaces of contestation?

In many ways, Red Power and Black Power emerged and operated in urban centers along parallel timelines, were precipitated by similar conditions, and shared similar ideologies. Both movements' largest groups, the Black Panther Party and the American Indian Movement, were established in late 1960s urban centers. The establishment of these organizations was precipitated by Black and Indigenous migration to cities at the mid-century, as well as emerging disillusionment that Black and Indigenous families and individuals developed after experiencing forms of racial violence, political disenfranchisement, and dispossession akin to those that they had experienced in the rural south or on Bureau of Indian Affairs (BIA) managed reservations. Within these particular urban contexts and amidst a global "Third World" uprising against colonialism and imperialism, Black Power and Red Power activists rejected the viability of social, political, and economic incorporation into the US nation-state, advocating instead for decolonization and varying forms of self-determination and sovereignty.

At the heart of Black Power and Red Power goals were matters of space and of security – the theme of our discussion tonight. When conceptualizing Black Power's and Red Power's central goals, I envision them to be: 1) the creation of places where Black and Indigenous life could flourish, free from various forms of violence and dispossession, and 2) the creation of mechanisms that could protect community members from various forms of state and white supremacist violence. For example, almost immediately upon its founding, the Black Panther Party initiated civilian patrols of the police in Oakland, California. The American Indian Movement initiated similar patrols of the police in Minneapolis, Minnesota upon their founding. Such police patrols were created with the intention of intervening in the surveillance and brutalization of Black and Indigenous urban residents by Oakland and Minneapolis police. Thus, in creating such patrols, Black Power and Red Power actors sought to create a community-controlled security apparatus capable of making the urban landscape safer for Black and Indigenous city-dwellers.

In my research, I'm also interested in investigating the ways in which Black and Indigenous forms of political action have historically informed each other. I'd like to close my remarks today by offering one brief example from the late Afeni Shakur, a member of the New York chapter of the Black Panther Party, a defendant in the Panther 21 case, and the mother of the late Tupac Shakur. Shakur, who moved to the Bronx at the age of 11, was actually born in Lumberton, North Carolina. Lumberton, a city situated on the traditional homelands of the Lumbee tribe of North Carolina, was a place where, to paraphrase a portion of Shakur's 1971 collective autobiography, there were always "three different bathrooms: bathrooms for the Blacks, for the Indians, and for the white people."[7] In her 2004 biography as recounted to actress Jasmine Guy, Shakur recounts a moment of Lumbee resistance against white supremacist violence that she remembers from her childhood:

> It was around my birthday, and the Klan had this rally near Maxton and in some open field. Up until the day of that rally, the Klan had been burning crosses and terrorizing folk in St. Paul's and were getting closer to Lumberton and Pembroke. They said they wanted to set the Indian straight, show 'em who's boss. Well, the Lumbees got guns and rifles and ambushed the Klan at their own rally. Folks say it was a mob scene. Shooting everywhere in the complete darkness of night. Black folk wanted to fight with them, but the Lumbees said they had it under control. They felt specifically challenged by the Klan, you know. They were like, "This is *our* battle." So we all just waited to hear what went down in Maxton and rejoiced with the news that they ran the Klan out.[8]

Here, Shakur is recounting the January 1958 Battle of Hayes Pond, an armed conflict between Lumbee tribal members and members of the Ku Klux Klan. Leading up to this conflict, local chapters of the Ku Klux Klan sought to expand their own reign of terror and restrict the movement of Black and Indigenous residents by implementing curfews, burning crosses, and holding rallies. According to some reports, as many as 1000 Lumbee men mobilized at the Battle of Hayes Pond to disperse the Klan rally that was taking place, capturing the Klan's flag in the process.[9] When asked about the significance of this event, Shakur characterizes the Battle of Hayes Pond as her "first taste of resistance."[10]

I close with Shakur's recounting of the Battle of Hayes Pond because this particular anecdote illuminates the ways in which Indigenous histories of self-defense and security strategy were integral to the formation of Shakur's own nascent political consciousness as a 10-year-old. Moreover, Shakur's recollection illustrates one way in which Black and Indigenous safety and security have historically been entwined, and the ways in which Black and Indigenous political actors have pushed back against white supremacist security logics of terror.

José Constantine

Having spent two days on a National Science Foundation (NSF) panel, evaluating science proposals for geosciences and hydrology, and hearing from
some of the great minds in our country, it's heartbreaking to hear and to see
how little of the problems they see – since the real and significant problems
that we heard Mary just speak to, and the problems that poor Black, Brown
and Indigenous communities face every single day, this very second, is
heartbreaking. There's clearly a disconnect between the world and the imaginations of many, and I would argue to say most natural scientists when they
think about what a just future and just futures might look like. I also think
about my role as an academic, and I generally question the role of myself
as an academic and the role of the academy – what role do we play beyond
commenting and studying and reflecting in terms of the lives of people who
are in crisis, this very moment, because of the ways that we have manipulated and mis-manipulated and harmed the environment?

At Williams-Mystic, where I was invited to participate as a visiting faculty,
I'd met folks from all walks of life – representatives of Indigenous communities in the Gulf Coast, representatives of Black communities in New Orleans,
working-class communities whose ancestors immigrated from Canada –
and hearing from them their daily struggles with regards to what climate
change is doing, not what climate change will do, but what it's doing this very
moment on their lives, inspired me to change what I do and how I think, and
how I conduct the work that I do as a natural scientist in big ways. That work
has inspired me to learn more about the history of environmental justice in
this country and beyond that, the very complicated role that natural scientists have played in perpetuating environmental injustice.

It's gotten me thinking about the ways that natural scientists might play
some role in securing or ensuring the securities of people, who I described
to my students as our brothers and sisters, who are struggling this very day
because of how we've mismanaged and harmed this world that we live in.
This journey has taken me to places across the country and has allowed
me to work with communities such as Centreville, Illinois, and Tallevast,
Florida, and most recently in Troy, just nearby; communities that suffer and
have suffered in full view of society, but with no mention or concern by
that society that lives around them. And I describe particularly the community in Centreville, the Black community who live right on the Mississippi
River floodplain, that they suffer invisible floods; floods that are a nuisance
to most people who are trying to get around and through the community
but are incredibly catastrophic to the people who live there.

There are 141 communities – that's what the Union of Concerned Scientists have identified – 141 communities that suffer chronic flooding as a consequence of climate change today. These are communities that have nowhere to go. That number's expected to increase by 60 to 70 in just 20 or 30 years. That number will only continue growing, and that's just along our coastal waterways and some of our inland waterways. When we think about communities across the globe, there will literally be millions of people – the most vulnerable in our society, those that have contributed the least to the climate change problem – that are going to be displaced. And I think about these issues because I work at an institution that sells itself in many respects, as a safe haven, as a place for people to escape the ills of society, a place to find peace in this bucolic setting, to escape those problems, and then to be free, to think big thoughts, to aspire, to be ambitious.

That disconnect, that insulation that we afford ourselves, that privilege we afford ourselves, can be bought for the time. And that privilege that is bought keeps us and, I would argue, many of my natural science colleagues whose proposals I reviewed these past two days, blind. It keeps them from perpetuating harm. But it can't last long. At some point, this problem's going to consume us all.

I'll finish my remarks by discussing work and progress that I'm learning about in an island nation that has a population that's not all that different from the population we have here in New England, and that's the island nation of New Zealand. New Zealand and the colonialist history that it has certainly caused tremendous harm to Indigenous peoples across the islands of New Zealand. But in 1975, a tribunal was convened to evaluate all the different ways that the New Zealand government and the Crown have broken promises, broken agreements that were made legal through treaties, that have perpetuated injustice toward the Maori populations.[11] That tribunal is, as imperfect as it's taken place, has led to some big moments, and the very recent one that led me to thinking about ways that we can learn and perhaps incorporate some of those philosophies, some of those brave considerations, here in this country. It took place in 2014, when the Whanganui tribal community fought for their rights, to not just inhabit a river system, to reclaim their ancestral homelands along the river system, but to also fight for the rights of the Whanganui River.[12]

They started that process in 1999, and it took 15 years for that process to conclude itself. But when it did, and the court sided with the tribal community, one of the big agreements that resulted from it was an agreement to acknowledge the Te Awa Tupua, which is the recognition that rivers, that nature, that all that we take for granted, has a right to exist. That acknowledgment that the river has a legal right to exist has made profound changes to the way that New Zealand manages its environment, whether it be mountain rivers flowing in the south, along the South Island of New Zealand, or environments in urban settings, where people coexist with natural processes. It's had profound impacts. I would hope, and certainly as a natural scientist who's only learning about this possibility, that the conversations that we're having today will only see themselves happen more and more and more often and that we as a society can incorporate Indigenous values, perspectives, and environmental ethics in ways that I think can only secure our future on this planet.

Meché

You've invited me to reconsider how I have a disposition to tense up at the word security. Given the things that I study, given my own research on militarism, I think each of you has offered a reconceptualization of security as emerging from the claims of different groups that are made vulnerable through all kinds of processes. It's encouraged me to open up how I think of security and not be so quick to jettison it or see it as this tool of empire, that it could actually claim to safety. I was really struck by the story that Mary offered of communities literally taking up arms in defense against white supremacist violence. How would we narrate those actions and what might that do to our reconceptualization of security?

Gallay

I was moved by what José said about the grant application reviews that he's involved in as a recent addition to the academic world. I know how important these NSF grants are. They are the holy grail, and to think of them as still being rooted in their history more than in their future is very concerning. I would like to ask José whether he has seen any glimmers of hope. I know that when I get my reviews back, a lot of folks seem to not quite understand where we're coming from with this community-oriented work and maybe not even see it as hard science, even hard social science. Have you seen glimmers of hope?

Constantine

I think the hope is that we're undergoing a generational shift in many respects, as an academic community at large, but certainly in the natural science community. Why demographics matter, I think, is unclear to me at the moment, but certainly among a certain cohort, it's becoming impossible to ignore and not to be affected by the problems that communities are facing. That's where I think my hope stems – is because of the way these funding bodies work, in many respects, the community decides what's important and what the present and future should be. I think we're hearing louder and louder voices, saying that the NSF should be funding different kinds of initiatives, and different ways that we are engaging with communities. I'm seeing from NSF different funding opportunities where they're acknowledging that they should be supporting different ways of doing science, different ways of doing academia.

We certainly are not there yet, as you just heard me say. I think there are so many impulses and pressures – capitalistic pressures, even – that academia faces, that lead to not only institutions, but academics, prioritizing the short-term instead of the long-term. But my hope is that more of us become engaged and are eager – as imperfectly as this process might play itself out – we're eager to do this differently. It's certainly not going to be soon enough, but I suspect that we're a decade or so away from a substantive change in the way that we do research.

I've been really interested in history, in the role – or trying to understand through the lens of history – that our modern management and misman-agement of the environment has come to be. It's gotten me to think about the forcible displacement of Indigenous peoples westward across the Mis-sissippi River, and the consequences of manipulating the Mississippi River floodplain to subjugate a people in the pursuit of riches. For someone like me, who's a novice and is trying to think about ways that the tools of histori-ans and the lens that historians provide us – just curious about how you see that in your work, Mary? How does your work help you understand and be a better advocate and activist?

McNeil

Personally, I'm very much a student of history. I came to history as an undergrad because I really had just this overwhelming question of why are things the way that they are. It's a very simple and perhaps reductive sort of question. As someone who was raised in the US South as an Afro-Na-tive person, just trying to make sense of the world around me, of particular things that were emerging in the news. I started college and my first year of college was the murder of Trayvon Martin. For me, history has always been an opportunity to understand the things that we encounter in our present moment – they're neither new nor novel. The contours of them may change a little bit over time.

There's specificity with each historical moment particularly. Scholars such as Patrick Wolfe and Saidiya Hartman and Tiffany Lethabo King have argued that when we're thinking about Black and Indigenous histories of the United States, that a lot of things are constants, particularly forms of settler colonial violence, or white supremacist violence, anti-Black violence. History allows us to track the development or evolution of these enduring forms of violence over time.

But what I find a lot of strength, and also a lot of interest in, is turning to history to also see what is the political imagination of folks. How have Black folks historically responded to these particular forms of violence, and imagined what a livable future could look like? And what were the very practical lessons that they learned and that future generations can build upon? Here, I'm thinking a lot about Robin D.G. Kelley's important book, *Freedom Dreams*.[13]

My goal as a historian is to always turn to the past, journey back to the past and to think about the importance of these political visions and how they might inform our current imaginings of a better world.

I have a question for the group. It seems security is operating on a couple of different registers across our work. A lot of the papers are thinking about security in terms of trying to mitigate climate catastrophe. My remarks are thinking about security in the form of anti-violence and trying to preserve human life from immediate bodily harm rendered by another force. I wondered if anyone from the group could talk a little bit about the relationship between what we might call ecological security and the security of the body?

Constantine

This is a big question. If I were to rephrase it in terms of the work that we're doing – I've got a colleague who I just saw is online with us, but the work that we're doing with the Black community in Southwest Florida called Tallevast for me speaks to ongoing and lived trauma in response to how we impact the environment. This particular community was found at the location of a turpentine mill, and eventually became a very close-knit community in rural Southwest Florida.

It eventually became cited as the location of a chemical processing plant that ended up polluting the drinking water for this community, and is now impacting the air that people breathe and the space that they live in. I'm just thinking about how you talked about impacts on the body, and on the bodies. I think it's so multi-layered. There's the actual impact on people's health and their well-being in terms of a physiological way, but in terms of the ongoing trauma of feeling besieged and feeling that sense of hopelessness creeping in response to that seems to be out of your control, taking place all around you, I think for me, it's hard to both fathom and it's hard to accept.

I don't know if that speaks to your question, but your question made me think about these wonderful people who, at this very second as we're meeting now, are breathing air that was poisoned by this contamination that happened over two decades ago, and living on land that was manipulated over a century ago – and on and on it goes this, this cycle of trauma.

Meché

I perhaps have a sideways entrance into that question. So much of my work is about a landscape that is oftentimes maligned. I work on arid environments, and there are narratives of arid environments as these wasteland spaces; of spaces that are inhospitable to human life. But in the West African Sahel in particular, Black communities have lived in that landscape for thousands of years. Then, there becomes this attendant narrative that there's something wrong with the bodies that would inhabit a landscape like this. I think that comes in multiple historical cycles. There's the kind of colonial moment when that narrative is jotted out. The narrative is jotted out again in the mid-twentieth century when the famines happen, but it's also being repurposed ostensibly as a climate justice protest move, which is to say that the West African Sahel is so vulnerable that perhaps in the future it will be uninhabitable.

I think that discounts the ways that Black Indigenous communities in that space have been attempting to craft lives, cultures, and agricultural practices. There's an inevitability that's oftentimes attached to the West African Sahel as this landscape that's always already a catastrophe is something that I'm actively trying to work against, while also still holding that there are very real and very worrisome trends taking place with regards to climate change. That relationship between certain bodies and certain landscapes is something that I'm trying to work through in my work.

Gallay

Brittany's comments really remind me of what I think is a fundamental challenge in the communities I work with. It's more about place than it is about body, but people are being told, "Oh well, you're going to have to leave your community at some point." The way they're being told that is both condescending and extraordinarily disrespectful, in that there are communities that are much more difficult to protect geographically or physically that are not being told to move – it's the communities where people aren't willing to invest what's necessary to keep them in the community. What I think is the most important thing for the communities that I work with is that sense of place and are they going to be given the resources and the consideration that more well-to-do communities are getting when it comes to whether they're being asked to leave.

For that matter, New York City is re-zoning neighborhoods in which people are being told they're going to have to leave at some point to allow the construction of new high-rise, market-rate housing that will somehow be invited to come in while others are being asked to leave – how extraordinarily unfair is that? Finally, is there any consideration being given to, if you must leave – for example, the famous example of Isle de Jean Charles in Louisiana, where an island that was 22,000 acres, because of subsidence and sea level rise, is now 300 acres. There's no choice; their community is being relocated. They talked for three years about how to do that the right way, and they're staying together. So, what is being done in these more difficult-to-protect communities in the New York, New Jersey Metro area, to ensure that they are given every opportunity to stay in their homes rather than being simply told "Your place is soon to no longer exist and your community must break up?"

Constantine

In terms of securing a future, what is it exactly that we're securing, given that more and more communities are going to be forced – displacement will be imposed upon them yet again, right, in response to climate change, what is it that we're securing? What is it that we hope to secure in the face of what seems incredibly ominous?

Gallay

What's at stake is whether we're ever going to redress these past injustices. Are we going to invest in communities that have been so fundamentally under-invested in that the asthma rates are through the ceiling and the own-ership rates are below the floorboards? And are people going to be given a chance to make their communities what they've always deserved to have, without being told "No, we're just going to give up"? It's existential. That's a word I almost never use, but it feels right for this situation.

Meché

I do sometimes wonder if there are things that we actually want that exceed the purview of security. Paul, to your point, is it about security or is it about redress? Is it about security or is it about justice? Is it about security or is it about care, or sustenance, or equity? I was just reading a book, *An Eco-topian Lexicon*.[14] It's all of these kinds of new, but also old, words that are being revived to sort of name something else that we might want. So maybe the terms under which we actually staged the debate are insufficient, and challenge us as thinkers or writers to imagine different terms that actually capture so many of the things that we would like to see in the world that perhaps aren't just reducible to security. But again, I'm not sure what kind of better terms might be on offer for that project.

Van Winkle

I think you've all touched on this in one way or another. Brittany, you talked about the importance of reckoning; and, Mary you talked about the eerie parallels of the present moment, and the 1960s and 1970s, and the Black Power movement. And then there was the conversation between Paul and José about involving the community in answers or the question of tribu-nals. What in your opinion – thinking as somebody who's involved in the academy, but thinking about community – are the processes that would be most effective to listen to the community? Do you have examples of where it's worked? It sounds like [in] New Zealand something's worked there.

Constantine

I think it's working. It certainly has worked much more slowly than I think many folks would've ever desired. But I was reminded, Tom, of some conver-sations that I've been a part of in Centerville, which is now called Cahokia Heights, in Illinois.

I think for me it's been absolutely vital to include the community and community leaders as collaborators, and borrowing natural science speak as co-investigators. And so, what we have been working on is involving them in articulating the questions that we should be trying to answer as natural scientists; that their voices are literally centered in proposals that we submit for funding.

But the reality is, when I'm there in the community, and hearing and listening, they're tired of talking. They've done the talking; they've talked and talked. They need something to be done. And what I hear is this desperate frustration for redress – we talked about that today – for acknowledgment, for recognition, and for help. Because the reality is that this community is drowning. Whenever it rains, the neighbors have to get boats out of their backyards and rescue each other. They need help. And I think what I'm eager to do is to find ways of listening without burdening, and ways of listening that can guarantee action – and that's a process. But that's what your question got me thinking about.

Audience Member 1

The possibility for governments to recreate colonial structures/processes for the sake of securing communities against climate change seems huge. Are there some positive examples for decision-makers or governments to offer equitable assistance? Does this go beyond effective community engagement to resource allocation?

Meché

I actually had this same sort of question in my work. What is the role of states and governments in both local remediation, mitigation, and adaptation, but then globally? If we acknowledge that so many of these violences are structural, then what kinds of structures might actually be large enough to respond to them? I would love to hear more, Paul, given your experiences in governments, where you've seen some of the most hopeful possibilities in that.

Gallay

I've heard some good things about the way the state of New York is trying to implement its 2019 climate law,[15] which not only proposed decarbonization on a very aggressive schedule that they're doing their best to live up to, but also promised the redress that we talked about, where 40 percent of their investments in climate would be invested in – the phrase they use is "disadvantaged communities." And, they've just come up with the definitions of disadvantages communities – with the partners that I have at New York City

Environmental Justice Alliance, and so many other organizations. They've done it over that same sort of year and a half of talking and actual dialogue that is transparent, and is building trust, and is requesting consent. The early reviews of how that money could be spent are relatively positive.

For a while, it wasn't even sure that it would translate to 40 percent of budgeted funds. New York's going to have a bond act for the environment this year.[16] And, if it passes, it'll be 3 to 4 billion dollars of spending. What New York has announced is that "40% means 40% of the money" and the definitions of disadvantaged communities. Unlike what's going on in Washington right now with Justice 40, where they've been trying to avoid being overturned by the Supreme Court, by trying to fix racial unfairness without mentioning race.

New York, which is a more uniformly blue state, is going there, and is talking about the need to address race and consider race directly, not indirectly. California has 55 percent of its spending of this sort going into these defined disadvantaged communities.[17] There too, they're avoiding the use of racial criteria, but even so, they're getting some good reviews. I think these are early efforts, but they have money behind them. Let's face it, if they don't, it's definitely not going to succeed. So, these may succeed.

Audience Member 2

How do you see building alliances, both international ones and ones that strengthen African/Black and Indigenous communities?

Meché

I think the attention to history and my own work has been important. I actually found a lot of resonance in what Mary was offering earlier. But in particular, finding both sources of inspiration and efforts in the 1960s and 1970s to build Black internationalist solidarities, especially with the Sahel, but also being mindful of the pitfalls.

In my own work, I've found that there is a moment of internationalist mutual aid. Local popup organizations were attempting to provide aid, but not in a formal aid way. Also, offering agricultural expertise from HBCUs around sustainable agriculture and doing mission trips to different parts of the West African Sahel at the invitation of local heads of state. But I think at a specific moment that was captured by the federal government and was woven into official diplomatic channels, making it complicit in a lot of ways in this kind of aid diplomacy that the US was amassing in the 1970s through the United States Agency for International Development (USAID) and different organizations.

I think as much as I've found inspiration in the moment of the 1960s and 1970s, and of thinking about Black global solidarities, there are also so many warning signs about some of the pitfalls of those efforts and perhaps some of the roadblocks to some of those efforts. And I think it's important to hold both at the same time and try to find places to build alliances.

Audience Member 3

I very much appreciate how each panelist has spoken about the power of stories, memories, and narratives, and advocating for social change/justice, and redressing harms. How are each of you bringing critical forms of storytelling into your own work? Scholarship, teaching, digital projects, mapping, more.

McNeil

I can speak briefly about that from a teaching standpoint. I think that one of the most powerful things that I've witnessed in the classroom is actually just giving students primary sources from the era and letting the people who wrote the sources tell the stories themselves. One day, I really want to teach a class solely on what we might call "movement memoirs," because when you look at the autobiographies that activists and organizers from Black Power and Red Power and other social movements of the 1960s and 1970s wrote, they are these amazing texts that are doing so much heavy theorizing work – really outlining what security looks like and what a better world might look like in the eyes of the storyteller.

In terms of my own research and writing, I suppose I am trying to decenter my own voice by paying close attention to the oral histories and primary sources that I draw from. I'm trying to allow these words to drive my interpretations and the frameworks that I develop in my scholarship instead of attempting to fit these sources and their words into my own pre-formulated framework or argument. And this is because, frankly, these writers and organizers have far more brilliant and in-depth insights than I could ever begin to have on my own.

Constantine

I can at least speak to how storytelling plays a role in my work. I teach a course on geographic information systems. I had a student, who was advised by both myself and a colleague who's here with us tonight, who really challenged me to think about mapping maps in an incredible, different way.

The student was from Brooklyn and spent a significant amount of time building a map. They didn't reimagine the places and spaces of his neighborhoods, but in many respects, it recaptured or undid what gentrification was erasing. It recaptured those places and spaces and re-centered them in a way that spoke to his history; the history of his family, and the history of his neighborhood. That really impacted me, and it's playing a role in the way I'm thinking about how we can move beyond what historical map makers have ever intended maps to be served for, and to do something very different with them.

I'm excited to see where this process is going to take us. Most recently we are in collaboration with the Historic Preservation Office here in Williamstown of the Stockbridge-Munsee Mohican Nation. I'm excited to see how digital map making and storytelling through maps can undo erasure and can recapture the various meanings and experience of place that we all share.

SOURCE NOTES

1. "Ali Sets Example." *Chicago Defender (Big Weekend Edition)*, March 15, 1975.
2. Ibid.
3. Ibid.
4. Packtor, Chrissy. "Racial Gaps in Children's Lead Levels." *Public Health Post*, July 13, 2019. www.publichealthpost.org/databyte/racial-gaps-in-childrens-lead-levels/
5. "NJ Environmental Justice Law and Rules." State of New Jersey, n.d. https://dep.nj.gov/ej/policy/
6. Zakirzianova, Zhanna. "New York City Waterfront Development in the Post-Sandy Era: The East Side Coastal Resiliency Project and Community Response." *ETD Collection for Fordham University*, 2021.
7. Odinga, Sekou, Dhoruba bin-Wahad, and Jamal Joseph. *Look For Me in the Whirlwind: From the Panther 21 to 21st-Century Revolutions*. Oakland, CA: PM Press, 2017.
8. Shakur, Afeni, and Jasmine Guy. *Afeni Shakur: Evolution of a Revolutionary*. New York: Simon and Schuster, 2010.
9. Ibid., 14.
10. For more information about the Battle of Hayes Pond, see: The University of North Carolina at Pembroke, "Battle of Hayes Pond: Routing of the KKK." *Museum of the Southeast American Indian* (n.d.). www.uncp.

edu/resources/museum-southeast-american-indian/museum-exhibits/
battle-hayes-pond-routing-kkk

11. Buchanan, Kelly. "Indigenous Rights in New Zealand: Legislation, Litigation, and Protest: In Custodia Legis." *The Library of Congress*, November 18, 2016. https://blogs.loc.gov/law/2016/11/indigenous-rights-in-new-zealand-legislation-litigation-and-protest/

12. Ibid.

13. With "freedom dreams," McNeil is invoking Black Studies scholar Robin D.G. Kelley's important history of the Black radical tradition of the same name. With "survivance," she draws from Native American and Indigenous Studies scholar Gerald Vizenor's theorization of the term. See: Robin D.G. Kelley, *Freedom Dreams: The Black Radical Imagination*. Boston: Beacon Press, 2002; Gerald Vizenor, ed., *Survivance: Narratives of Native Presence*. Lincoln: University of Nebraska Press, 2008.

14. Schneider-Mayerson, Matthew, and Brent Ryan Bellamy. *An Ecotopian Lexicon*. Minneapolis: University of Minnesota Press, 2019.

15. "The Climate Leadership and Community Protection Act of 2019 (CLCPA) commits to 100% zero-emission electricity by 2040, and a reduction of at least 85% below 1990-level GHG emissions by 2050," from Climate Leadership and Community Protection Act (CLCPA), n.d. https://climate.ny.gov/

16. Julien, Sydney, and Laura Rabinow. New York's Environmental Bond Acts. *Rockinist*, April 28, 2022. https://rockinst.org/blog/new-yorks-environmental-bond-acts/

17. "California Climate Investments to Benefit Disadvantaged Communities." *CalEPA*. Accessed July 11, 2023. https://calepa.ca.gov/envjustice/ghginvest/

3

Sovereignties

Brad Lopes, Katy Robinson Hall, Ernest Tollerson,
and moderator Ngoni Munemo

April 12, 2022

Brad Lopes

I'm going to talk to you all about tribal sovereignty and address the right
to self-determination that we as tribal nations have here in what is now the
United States, but also what is now known as Mexico, Canada, and elsewhere
across the globe. We do not necessarily call these locations those names. I
tend to call North America Turtle Island, and the island in which my tribe
is from, which many people know of as Martha's Vineyard, is called Noepe.

Today, there are over 570 federally recognized tribal nations here in what
is now the United States. There is no one Native American group. There
are actually 570-plus independent, sovereign nations within this country's
borders. My nation is one of those. In fact, just two days ago, we marked our
35th anniversary of being a federally recognized tribal nation here, despite
existing in Noepe for over 12,000 years based on archeological records that
we do have. Federal recognition is something that happens to a lot of tribal
nations as we have sought to extend our sovereignty and ensure that our
rights are recognized and that we are respected as people and as the original
inhabitants of this land. Yes, we are still here.

Some of us are unfortunately not in our homelands, but some of us are.
Often, I even encounter people who say they've never met a Native person
east of the Mississippi. They thought that we were all gone. And that is far,
far, far from true. Today we are considered under the United States legal
code as US domestic sovereign nations.[1] And that phrase is interesting
because it's a slight oxymoron, to be both domestic and sovereign, because
to be domestic means that we are within the United States and that we, in
some way, are underneath the United States legal jurisdiction so much so –
and some of you may not know this – federally recognized tribes have tribal

IDs. So not only do I have a state ID for the State of Maine or a social security number for the federal government, but I also have a tribal ID, which is something that I carry around and use as much as possible.

Unfortunately, this is not an even relationship. In fact, the United States' legal system and the Supreme Court have actually cited the papal bills issued by the Pope in a series of decrees in the 1450s and onward as the essential legal justification for the existence of the United States today. In 1823, the papal bills were cited by the Supreme Court in *Johnson v. Mcintosh*, and essentially ruled that Native people here in the United States did not have a right to own land, we only had a right to occupy it.[2]

This is something that still today breaks my heart as a Native person, as somebody who's very connected to the land of which I'm a part. In our language and in our culture, we are a part of the land.

I said to somebody the other day: there are clay cliffs that exist in Aquinnah and they're spiritual. They're a part of us. When those cliffs eventually crash into the sea because of erosion and climate change, for many of us, it will feel like the end of the world. And that's true because it's an extension of who we are. Now, there are tons and tons of non-federally recognized tribes here in the United States. Some are recognized by states, and some aren't, unfortunately. Those that aren't recognized by the federal government primarily do not have access to many of the rights and funding and other sources that federally recognized nations do. And there are some other examples currently here in Maine, the four Wabanaki tribes, Penobscot, Passamaquoddy, Maliseet, and Mi'kmaq are currently engaged in looking at the 1980 Maine Settlement Act[3] and trying to pass legislation that would reverse some of the decisions made in that Act.

That Act, unfortunately, took away part of the sovereignty of the tribal nations here in what is now Maine in Wabanaki territory. As a result of that decision, the Wabanaki tribes essentially became wards of the State of Maine. They are basically treated as children without parents, and the State of Maine has, unfortunately, used this at times to its advantage regarding certain legal matters and certain matters of cultural practices and lifeways. This is something that has happened in my nation in Massachusetts as well in the past. Now, when we're talking about federal recognition and tribal sovereignty, it's important to recognize too, that there are Indigenous people in what is now the United States who don't want to be federally recognized. I'm talking primarily of some Indigenous Hawaiians who would much rather be independent than be federally recognized.

Another thing that comes up with tribal sovereignty is not just this right to self-determination, this right to govern ourselves – we have our own constitution, we have our own elections. We have our own governments – but it's also this right to cultural practices and lifeways. You'll be surprised to learn that for many Native folks, we did not actually have religious freedom until the 1970s when the Native American Religious Freedom Act was passed.[4] Prior to that, there were many, many ceremonies or practices that actually may have been legally justified as outlawed.

Another thing is access to sustainable fishing and game sources. We are seeing consistent pollution, consistent threats to our sustainable living sources. Here in Maine, the Penobscot Nation has fought a decade-plus-long conflict with the State of Maine, and perhaps potentially taking it to the Supreme Court of the United States, for their access to the Penobscot River.

Just like the Aquinnah cliffs are a part of us, the Penobscot River is a relative, it's an extension of the Penobscot people. They have fished on this river for thousands of years in a sustainable respectful way and they are constantly faced with issues of pollution and the misuse and mismanagement of species along the river. We are also dealing with environmental protections. For example, in the Bay Area of Massachusetts, there have been some notions of possibly even nuclear waste being dumped in some places, places that might affect Native ecosystems, in which we are still ingrained. And speaking of nuclear waste, unfortunately Indigenous nations have often had to deal with environmental attack, whether it's actually been here and what is now the United States or in some places such as Southeast Asia or the Pacific Islands – in the case of the latter they dealt with nuclear waste being deposited largely by the US army, in some cases by the Soviet or Russian military, and they have become receptacles, sometimes becoming unlivable.

Another way that we have been able to reassert our cultural sovereignty is by recovering languages and advocating for language practices. We speak Wampanoag, and it is a language that has been recovered, thanks to the work of Jessie Little Doe Baird and folks at MIT and a bunch of people who have been involved with the Wampanoag Language Reclamation Project. Today, we have a school, the Weetumuw School, which teaches Wampanoag for grades one through three, and it also teaches a lot of our cultural practices.[5] Additionally, we are also seeking to advocate more and more for our practices and our holidays – which you might call them holidays, we call them ceremonies perhaps, sometimes. This is an issue I run into as well as a public-school teacher. I do not have any Christianized, or traditional American holidays that I practice anymore. Because of that, there are some holidays such as Cranberry Day in Wampanoag that I need to necessarily ask for time off. It's a time period we've traditionally used to collect cranberries and be with our community. Strawberry Thanksgiving would be another time period, or the equinoxes or solstices.

Often, we've had to reassert our own sovereignty in our own backyard. One example of this is in Mashpee Massachusetts, where my brothers and sisters of the Mashpee Wampanoag live and have lived for thousands and thousands of years. There's a great book and a documentary about a period during this time, it was called the *Mashpee Nine*, similarly named to the *Central Park Five* [documentary by Kevin Burns].[6] The Mashpee Nine were Mashpee tribal members and other Wampanoag tribal members who were targeted by the Mashpee Police Department. Unfortunately, we're exposed to police brutality and discrimination. As a child, I was told, "Don't drive while Indian." That's true for many of us who grew up in this kind of environment, in this culture in the United States today.

Another thing I'd like to talk about is our rights to our children and our ancestors. I bring this up because I knew I had to say something about two pieces of legislation that should be known by every American citizen. The first one is ICWA, Indian Child Welfare Act.[7] After a lot of child agencies were, unfortunately, placing Native kids, not with Native families, primarily with largely white families in the 1960s, 1950s, and prior to that, into the 1970s as well, ICWA was passed.

ICWA basically makes them go through the process of identifying, if there is a tribal family that this child should live with? Is there anybody within the tribe that they could live with? And then you go outside the tribe, recognizing that many of us have a hundred aunties. I have a hundred different kinds of people around our nation who I would not hesitate to leave a child with, a child of mine, which would be the dearest thing to my heart. And that's how a lot of our cultures work, especially here in Algonquin territories on the East Coast. And in a lot of these cases, we want to make sure that the child is protected. ICWA is currently being challenged by the State of Texas, which has described it as being racially based, and so, unfortunately, this law could potentially go away.

As some of you may also be aware, this is tied to boarding school experiences that happened earlier on. Some went right up into the 1990s in which Native children were sometimes forcibly taken away. So even when we're talking about tribal sovereignty, sometimes we're talking about just the right to assert the decisions that we make over our own family, our own kids, and sometimes our ancestors.

The other piece of legislation I'd like to talk about is NAGPRA, which is the Native American Graves Protection and Repatriation Act.[8] This act was passed in the 1990s, and was essential for protecting Native grave sites and Native ceremonial objects. Prior to this law being passed, unfortunately some of us had our ancestors on display in museums. Some of us had spiritual objects on display in museums. Unfortunately, there are still institutions that are not compliant with NAGPRA.

There is something you can do to address tribal sovereignty in your area, no matter where you are. And that is to do very much how we started off this meeting, which is to acknowledge whose land you're on. Land acknowledgments have kind of become very popular – and I use that phrase loosely. There's something that I've been asked to write, I've written some, and I would just like to share with you all that Land Acknowledgment should and can lead to very authentic relationships with Native people and their people that are currently living there today. And this can be done in a variety of ways. Brown University and Mystic have done a good job of putting together what will be eventually an amazing exhibit. I'm a part of the committee that's planning that exhibit. To me, this is an example of an authentic relationship. It is an example of: we acknowledge this land, but we are also working toward telling this story or contributing in some way.

I always say Land Acknowledgments are just a baby step. If you are curious about whose land you currently live on, you can head to the website native-land.ca.[9] It's also an app on your phone that you can get, and it will tell you effectively whose land you're on and this database is consistently updated. You can contribute to it yourself as well. And they're currently actually working on Africa, and they have some other places mapped out. The Americas are very detailed, very mapped out.

People forget there are Indigenous folks in northern Finland, northern Japan, and more. Just know that whoever or wherever you are, there is likely a Native folk, or a Native tribe, or a Native nation very close by. And I think that's important to be aware of as well as how you can work toward authentic settler and Indigenous relationships that respect tribal sovereignty.

Katy Hall

I want to share a story tonight about a lawyer-educator learning humility, and then end with what I hope is a shared vision for a just future that's grounded in traditional values and knowledge and authentically collaborative work. Essential to our experiential educational model at Williams-Mystic, we are fortunate to travel and meet incredible leaders in communities all along our coast, many bearing the direct impacts of climate change. Amid facing dire sea level rise, and a steady loss of their coastal lands, their homes, and their livelihoods, these frontline coastal community leaders make time to graciously share their passion and their expertise with our students, educating and inspiring all of us.

They are tenacious. They are brave, and they are generous to the core. And in these coastal areas, all of which are facing disproportionate impacts from our changing climate, the leaders we engage with also share their sense of grief and loss for what they thought was the future of their community in a place that is sacred, beloved, and intricately tied to who they are. It is powerful learning. It is a shared intimacy, and it's part of the trusted relationships that we try to forge and honor with our field seminar partners.

A few years ago, the Chief of an Indigenous community in southeastern Louisiana, one of our field seminar sites, reached out to us and asked if we could work with them to help them assert their legal rights as a sovereign community, hoping to thwart persistent biases and discriminatory practices against their community, which are now hugely exacerbated by climate change. Lack of sovereignty is akin to invisibility, and being invisible is heart-wrenching. It's cruel, and it's untenable. When you are facing the kinds of changes to your environment that threaten everything you know; your livelihood, your way of life, your traditions, your cultures, your very sense of your place in the world, it is the painful and true reality of lack of self-determination, and it is real. Frontline coastal Indigenous communities in the US, including those along the bayous of southeastern Louisiana, bear a long and painful legacy of discrimination, which is perpetuated by a lack of agency and lack of self-determination, particularly in climate adaptation and decision-making. They suffer from deficient access to robust disaster funding, disaster mitigation planning and a true lack of sovereignty that persists along our country's coastlines today. As a result, they are facing difficult decisions about the future of their communities, their homes, their lives, and their way of being.

As a friend and colleague of the tribal Chief of this Louisiana bayou Indigenous community, I shared her passion and was eager to work with her, to help support her work to correct long-standing injustices. And as a litigator, I also was anxious to roll up my sleeves and help her engage in what I imagined would be a full-throttled assault against these persistent injustices faced by her community. The cause was urgent and important.

We dove into the work together, building a strong legal case addressing federal discrimination, seeking to increase the tribe's self-determination, honor its sovereignty, and seek redress for long-standing harms caused to the Chief's tribal community. We had a shared passion for the work, and we were guided by the end goal, which was solely informed by the clearly articulated needs and desires of the Chief's community. But I was also guided by the bedrock mindset of a litigator which is to be a tireless and zealous advocate for my client; that "all-in" mentality that drives and energizes my lawyering, with a focus on result-driven outcomes.

However, in the zealousness of my advocacy, I overlooked a basic tenant of the kind of true collaboration that's necessary for a lawyer–client relationship when working to increase and honor a client's tribal sovereignty. I needed to stop and consider if the form and manner of my zealous advocacy was how my client, the tribal Chief, wanted to proceed in the case.

Although we both were working toward the same outcome, applying the litigation mindset, and deploying the typical tools of litigation such as discovery and motion practice were not in line with the manner and traditions of my Indigenous client's form of leadership. Although our work and passion for the outcome was aligned, I had much to learn on how to get to that outcome while honoring Indigenous ways of knowing and working.

I shared the Chief's desire to attain her community's goal for sovereignty, for true agency, and the self-determination that results from both. But I didn't recognize that the manner or the processes that I naturally leaned on to achieve that outcome was wholly out of sync with just about everything my Indigenous client valued. Guided by the Chief's patient and unexhausted mentoring and teaching, I gradually understood that my litigation mindset and the tools I was accustomed to deploying in my zealous advocacy were not in line with how the tribe functioned and not the kind of support she wanted. Over weeks of late-night conversations, the Chief and I discussed our growing legal case, and strategized over the process and manner of proceeding in the case. I leaned heavily on my "take-no-prisoners" approach to the litigation, seeking her permission to make discovery requests, interview tribal members and leaders for more evidence, and make further petitions to the court. During one of these sessions as I listed some of the litigation tools we could deploy, the Chief stopped me. With enormous patience and grace that still inspires me today, she simply said,

Yes, yes, Katy, this is painful. This long-standing discrimination that we are fighting together, it's hurting my community. And yes, absolutely,

Katy, I share the same burning desire that you are advancing to me for this just result. But achieving that justice, that sovereignty, that voice, it can't come at the expense of our community's shared cornerstone and key values of peace, love, and light.

These values were, and are, my client's tribal community's guiding bedrock principles. These principles guided every facet of the Chief's leadership, her decision-making and how her community engaged with each other and their surrounding communities and government leaders. I could not imagine how the Chief and her community could retain a sense of peace, love, and light while enduring and fighting the persistent injustices faced by her community. In fact, considering how to apply these principles to our litigation turned everything I knew about being a zealous advocate on its head. Peace, love, and light – they're not exactly lawyering terms; honestly, they're not. They don't normally frame the work of a zealous advocate litigating and advocating on behalf of a client. That is not what guides the zealous advocate lawyer.

We don't do our work in the absence of these values, but they are not the guiding principles to zealous lawyering. However, for the Chief's community, a community that was fighting for persistent and resilient sovereignty for their future, the Chief believed that framing our work as a battle was not going to lay the groundwork needed to sustain the strength, resilience, capacity, and credibility for her community to envision and achieve a just future in this incredibly changing and unpredictable time of climate change. The journey itself, not just the end goal of attaining a just future, had to walk that path crafted from the cornerstone values of the community; those of peace, love, and light. For my contribution to be useful to support the Chief's work, I had to set aside the zeal of my advocacy, the zeal of my training, and ground our work fully in her community's values.

Together, in that grounding, we have continued to support the Chief's work to correct and mitigate flawed and unjust decision-making by the federal and state governments. We continue to support her successful promotion of her tribe's agency as well as their meaningful participation in processes that are critical to her community's vision for what their just future will be in a time of a vastly changing environment and climate. And we're doing it in a way that truly continues to honor fully collaborative work. And while I still bring my passionate lawyering to support the Chief's goals for true and lasting sovereignty, we call that lawyering what it truly is, zealous collaboration.

Ernest Tollerson

How many of us are taking off October 18 to celebrate an important human rights milestone? If October 18 doesn't ring a bell, that illustrates how low water sovereignty ranks in the world of compound crises with the existential crises of wealth and in income inequality, climate emergency, and woefully dysfunctional democracies under attack at home and overseas – all this can be forgiven for not planning to observe the 50th anniversary of the Clean Water Act, formerly known as the Federal Water Pollution Control Act.[10] It's not really important whether you celebrate the 50th anniversary of the Clean Water Act. It's important for folks on the Eastern seaboard and in the 13,000-plus square miles of the Hudson watershed to assess the state of water sovereignty, and then have a long-term plan of action. Like the state of the nation, the level of water sovereignty is not good.

The Clean Water Act, signed into law in 1972, envisioned achieving the following goals: "to make all US waterways fishable and swimmable by 1983," "To have zero water pollution discharged by 1985," and third, "to prohibit discharge of toxic amounts of toxic pollutants." None of those congressional goals have been achieved.[11] In our region, and nationally, gains have been made in reducing point sources of pollution, but when it comes to non-point sources – think agriculture, industry, large and small stormwater runoff from urban suburban communities – not that much has been achieved. Most of us, if not all of us, are within walking, biking, or driving distance of some egregious example of our water sovereignty deficit; a deficit, which hits low-income, low-wealth communities and Indigenous communities harder than the middle class, harder than the wealthy.

I want to focus tonight just on three brief examples. The waterfront city of Newburgh continues to get its drinking water from New York City's water system because Newburgh's primary drinking water source, Lake Washington, remains contaminated with a firefighting foam used by the military at Stewart Airport. The firefighting foam contains the toxic PFAS chemical, popularly known as a forever chemical. The timing of the cleanup is totally at the discretion of the Pentagon. It took this ongoing, clean drinking water crisis to make it clear that Newburgh's residents, predominantly people of color, lack water sovereignty.

As a city, Newburgh doesn't control Lake Washington or the runoffs that end up in Lake Washington. Nor does Newburgh control its second source of drinking water, Browns Pond. To save Browns Pond, Newburgh and its allies, including Riverkeeper, are working to come up with a watershed protection plan, a plan that would be similar to New York City's landmark watershed protection agreement signed in the 1990s. Note that this first example has quite a cast of villains: the US military in the region, the Pentagon, and suburban development pressures that could befoul Brown's Pond.

Now the second example. In the popular imagination, the Hudson River occupies a rarefied space in culture and history, rightly or wrongly. The Hudson-inspired painters who became emblematic of the Hudson River School. The Hudson provided literary inspiration for Washington Irving, Edith Wharton, Mark Twain, Walt Whitman, and many others.

There's also the Hudson River Pier where Frederick Douglass probably landed when he escaped from slavery in Maryland. Hudson waterfront communities served as stops in the Underground Railroad. Sojourner Truth escaped from slavery in the Shawangunks' region. And now, folks living in the Hudson watershed – which is a lot of people, north of 10 million people – are beginning to learn the Lenape, Munsee, and Mohawk words for "the river that runs both ways." The Hudson's significance, however, is overshadowed by its dismal ecological status. For some 200 miles between the Albany-Troy region, all the way down to the battery at the tip of Manhattan, remember, the river remains a long-winding Superfund site. Even though General Electric finally performed one round of dredging in 40 miles of the river above Troy, the PCBs remained a threat to human health and the health of the river and tributary ecosystems.

GE's dredging had little to no effect on PCBs below the Troy dam. Now, talks have opened on the need for a cleanup of 150 miles below the dam. The tidal section of the Hudson is the part of the Hudson known as the Hudson Estuary. EPA is considering a voluntary study instead of a remedial investigation, a remedial investigation would have more teeth. And that distinction between a voluntary study and a remedial investigation, it's just another demonstration of a water sovereignty gap. And, as we all know, it'll be generations before fish from the Hudson will be safe to consume.

A third and final example of water sovereignty deficit. New York City's water supply, known as the Cat Del system, serves more than 8 million New Yorkers and folks in Gotham's Metro region. It enjoys a reputation as the "champagne" of potable water supplies.

A tiny share of it, the Croton system, goes through a filtration plant, the rest is unfiltered. But there's an ugly backstory; New York City's Department of Environmental Protection, New York City DEP, routinely dumps turbid water, muddy water from the city's Ashokan Reservoir into the lower Esopus Creek, which flows into the main stem of the Hudson. New York City DEP releases muddy water from the Ashokan to preserve drinking water quality. But the release of turbid water shifts the cost and consequences of turbid water onto the backs of lower Esopus communities, farmers, and businesses. The culprit, New York City DEP, hasn't inadequately managed the Catskill Mountains sediments that wind up in the Ashokan Reservoir. After a decade of agitation, New York's Department of Environmental Conservation, New York State DEC, has just ordered the city to find alternatives to dumping sediment-laden water from the Ashokan into the lower Esopus.

Now these and other water sovereignty deficits – in the Hudson, on the Eastern seaboard, and elsewhere across the nation – could be with us for another 50 years, unless we act and begin to see ourselves as citizens and stewards of watersheds, not just citizens and voters in political jurisdictions. The centrality of ecological citizenship and stewardship got a boost last year when New York State voters overwhelmingly approved amending the state Constitution's Article 1 to make the right to clean air, and clean water in a healthful environment, a constitutional right, part of New York State's Bill of Rights.[12]

This new constitutional right, which mirrors those in Pennsylvania and Montana, will only be significant if folks who want to achieve just outcomes for people and ecosystems activate that right. Perhaps during the Q&A, we can grapple with the question of applying a water sovereignty lens to the USD 2.6 billion New York State is supposed to receive over five years for water infrastructure.

While my remarks have been devoted to water sovereignty, I did want to give a shout-out to one intersectional sovereignty issue we also ought to be focused on in this decade and the next, and that's energy sovereignty, or what many people call energy democracy.

Hall

I have a follow-up question for Brad regarding the ICWA, the Indian Child Welfare Act. Are you seeing more generalized advocacy with all of the recognized tribal nations inputting the Child Welfare Act and justice in that realm to the forefront in their communities?

Lopes

Absolutely. I have seen a lot of people, especially ever since the motion out of Texas kind of came, advocating for ICWA. ICWA is something that a lot of Native people from a variety of tribal nations have advocated for, whenever it has been threatened. In fact, there is a great documentary called

Dawnland.[13] Dawnland is a traditional name that sometimes you might hear either in Wabanaki, Wampanoag, or Piqua – we all kind of call this area, the place where the sun first comes up, Dawnland, the land of the dawn, the land of the sun. *Dawnland* is about how some kids in Maine were still taken from their families, even with the passing of ICWA. The State of Maine did conduct what is called a Truth and Reconciliation Committee, similar to what South Africa did after Apartheid. And the goal of this committee was to hear from these stories, hear from these people, and to collect that information, and to make a series of assessments to the State of Maine. There were several tribal members, but also non-tribal members involved in that. There was a significant amount of advocacy that came from that, and that has continued to come from that. Wabanaki Reconciliation, Engagement, Advocacy, Change, and Healing (REACH) is another group that is constantly advocating for ICWA protections and for knowledge about ICWA too, and ICWA practices.[14] Each tribe has somebody responsible, almost solely, for what goes on with ICWA just because of how important it is.

Tollerson

Brad, you briefly mentioned Massachusetts and the dumping of nuclear waste and waters off of Massachusetts. Can you just bring us up to date on that? Constantly, I find that when you're thinking about either estuary rivers or the ocean right off of an estuary, it is very hard to get people to focus on the web of life in the estuary or in the ocean because they can't see what's going on there and they discount its importance.

Lopes

Absolutely. I have seen most of it on social media so far. A lot of it has been efforts to prevent a proposed dumping of what I believe is like nuclear waste, but also what just appears to be a chemical waste of some sort. And so, one of the things that I know Herring Pond, which is another Wampanoag community has been heavily involved in is also the dumping, too, as well, or the potential to stop the dumping. I forget which company has been responsible for that particular dumping, or proposed dumping, I should say, but it wouldn't be the first time that Native folks and waterways have been targeted. In the 1990s, a lot of tribes were asked to take on nuclear waste.

Ngoni Munemo

I was struck, Katy, in your presentation by the juxtaposition you drew between the zealousness of advocacy, your training as a lawyer and the guiding values and ethos of the community you were working with: love, peace, and light. Could you describe in a little bit more detail what your lawyering now looks like as a result of its interaction and encounter with a very different disposition?

Hall

The first thing I do is I keep a sticky note with me all the time because honestly it is a matter of retraining. We're required to be under our code of ethics, we're obligated to be a zealous advocate. It is actually something that we can be disciplined for in the bar if we do not retain and work toward zealous advocacy. But what that looks like for different clients, it's going to look differently.

While we grounded the outcome, and the goal of the outcome, of increased sovereignty in agency that was grounded 100 percent in the value of the client in the community, which is the norm, anyhow, for this type of work, what wasn't the norm was that normally clients leave it to you to get there.

They leave it to the lawyer to find, to put together all the pieces of the litigation puzzle to get to the result. In this case, that was so critically important that she understood well, what does that look like? And you know what? It can't look like that. It can't look like barnstorming. I had, for example, the idea that I was going to have this particular, very laser-focused evidence and affidavits, and all of these things that were really supercharged for this outcome. And she was like, "Oh, there's a whole different way we're going to look at this. We're going to get to the outcome, but that's not going to work for the longevity of our credibility with the sovereignty that we're hoping to gain."

That was really different for me because I feel like these are the tools that get the job done. And now it's like, I can't use the tools? But it wasn't that. It was, we're going to use the tools, but they're going to be shaped differently, they're going to be shaped by our value of the love and the light. The words are going to be different. They're going to feel different. We're going to get rid of the edge that is customary for litigators to use. And it didn't in any way take away the opportunity to reach the desired outcome. And we have achieved some of the goals and outcomes that we wanted. And it was really pivotal for me as an attorney, as an advocate, to be thinking about this really holistic process, this holistic way of looking at the practice. A holistic way of looking at the work.

It is all in the journey. I used to feel that this is the path because this is how you get stuff done. I don't think about it like that anymore. It is a bigger holistic picture. When you take the process and you also ground that in the values of the community you're collaborating with, it's totally different. As practitioners understand, we ground the desired outcome and the goal in the values of the community, but that's not enough. How you get there also has to be 100 percent how the community wants to get there.

Munemo

I have a two-part question for Brad. For those of us who are less familiar, what does it take for Indigenous and Native communities to become federally recognized? Brad mentioned that there are 570-plus recognized nations, but many which are not. What does it take for recognition? And then, Brad, could you say a little bit more about that curious designation of US domestic sovereign nation member? As a political scientist, this sounds a little bit like an oxymoron. How do you work within those parameters which seem to both give with one hand and take away with the other?

Lopes

That's a beautiful way of describing it: give with one hand, take with the other. I've heard tribal federal recognition sometimes referred to as having your shackle cut from your ankle, but to be weighed down with a weighted ball anyway. The federal recognition process is quite complex and can be quite lengthy. From my understanding, we were working on it for at least like a decade before we were actually able to become officially federally recognized. And it requires a lot of legal counsel, requires a lot of assistance from both the state and your tribal, historic preservation officers.

We had to prove, for example, that we have existed in this area continuously for 5000, 12,000 years. We had to come up with an archeological record of ourselves, which we know already was there and already existed, but we had to prove it in a way that Western governments, Western sciences would also accept and honor and recognize. The first part was actually proving our existence as Native folk. Native nations were also largely given options on how to deal with their membership afterwards. There are primarily two methods that have been recognized and utilized.

One's a genealogical record. And one is notoriously blood quantum, judging how much of your blood is Native American, which is unfortunately a very Western concept in a lot of ways and borderlines, for some of us, the concept of eugenics. Additionally, we use genealogy. I have our family history mapped out to the 1700s at least. And we know everybody, it's kind of a joke that we're all related in Aquinnah. In some weird ways, a lot of us are. Additionally, we had to go through a land settlement claim afterward, so we actually had to give up territory within Aquinnah for them to agree to our federal recognition.

This includes some sacred sites as well, as very important sites. The first one that always comes to mind is Toad Rock, which is a rock shaped very much like a toad. We say that it's Mashap's, and we often tell stories about his pet toad. And when Mashap left the island, he became solidified. And we used to use it as a community meeting center, but also a place where you could leave notes for other tribal members. It was like a pre-post office. We went through the Land Settlement Act and had to clarify, what is our land that is being held in trust? We don't have a true and blue reservation as the US legal system would call it, we have land held in trust. The land is still technically within the State of Massachusetts's ownership in some way.

It's very, very tricky navigating that kind of relationship. For the second question, it is very much an oxymoron. It's very much a strange concept. And because of that, it's oftentimes even the product of jokes for us. What does it mean to be domestic and sovereign? I think of one scene from *Smoke Signals*[15] where they're driving off of the reservation in the movie, and one of them makes a comment, "Oh, you're going to America, that's as foreign as it gets." And it's true in a lot of ways. For example, I saw a person speaking Penobscot on a *Netflix* show. Instead of saying "Penobscot" or "Native language" or "Indigenous language," [*Netflix* stated] "language," or "speaking foreign." That was like a hit on the head because I sat there and I said, "Well, English is actually the foreign language we're going to get through here."

… I think about it often. It's very paternalistic. We are seen in many ways, or at least in my opinion, as the children of the federal government. They couldn't get rid of us, so they paternalized us in a lot of ways. COVID-19 was probably a good example of the trickiness of the situation because a lot of funding became available and a lot of our communities were hit very, very hard. We did need to depend on federal funding to survive. It's kind of these illusions of choice that we're constantly faced with because of our status.

Hall

Brad, you mentioned this with losing some of the cliffs of the lands out on the islands in terms of erosion and climate change. The seven criteria that a tribal community has to prove, includes as one, that the community has inhabited a specific area that their community has been in this place and that the places that they have been are underwater.

In many of these communities, there are these preposterous criteria, developed by a colonizing nation for these communities to have to jump through these hoops are exceedingly burdensome, but they're also 100 percent out of line with climate change. It is exceedingly difficult to meet these criteria at this time without addressing or acknowledging these massive changes to our environment, including the absolute loss of land and place.

Many of these communities in our United States have been pushed into these fringe areas of these swamps and these communities down in the bayou in particular, in the southeastern part of the country, that land is disappearing at a rate of a football field every hour. And the land loss in those communities is far and away in excess of the land loss rate of other communities that are not disproportionately impacted. It is just a one-two punch constantly, and then to try to achieve these criteria that are, I just don't know what people they're made for.

Munemo

I'm wondering how do we mobilize around these concepts and ideas like water sovereignty, and energy sovereignty, when it looks like as citizens of this country, we are blind to the legislation and the basis on which we might actually organize. I think many of us can think back to the mobilization around access to clean drinking water that happened in the aftermath of Flint [Michigan, 2014-]. Major catastrophes, yes, but until such a time it seems like we are otherwise ignorant. I'd be curious to hear from Ernest in terms of the work that your group is doing around these issues.

Tollerson

One entry point is to follow the money. One of the things that's come out of Washington that the Congress and Biden were able to achieve was these billions and billions in infrastructure spending. New York State's share of that infrastructure spending will be something scored as, something like 2.6 billion over five years. So, north of 500 million is coming into the state for water infrastructure. The question becomes, particularly if you apply a water sovereignty lens, how's that going to be spent? Is it going to be wasted? Will that spending get rid of all lead service lines going into homes with young children and into schools? We all know about lead and the impact of lead on the development of a child in the womb, and of course, a child from birth to about age 5. Lead is not something you want any child to have to deal with.

If you care about water quality, you care about the conditions of the waterways near you and ones that you admire and can get to, you want to know how that money's going to be spent and you want to put pressure on both your local officials and your officials in Albany to get an accounting. The amount of money for water infrastructure in the Biden Infrastructure Law, I believe totals about $15 billion. That $15 billion is thought to apply against the problem that's more like $45 billion. Once again, the money flows in, but how much of the problem will be solved region-to-region since you know that the appropriation coming out of Washington can only address a third of the problem?

That gives people – at a local, regional, and state scale – something to organize around. If the federal government is giving you a third of what you need in infrastructure funding to get rid of lead lines, you want to ask the governor and the legislature to come up with the other two-thirds. And, in a country that's failing to collect taxes from people in corporations that could be paying taxes, there are places to get the money. That's certainly one way.

Joy James

Could you speak a little bit more about ways of building alliances between and among Indigenous communities and Black communities?

Lopes

In Martha's Vineyard, we have a very, very rich Black community. We also have a very rich Wampanoag community. There's a very rich variety of communities on the Vineyard.

There's not only a lot of vulnerabilities that can be highlighted but a lot of strength, too. The entire whaling industry, in my opinion, of New England is built on the backs of Indigenous, Black, and Afro-Indigenous people.

For example, Paul Cuffe was a very famous whaler.[16] Paul would usually only keep a crew of Black and Wampanoag, or Black and Indigenous sailors. It's important to also recognize that Paul was also recognized, and welcome, and considered in many ways to be Wampanoag.

When we're talking about some of these sailors, and these whalers, too, as well, some of them were sharing that identity of being both Indigenous and Black. It's my great, great, great-grandparents, where the name Vanderhoop first pops up. And if you've been on the island, you have probably met a Vanderhoop. There are many of them in our tribe, and Vanderhoop, many people will point out, seems like a Dutch last name, or has Dutch roots. It's because the name comes from Suriname and it comes from when one of them moved up into the Vineyard and married my great-great-grandmother. They had an Underground Railroad stop on the island.

Our tribe was very intricately involved in helping people escape slavery. Largely, it had to do with being on the island, because we could hide people much more easily on the island. And we, ourselves, had always been enslaved in some way. It's something that we tried to talk about a lot in our own exhibit we published this past year at the Aquinnah Cultural Center. We now know of at least 2 million Indigenous slaves. We're talking about – one thing that people don't know is, for example, why does Tisquantum (known as "Squanto") know English? It's because he has already been to England. He'd been enslaved in England, and Spain, as had Epenow. Epenow was from our island.

Epenow, eventually, was able to convince them that there is gold as far as you can see in the Vineyard. The English brought him back to the island. And when he is within sight of the island, he jumps off the boat, and swims back to the island, and there are people waiting for him, and he later becomes a leader on the island. There's a lot of ways to use stories like this, and a lot of similarities. I'm working with Akeia de Barros Gomes and the exhibition committee through Brown–Mystic, their partnership, to really help tell some of these stories.

The ocean can be many things. It's an extension of who we are as Wampanoag people, but it's also the same water that carried us away from our home. There's Wampanoag people in Barbados, for example, because of the British slave trade. For many West Africans and Central Africans, even though many of the ports were in West Africa, people were kidnapped from all across the African continent, and brought to West Africa on slave ships.

There are many, many things that the ocean represents; death, and genocide, but also in a lot of ways, it's part of our cultures, both in West Africa and here on the east coast of Turtle Island. It's something that can connect us in life, as well. There are a lot of opportunities for our communities to come together and build very effective alliances, understanding that we often share many of the same struggles, even when it's through different perspectives, and different standpoints, and understanding our relationship. Where do we fit in, in this grand scheme of what is the United States? Where do we fit in? I'm not sure if Indigenous people or even Black people, or even just Afro-Indigenous people, were a part of the long-term vision of the United States in a lot of ways. But we're here, and we're still surviving. We're thriving in many, many ways.

That's why I believe there needs to be much more education around both Black history and also Indigenous history of the United States. I think that's another way to build very effective alliances, too, to tell a more truthful history, a real history.

Tollerson

At Riverkeeper, one of our recent board members is Chief Dwaine Perry of the Ramapough Lenape. The Chief is a moving force behind a new spiritual center in the region, which I think that the spiritual center will end up being a place where a lot of people who are not Indigenous, whether they're Black or Hispanic or people of color, the mainstream community will get to kind of engage with Indigenous communities on the terms of the Indigenous community.

I can't underestimate the value of having Chief Perry on Riverkeeper's board because that's essential to Riverkeeper deepening its relations with Indigenous groups in Canada who have to deal with Hydro-Québec.[17] The whole battle that's going on now in New York State over bringing greener, cleaner electrons into the state, how do they get there? Are some of the projects proposed reasonable projects when you think about their upstream impact on Indigenous people in Canada where, given demand, Hydro-Québec might end up seizing more land to build more dams, which would be bad for those Indigenous communities in Canada?

Hall

Touching back to Joy's question, and on the federal recognition process, as one example of a way to build alliance within the communities is to have a system within the federal government that doesn't pit one community against the other through a political process.

Brad, you said it took your community ten years to be recognized. The communities that I'm working with are in their 21st year of filing for tribal recognition. That's absurd, but it comes to the same thing where there's strength in these communities that's beautiful, and to honor the cohesiveness of that strength. I think the political, the legal system has to honor it. This political system that's been created for a time that does not exist now. There has to be a change in that system, and in that process, and in those laws because that change can foster, and celebrate the diverse strengths of these communities.

Lopes

I'm a huge advocate of a national reconciliation commission, a national federal reconciliation to address policies toward Indigenous folks, but also policies toward Black folks, and a variety of others, as well. I was just working on a film that's about Indigenous people who are reclaiming, and bringing water back to Manzanar, which was an internment camp for the Japanese Americans from Second World War.

It's a very powerful alliance and collaboration between those people who are descendants of the folks who were, in my opinion very unjustifiably, put into camps, and the Indigenous folks who have traditionally called that land home but have since seen much of that water diverted elsewhere to go to large city centers. An amazing example of alliance and how alliance can lead to these kinds of reconciliatory moments where we're able to reconcile the past. We're able to tell the truth. South Africa today still has many, many issues, but at the same time, South Africa acknowledged, through Desmond Tutu, and all the other folks involved, that before they could heal, they needed to tell the truth. That included victims and perpetrators. I think the same thing needs to happen in the United States.

Audience Member 1

For Katy: Do you find that you now take that different mode of lawyering to your other clients, not just this community?

Audience Member 2

For Brad: Can you share a little bit of how Martha's Vineyard is engaging with the now reasserted recognition and thinking about the treatment of Black folks in this country as a result of Black Lives Matter?

Hall

Yes, there is a shift in terms of holistic practice. It has shifted my mindset, but really importantly it has added more urgency to the work itself, but also urgency to the way I educate the students that are going to carry this forward. Holistic listening is not just the ethic of peace, love and light; it's the way in which it was imparted to me. I was carrying something into this collaboration that wasn't as collaborative as it could have been, it just was an unconscious part of me, the role of the advocate.

Tuning into how you come into those relationships, and how you come into issues that are fraught with controversy, and hearing really disparate perspectives, but also the way the process is carried out, entering into that with a different mindset. Entering into it with a big dose of humility in the backpack, and in your pockets, and in your mug, and carrying it with you all the time. That's really the urgent message that I'm still learning, but hoping to learn, to continue to learn, to be able to pass that on to our students, as well as carry it in the work. The students are the key to the future – that's the most important thing, is how we can communicate that to our students because they are everything, and what they take out, and away from their education is going to make all the difference going forward.

Lopes

One of the cool things that has happened in the Vineyard, in the last five to ten years, is that there have been a lot more initiatives from the variety of non-profits on the island to actually acknowledge and celebrate the diversity of Martha's Vineyard. To acknowledge that Martha's Vineyard is one of the most diverse communities in New England, and how it has actually served as a refuge, not only for my people, but for other people throughout history. That's very important to celebrate and to acknowledge, whether it's the Martha's Vineyard diversity commission, or even just the work that I've done through the Aquinnah Cultural Center in the very short time I've been there consistently, have people been reaching out, have been working on collaborations that may take a while for us to unveil.

What it's doing is building very strong alliances, and leading toward what I believe will be very, very powerful narratives to tell a new history of Martha's Vineyard, a history that's inclusive, and a history that's honest and true. A history that acknowledges our presence on the island and acknowledges many of the people who are brought to the island either by force, or by choice, and have since also viewed it as a refuge.

During the second Anglo-Algonquin War – which is a phrase I used to indicate King Phillip's War, many of our people in Aquinnah stayed in Aquinnah, and did not engage in the conflict directly. We treated the island like a refuge, to hide away. And many, many people still love our place because of that. Many of you are probably familiar with how much Martha's Vineyard is a vacation spot. And since then, it has largely, unfortunately, become in some places too gentrified for many of our Wampanoag youth, and for many, many youths from the global majority.

For example, it's impossible to find a house, unless you have significant resources, on Martha's Vineyard. So, it creates some challenges, but I see some really amazing things happening on the Vineyard about how to engage with this difficult history. And it needs to be engaged with. It's not something we should look away from. A lot of people have had a lot of fortunate privileged experiences where they're able to look away from some of this. For the people who have called Noepe home, there is no privilege to look away from. It's just our reality. It's the truth. And so, we need to accept each other's truth, and acknowledge them. And I think that's very important, and I see that happening in the Vineyard. And I know I'm part of that through the Aquinnah Cultural Center, and trying to engage people in those kinds of conversations.

I've been meeting with groups of ministers and pastors throughout Massachusetts who are very interested in how to rebuild that relationship between the Catholic church and other church systems in Massachusetts, and Native folks, as well. That's another thing that we're looking toward in a way to potentially address the past. I would just advocate that you continue to ask these questions and continue to seek out answers.

SOURCE NOTES

1. "Native American Policies." *Office of Tribal Justice*, June 15, 2022. www. justice.gov/otj/native-american-policies
2. "In *Johnson v. McIntosh*, the Supreme Court under Chief Justice John Marshall upholds the McIntosh family's ownership of land purchased from the federal government. It reasons that since the federal government now controls the land, the Indians have only a 'right of occupancy' and hold no title to the land," from "Tribes – Native Voices." *US National Library of Medicine*. Accessed July 11, 2023. www.nlm.nih.gov/nativevoices/ timeline/271.html#:~:text=In%20Johnson%20v.,no%20title%20to%20 the%20land
3. H.R.7919 – Maine Indian Claims Settlement Act of 1980. Accessed July 11, 2023. www.congress.gov/bill/96th-congress/house-bill/7919
4. American Indian Religious Freedom Act of 1978 (AIRFA) (42 U.S.C. § 1996). Accessed July 11, 2023. www.law.cornell.edu/uscode/text/42/1996
5. Walker, Jack. "Wampanoag Language Immersion School Navigates Linguistic, Cultural Education Remotely." *The Brown Daily Herald*, April 7, 2021. www.browndailyherald.com/article/2021/04/wampanoag-language- immersion-school-navigates-linguistic-cultural-education-remotely/
6. Wisecup, Kelly, and Paula Peters. "Telling Our Story: An Interview with Paula Peters." *Early American Literature* 56, no. 1 (2021): 209–218.

7. S.1214 – Indian Child Welfare Act 95th Congress (1977–1978). Accessed July 12, 2023. www.congress.gov/bill/95th-congress/senate-bill/1214/text

8. H.R.5237 – Native American Graves Protection and Repatriation Act. Accessed July 11, 2023. https://www.congress.gov/bill/101st-congress/house-bill/5237/text

9. Native-land.ca: Our Home on Native Land, October 8, 2021. https://native-land.ca/.

10. "CWA 50th Anniversary Landing Page." Potomac Riverkeeper Network, March 24, 2023. www.potomacriverkeepernetwork.org/clean-water-act-50th-anniversary/

11. Pelton, Tom. "Clean Water Act's Promises Half Kept at Half Century Anniversary." *Environmental Integrity Project*, March 17, 2022. https://environmentalintegrity.org/news/clean-water-acts-promises-half-kept-at-half-century-anniversary/#:~:text=The%20U.S.%20Congress%20passed%20the,into%20navigable%20waters%20by%201985

12. "New York Proposal 2, Environmental Rights Amendment (2021)." *Ballotpedia*, November 2, 2021. https://ballotpedia.org/New_York_Proposal_2,_Environmental_Rights_Amendment_(2021)

13. Satz, Martha. "Dawnland by Adam Mazo and Ben Pender-Cudlip." *Adoption & Culture* 8, no. 1 (2020): 119–121. https://doi.org/10.1353/ado.2020.0015

14. "We support the self-determination of Wabanaki people through education, truth-telling, restorative justice, and restorative practices in Wabanaki and Maine communities. We design our structures and processes to be responsive to Wabanaki communities and beneficial to Wabanaki people." ("Mission, Vision & Values." *Wabanaki REACH*. Accessed July 11, 2023. www.wabanakireach.org/mission).

15. Hearne, Joanna. *Smoke Signals: Native Cinema Rising*. Lincoln: University of Nebraska Press, 2012.

16. "Biography." *Paul Cuffe*, September 6, 2022. https://paulcuffe.org/biography/

17. "Hydro-Quebec and Native People." *Cultural Survival*. Accessed July 11, 2023. www.culturalsurvival.org/publications/cultural-survival-quarterly/hydro-quebec-and-native-people

II

"Study and Struggle"

4
Freedom

Anthony Bogues, Barbara Krauthamer, Kyle Mays,
Jasmine Syedullah, and moderator Joy James

May 10, 2022

Anthony Bogues

My remarks will be in thesis form.

Thesis 1: The arrival of Europeans into the Americas marked the opening of a series of human encounters based on genocide and dispossession. The logic of settler colonialism in the Americas was central to the emergence of a form of colonial capitalism. This is a form of capitalism that became deeply rooted in the European colonial project post-1492. In this social and economic system, the transatlantic slave trade and then plantations in the "Americas" very quickly became central features. Early settler colonialism in the Americas, therefore, should be understood as a form of colonial capitalism based primarily on war, genocide, and dispossession along with racial slavery and white supremacy.

Thesis 2: in the New England region, before the arrival of the African slaves, there were slaves, both slaves and indentured Indigenous people. In 1614, we have reports of Indigenous people being taken from the New England area and being sold as slaves in England. Settler colonialism, and settler colonial capitalism, engaged in various forms, not just of genocide and dispossession, but also forms of slavery and servitude. The British Atlantic world was deeply linked to the New England area and considered an outpost of British colonial and settler colonial region, with Jamaica and Bermuda, Barbados, and other British and indeed Spanish colonial as well as French colonial territories. The point is that prior to African enslavement, there was both Indigenous dispossession as well as Indigenous slavery, particularly in the New England area. There are consequences for this historical formation.

Thesis 3: Racial slavery was mapped upon this form of Indigenous servitude and slavery. It is clear to see when one examines the codes of Barbados, the racial codes of South Carolina, and the ways in which these particular racial codes in the early and late 1600s began to characterize people. In the first instance where what happened was that Indigenous people were characterized as heathen, along with Black people, and then Christians were characterized as primarily white people in the early versions of the code. By the late 1600s, there were three different characterizations in slave codes of people who were Indian, Blacks, or white. My argument is that racial slavery has to be seen as being mapped upon – not separate from, but actually related to and mapped onto – certain forms of slavery and indenture that was happening particularly in the New England area. For this thesis, we should recall that the Barbados slave codes became the prototype for slave codes in the British Colonial Atlantic World.

Thesis 4: Historically, genocide and dispossession and racial slavery – and notice I don't say chattel slavery – generated colonial violence, and this violence over time was then based on racialized Black bodies. However, the relations between Indigenous peoples and Blacks today are sometimes considered in the following way: a relationship of antagonism; a relationship in which the struggles or the different forms of oppression are seen as incommensurate; lack of a certain commonality. Thus, there is a political claim about the necessity for solidarity.

Thesis 5: Some scholars working through Edouard Glissant, the Caribbean thinker, argue that rather than thinking about exceptionalism and solidarity, we should begin to think about questions of relationality. For Glissant in particular, this concept of relationality comes from his book, *Poetics of Relation*. However, Glissant also says that the idea of relation does not actually limit relation, and that the idea of relation does not actually preexist, which means that the question of relationality is something that is always and consistently being worked through.[1]

I want to start from this position of thinking of relationality, but end at a different destination; a destination of common association, because as Glissant says, the idea of relationality demands work, and because it demands work, I would argue, it becomes the work of freedom.

Thesis 6: to grasp this relationality, in the words of this particular webinar of *Entwined* (a concept developed with Mystic Seaport Museum and Brown University for the Mellon grant), perhaps two things among many other things are necessary. First, a certain kind of the history of both groups – Indigenous as well as African Americans – but from a perspective of a certain kind of relationality itself. Second, a mapping of the relations of domination, the relationship between slavery, servitude, and then the relationship around racial slavery, and to examine them as relations of domination, mapping their relation, but also mapping the historical signs of refusals. I'm not talking about questions of rebellions nor war, but trying to map the everyday and how it is lived, and how in these experiences of the everyday – the quotidian, if you wish – the business of freedom is organized and thought about. How is freedom lived, and how does it have a change in character that is not normative, and that is not a kind of normative installation in the way sometimes it is often thought of? What I'm arguing for is mapping relations of domination between the two – how relations of domination worked in between the two groups – while talking about the practices of freedom.

Because, what one wants to think about – again, just in terms of relationality – is how this kind of mapping can show us the shapes and influences between each other. But also, there's the aspect of anti-Black racism. I'm not talking about overlapping histories, but rather, about forms of domination and how different forms of domination operate, and what are their specific relations in what is colonial capitalism, within a settler colony ideologically undergirded by white supremacy.

We know that racial slavery created an anti-Black racial order. It made Blackness at the bottom of the hierarchical human codes and classification schema. We know now that settler colonialism was really colonial capitalism, and that this is also generative of racial slavery. Therefore, what I would want to suggest, is that before the transformation of colonial capitalism into racial capitalism – and I think this is important because it's an argument with a lot of literature today around the question of racial capitalism in America – what you had was colonial capitalism, which once race enters into it, then you begin to get the business of racial capitalism. This is very important in trying to think through this business of not just America, but the Indigenous and Africans in the Americas itself.

What that means, is that America is today a settler colony state, but that is, as a settler colony state and an imperial one on which the material foundations are of racial capitalism. Let me explain what I mean by an imperial state, and how thus this imperial state draws internally from the ways in which it has treated and the way it has dominated Indigenous people. I want to just make reference to two particular islands in the Caribbean. One is Puerto Rico, and one is the Virgin Islands. Both today are American dependencies, although they are not called so formally. However, I would suggest to you that the juridical frame for these American "colonies" drew from the nineteenth-century legal language of "dependent states," which draws from a set of court cases in 1831, when Justice Marshall described Native Americans as independent political communities who were "subject to paternalistic powers of the United States."[2] From this ruling there emerged the concept of "dependent domestic nations." Surely, the imperial drive of the US state can be discerned at this moment.

Thesis 7: I return to the business of common association, and I would argue that one of the central questions – not the only – but one of the central questions of our times is how we live together in difference. That is, how do populations that do not have overlapping histories, but in some ways have common history, how do we rearrange and organize life and politics as a kind of practice of common association to live a human life? Because, in the final analysis, what faces us, in the contemporary moment is the quality of human life on Earth, and therefore a kind of life that is not structured around difference, around sets of structured hierarchies, around forms of domination, but rather a set of practices about human life which are done in what I've called common association, which would allow common association to be a practice of freedom. Not a practice of liberation, nor a practice of emancipation, but actually a practice of freedom itself. That practice of freedom is absolutely antithetical to the racial capitalist settler colonial state, which we now inhabit.

For this to happen, there are many things that need to be done, obviously, and one is not in the business of saying, making a list of things that need to be done, but I would just suggest from where I sit that two things might be necessary as part of the many things that need to be done at this point in time, in our history, in this country. One of them is about trying to rethink and reimagine the history of the Americas, to understand its settler colonialism, to understand it as part of colonial capitalism, and to understand how it produced certain kinds of violence, and how ideologically, it produced white supremacy, which then has become the deposit, the ideological sediment, the ideological deposit in which the right-wing actually goes back to reactivate in terms of trying to develop certain kind of politics in this country. Second, to begin to talk about how we can explore the various forms of common association that have occurred both in history and in the contemporary moment, but also quite frankly, to move away from certain kinds of ideas about things that are not around incommensurability, around ideas of solidarity, but rather, to think through questions of a certain kind of relationality, of beginning to think about how, in living in relations, what does that mean in a particular state, like the imperial state of the United States?

Barbara Krauthamer

I want to talk briefly about some of my work on the history of African and African American enslavement in southern Native American nations, because from my vantage as a historian of African American enslavement, this history presents a nicely encapsulated case study, if you will, for understanding the complexity of settler colonialism and precisely those kinds of overlapping and intertwined histories of enslavement of African peoples, and a colonial campaign of domination of Native peoples. How did Native peoples and peoples of African descent interact, encounter each other and interact? One of the first interesting things to remember, of course, in this long history is that until approximately the 1730s, more Native Americans were captured and enslaved and exported from North America to Caribbean colonies than African captives were brought to North America. When we think about the history of slavery and those intersecting histories of Native peoples and African American histories, there's no single set of definitions or no single narrative that neatly encompasses people as enslaved people or free people, but those categories are always unstable and shifting over time.

I'm particularly interested in understanding the complexity of Black life beyond what I still think predominates in much of the scholarship as a Black–white binary, with the exclusion of Native peoples or the flattening of Native peoples to kind of a generic, "and Native Americans," without taking into full consideration the vast diversity of Native cultures, linguistic groups, and regions across North America, for example.

One of the problems that continues to plague scholars, that's sort of inescapable, or the nature of the beast of the work that we do with historical research, is how to understand the sources that we're left with. Again, as a historian of African American life and African American women's lives in particular, this is a real challenge. Sources from the eighteenth century, and the nineteenth century, written by Euro-Americans, are fully suffused with and created by the products of a colonial settler regime, both by colonists themselves and then later in the United States, primarily by either missionaries or government authorities who are invested in a regime of domination, both domination of enslaved people of African descent, but also enslaved people of African descent and Native Americans, in my case, in the southern states. Trying to tease out the reality of slavery and colonization to uncover the traces of real people's real lives – it is always challenging, and I think requires a constant reading through the layers, reading through, reading against the grain, if you will. One of the challenges I think that we can now have a conversation about is how to hold Native American history and African American history in their full complexity and humanity, and how do we hold them together side by side?

I'll give just a couple of examples of this. In the nineteenth century, white missionaries in the Choctaw and Chickasaw nations, which I know best, owned enslaved laborers and hired enslaved Black laborers from Native American slaveholders to work at mission stations, and the point of the mission stations was to "educate" and "civilize" Native American youth. Tensions emerged with wealthier, more powerful, more prominent Native families who didn't want their children being trained in the arts of the dominant society, whether it was gendered labor, like spinning and weaving for women or agricultural labor for boys and men, because that went against traditional Native gender roles in the case of the Choctaws and Chickasaws. This type of training also put Native children in close proximity to Black laborers at the mission stations. There's this tension, on the one hand of Native peoples wanting to maintain cultural traditions of their own in the context of gendered labor, and understanding that gendered forms of labor were also racialized in the world of white missionaries, white settlers, and trying to reconcile both of those competing ideas of gender and competing ideas of race and racial hierarchy and racial identity.

We see it in a story in the *Choctaw Telegraph* of a Choctaw enslaver named Harkins who's killed by an enslaved man named Prince, and depending on whose account you read Prince is cast as a savage and Harkins' widow as bereft – if you read a missionary account of it.[3] Then in the end, Prince takes his own life and other enslaved people are interrogated and then put to death as accomplices in the murder of Harkins. Some scholars writing about the Native enslavers have said that putting enslaved people to death was really part of a traditional way of exacting vengeance against enslaved people. There are other sources, however, that suggest that these are families who otherwise were ready to break with older Native traditions of servitude by purchasing enslaved African American laborers, such as Prince.

All of the complexities of trying to understand both Native history on its own terms and African American history, and seeing African American gender roles that were imposed on Black people through systems of slavery, have been at the core of what my work. I've looked at these histories to understand how Black women, in particular, saw themselves as enslaved people, as laborers, as mothers, as wives, as daughters, as kin, and how they attempted to define themselves and define their freedom after the Civil War. I will wrap up with just one more thought, which is that the history of the Civil War and the history of emancipation in the Native nations, again, presents us with these intertwined competing claims for freedom and for sovereignty. For some Native nations, defending chattel slavery was often part and parcel with defending their sovereignty. After the Civil War, there was a tension in how freedom is defined, but for some Native leaders, it's defined as the freedom to exclude people of African descent from citizenship in the Native nations, where they were enslaved and emancipated. For African Americans, their freedom claim is to be included – and that inclusion and exclusion is the legacy of slavery that we're still struggling with.

Kyle Mays

One question – I'm talking about the Black and Red Power era – around Black and Native solidarity: How can we build a world on the way to the aftermath of settler colonialism and white supremacy? What role can expressive culture play? And what are these possibilities, again, for kinship in the aftermath of settler colonialism and white supremacy?

It's always important to just mention the people I'm connected with, family history. My great-grandmother, Esther Shawboose Mays, came from the Saginaw-Chippewa reservation to Detroit in the spring of 1940. She married an African American man, for which she received a lot of hate from the Native community in Detroit, and she had these Afro-Indigenous children. She became a well-respected elder around culture and education and activism for youth in particular and co-founded what was called Detroit's Indian Education and Cultural Center.[4] She is what I like to describe as an urban Indigenous feminist, and subsequently my Aunt Judy formed what was called Medicine Bear American Indian Academy in the early 1990s, and it was the third-ever public school with a Native American curriculum.[5] There are still a lot of activists, artists, and cultural workers, who are still very much appreciative of that school and the work that either my great-grandmother or my Aunt Judy did in the city of Detroit for Detroit's Native community.

The enslavement of Indigenous Africans is a part of the history of settler colonialism. We often mark Indigenous peoples as simply African or Black, but those are Indigenous peoples having their own language, thoughts, cosmologies, and so forth. Many people approach this, or at least write about this in some capacity, but it's taken for granted that you have really the collision of these two Indigenous groups, exploited and dispossessed in a variety of ways. Typically, in many Black communities, you hear the discussion of the Five Tribes.[6]

I always hear this thing, and the other one is the Buffalo Soldiers, which is certainly a very complicated discussion and narrative. While they are in the aftermath of getting their freedom after the Civil War, there's also this matter of genocide that they are participating in – promoted by the United States government, but they are participating even if they had their own reasoning for doing so.[7] This is kind of the lens through which we often see Black and Indigenous relations.

One of the most important, if not the most important writers during the Black and Red Power era is Vine Deloria Junior, who wrote *Custer Died for Your Sins: An Indian Manifesto*, published in 1975, and he said,

> Minority groups are often astounded to learn that the Indians are not planning to share the continent with their oppressed brothers once the revolution was over. Hell, no. The Indians were planning on taking the continent back and kicking out all the black, Chicano, Anglo, and Asian brothers who had made the whole thing possible.[8]

I think this is important to say, because solidarity at this particular moment in time – as much as we believe that it is important – was not always inevitable, and it was not something desired, necessarily, by many Indigenous peoples. This is one person saying this, but I think this was, for a majority, more of a sentiment than realized, although today I'm going to talk about a least a few exceptions.

This whole notion of land has been central to the African American, or people of African descent, desire for sovereignty, of freedom, of humanity, in some particular way. For instance, in 1968, with the Republican of New Africa, I think there's an important discussion – historically and today, although some of those things are certainly changing and this conversation is one of those that's helping. What do they imagine about returning land to Indigenous peoples? Even if they wanted the five southern states, how does that perpetuate the dispossession of Indigenous peoples who are many, largely removed from the area, but some did in fact remain. This is a discourse of nationalism, and sovereignty, that can easily, and did, lead to the erasure of Indigenous peoples on that particular land.

Are there shared values between the Black and Red Power eras? Importantly, a critique of US democracy. Anytime we say Indigenous sovereignty or in honor of the treaties, that is certainly a critique I think is worth mentioning. And returning land is in many ways, if we re-conceptualize our conception of land, is about anti-capitalism in some capacity. Now, to the extent that every group shared this, of course, that was not every group, but returning land to Indigenous peoples would certainly disrupt, in some capacity, the notion of US racial capitalism. Stokely Carmichael, who I highlight here, says,

> All of us must struggle against capitalism. The red man is struggling against capitalism. Certainly, he is! He must! He has been a vicious victim of capitalism. It is on his land that the most powerful imperial system has been built at his very expense. Of course, he must struggle against it whether he is conscious of it or not.[9]

Here's Stokely again – he's one of the few Black activists during the time who very explicitly stated that this is Indigenous people's land – in 1975 in St. Paul, Minnesota, speaking at a particular rally in support of the American Indian Movement. What happens when we center land and think about land differently outside of this extractive and exploitative process? A particular moment of solidarity here on the White Earth reservation in 1981, or certainly a precursor to the Declaration of the Rights of Indigenous peoples, in which we have Black and Indigenous peoples from North and South America fighting for recognition from the United Nations? This is a particular moment at the International Indian Treaty Council here, and I wish there was more scholarship on this particular history, which is super important.

One group doing this is the Land Back Indian Collective and their discussion of Land Back, including Black people, Indigenous peoples from Central and South America who have been removed and forced from their homelands, often because the United States has neoliberal policies that influenced that area.

Finally, what can some of these things look like? Audre Lorde said, "Any future vision which can encompass all of us by definition must be complex and expanding, not easy to achieve," and it requires a lot of various forms of solidarity.[10] Anything from eating together, to reading together, and hanging out, are some very important things.

Jasmine Syedullah

My contribution is coming from a perspective of practice, trying to think about practices of relationality that help us reckon with things as they are, with the fever dreams we inherit, their dystopic trajectories, and the long shadows those unfortunate futures cast on our present reality. I am learning with my students to know what time it is and create space in classrooms for the practice of more truant protocols of relation, the curricular version of inciting a riot, to invoke the pedagogy of Audre Lorde.[11] One that actually centers, for example, Indigenous Studies within the framework of critical race and ethnic studies. Or, one that is as embodied as it is analytic. I came out of a student movement in Santa Cruz to create a Critical Ethnic Studies Department, and after a 40-year struggle for ethnic studies in Santa Cruz, once we saw we were winning, one of the most contested conversations that we couldn't get past asked, what is the role of ethnic studies in relationship to Indigenous Studies?

What Professor Bogues was talking about in terms of relationality, and the other panelists as well, is not just a political question, not just a cultural or sociological, or even a historical reckoning question, but is also a question of pedagogy, which entails thinking really expansively about how we occupy classroom space in ways that can disrupt carceral, colonial logics of learning and knowledge curation and creation. I was drawn to tap into my own contemplative practices and begin to see how I can use a combination of contemplative practice, embodiment, poetry, music, conversation, and the scholarship of abolitionist movements, through time, to really begin to invite people to have their whole selves be present in the work that we're doing together in the classroom. I was invited to rethink pedagogy through a lens of abolition and contemplative work through the work of Stefano Harney and Fred Moten in their piece about the Undercommons, when they say,

> It cannot be denied that the university is a place of refuge and it cannot be accepted that the university is a space of enlightenment. In the face of these conditions, one can only sneak into the university and steal what one can, to abuse its hospitality, to spite its mission, to join its refugee colony, its gypsy encampment, to be in, but not of. This is the path of the subversive intellectual in the modern university.[12]

I really wanted to run with this idea and think of it not just as the work of a single individual, an exceptional fugitive, but as the work of us becoming more fugitive, or perhaps just more truant together, as collective communities, potentially, working across silos, across departments, across disciplines to create, invoking Audre Lorde, "another kind of open." In the poem "Coal," she says, "Love is a word, another kind of open. As a diamond comes into a knot of flame, I am black because I come from the Earth's inside. Take my word for jewel in your open light."[13] As activist academics it can be easy to get caught up in fighting the external forces of opposition to justice, equity, and liberation, but my practice teaches me that authority is embodied in all living things, from the places where our feet greet the living Earth. The struggle begins within.

I'm led by poets like Lorde, by political prisoners, and those poverty scholars who risk it all to keep their own account of what counts to put the protocols of relation they model out of necessity into practice in my everyday life. The choice to confront what abolition teaches us about feeling ourselves beyond the conceits and comforts of capital and integrating it not just when we are winning but when we are alone and up against a wall is a practice. To reiterate the question from my essay's abstract, we begin by asking, how might a Black maroon politics of care reorient to disorient the present political time, or temporal trajectory of democratic development toward something else, a different vision – another horizon? My practice begins with knowing how to find my feet, finding my feet as a way to honor my relationship with the Earth and beginning to understand what knowledge transcends from that relational consciousness first. It begins by putting that mutuality, that relation of care at the center from day one.

What freedoms might we find when we "reprogram, deprogram, and get down," in the words of Janelle Monae's "Q.U.E.E.N" (ft. Erykah Badu)? I borrow an example of what this might look like from Christine Anne Smith's work on Quilombos. Quilombos are simultaneously spaces of escape and refuge, and war encampment, Smith teaches. She says,

> For decades, Black Brazilian scholar-activists have looked to the liberation model of the Quilombos for political inspiration. Quilombos are the physical spaces where enslaved Africans encamped to escape from bondage during the period of slavery and the contemporary communities of their descendants that still occupy these historic encampments, yet, in the Black radical tradition in Brazil, Quilombos are not only physical spaces, but also the practice of finding refuge from the total condition of slavery, including those conditions that extend beyond the temporal boundaries of physical bondage, like racism and the erasure of Black history. Quilombos are not only physical and cultural spaces, but also trans-temporal, trans-spatial spaces of Black liberation that Black people in Brazil have articulated in response to the conditions of subjugation.[14]

The practice of finding refuge from oppression has its roots in traditions of Indigenous resistance to slavery that predates, according to Afro-Brazilian academic and activist Beatriz Nascimento, the Middle Passage.[15] As a practice passed down from nomadic warriors living in the colonized lands we know now as Angola, maroons did not merely resist oppression in the wake of the transatlantic piracy of a people, they were fighting Portuguese incursion even before they became stolen peoples on stolen lands. Drawing from the embodied scholarship of maroon abolitionist feminisms, past and present, we might think about present-day abolition, prison abolition movements as the new enlightenment, with fire this time, the unfinished work of nineteenth-century maroons and fugitive abolitionists, the ongoing reparative work of waking the dead, walking with ancestors, fighting to feel haunted, or, rather more than haunted. To become more than hunted, more than humiliated, dispossessed, and abject, becoming more collectively than possessive individualism could ever hope to contain on its own.

Embodied praxes of finding refuge and centering otherwise futures are prophetic in their passage from generation to generation, burning hot enough in the flesh of Earth to turn coal to jewels that quake and crack the foundation from below, to invoke the poetics of Lorde, cited above.[16] For Lorde, like many of us who strive to teach liberation as a theory and a practice, classrooms become something more than spaces of intellectual mastery, consumption or mere contemplation. They become spaces of refuge, protest, and mutual education, extensions of the maroon formations, riotous congregations, even as we find ourselves, as Smith writes, "teetering on the edge of invisibility, disease, and insanity." The classroom is an alchemic catalyst for change, for us to practice a protocol of relation willing to retreat from the kinds of futures so-called free people yearn for and imagine more.

When contradictions are revealed, something new can enter the frame. Sometimes teaching feels like this, like exorcism, helping teach students to notice how we learn, not just with our minds, but with our whole bodies, feet first, on the ground, absorbing lessons we may or may not have chosen for ourselves, then creating the conditions that can support them in shedding what no longer serves the kinds of learning they notice they're missing. Lorde called this pedagogy confrontation teaching.[17]

Many of us are learning to confront these overlapping histories of poverty, racial, gender, and Indigenous violence, dispossession, and decreased life chances as they become known to us, but how are we noticing how these truths land on our flesh, in our bodies, in the spaces between us, on the land, on our tongues, in the places we call home? Can we notice and shift our protocols of relation accordingly without punishment or policing? I'll stop there, but I think this kind of not knowing resonates with a tradition of Dharma that includes mastery but begins again and again with not knowing, also known as beginner's mind. Beginner's mind is a practice of Zen Buddhist understanding wherein returns to even the most familiar and predictable sites of relation are saturated with nearly imperceptible bits of charge, sensations to note, information that was, until now, gone missing. The beginner's mind is an embodied practice of mutual learning and teaching that resonates between beings. Beyond the bare-life kinds of survival that all beings deserve, what kinds of open are born of all these feet on this land at this moment? How will we practice relating to one another, not just as citizens, subjects, captives, or fugitives, emancipated or liberated, but as kin to another world of possibility?

Joy James

It seems to me that radical traditions become the nexus or the crossroads that we are seeking. If the communities do not want to be intertwined holistically in terms of the majority, is there a radical tradition then that would allow slices of the community to merge and to create the kind of visions and analyses that you've offered us today?

Krauthamer

I don't have an answer to your question, but it makes me think of two things. Kyle, your idea of the labor of anticolonial solidarity really stuck with me – thinking [that] what we're talking about is work. The kind of work that we have to do as scholars, as people, as community members, and it's challenging. Jasmine, I think you misspoke – and then corrected yourself – but I liked the misspeaking better, when you said something like, "We want to be more haunted." I feel like maybe we do want to be more haunted. Maybe we do need to actually feel the presence of the past. To feel the weight of the past more in order to do that anticolonial work. I liked the idea of being more haunted and not trying to create something new, but to really looking back while we're thinking about moving forward.

Syedullah

That is exactly what's been happening in the classrooms this past couple of years. One of the comments one of the students shared last week is that when they're walking with their peers, but they're not necessarily walking with previous or future generations. Their sense of being in time is challenged by the kinds of media and conversation that they are a part of and are keeping younger generations in tension with each other on the level of discourse, as opposed to place or land, and then that kinship becomes impossible because the artificial barriers are so sedimented and entrenched.

When they began to think about what time it was and how their moment is built upon the gifts and struggles of generations past – both the lessons learned, and the desires and dreams – they started to get a little bit more curious about what it means to be in solidarity, not just with people across lines of class and race, because that's kind of a script that they're familiar with, but being in solidarity with previous generations was something that they had not considered before. It does make me think that it begins small. It begins in small ways with the communities that we can leverage ourselves into, beginning to introduce this different practice of relationality that isn't based exactly, as Bogues said, on competition or domination, but on mutual survival.

Bogues

In relationship to Professor James' question, the way I've been trying to think about it is that it is really through relationality, rather than overlapping histories, and then trying to think about, "Okay, let's then see if we can put together people for solidarity or call people for solidarity, action, and so on," but that if we think about discussions of relationality, where there's no template, there's no kind of preexisting form, then everything needs to be worked through. It has to be worked through toward freedom, and it's the working through that becomes the actual key, which means that there will be difficulties, differences, quarrels, breakups, all sorts of things, massive things, as people try and work through a set of relations. Because, I think in the end, the question is, how do we have a kind of common association where we live, but we actually live with different sets of histories, even if sometimes those issues are common and complicated? Then, how do we construct a kind of democracy, that is not an electoral democracy, but one in which people have voice and speech with a certain kind of plurality, so that there's no one single narrative voice that says, "This is the truth, and this is what you must do."

Those are such practices that one has to engage in and work through and quarrel through until we get to what we, I like to put it, until we get to the other side of the River Jordan.[18] To cross the River Jordan is one of the most fundamental, one of the most difficult things to actually do. I appreciate the ideas of the 1960s and so on – I myself being a kid, a high school student in that period, and growing up in the early 1970s with all those things in my head, but I also understand something which has happened, which is that the way in which neoliberalism in this particular order of racial capitalism has operated is that it has actually created historical amnesia; first, around those kinds of moments of "solidarity," and second, it has constructed a set of categories of recognition and actually put people in competition in relation to each other, about questions of recognition. That means that recognition then becomes a kind of misrecognition of a certain way in which we think about capitalism.

You read a lot of literature today about settler colonialism and I quickly went through some of it, again, for today, and very few people ended up talking about capitalism. It's as if you are struggling only against white supremacy, but we need to think about how to tackle a society that has been constructed historically and that has shaped all of us who live in it. To me, the question is working through and relationality and relationship.

Mays

One thing that I remember is doing oral histories with family. I would ask some things like, "What was activism like for you all back in the day in Detroit?" My Aunt Judy responded to me that they used to either go straight from a Native protest and then go right over to, say, the League of Revolutionary Black Workers or whatever protest that they were doing, but they didn't see that as a form of competition, and so I'm glad Professor Bogues brought that up. It wasn't a competition for them. It was simply that they were growing up in the Black and Indigenous radical space, and they were educated and encouraged to struggle against all forms of issues happening within their city. That is probably an exceptional and rare occasion, but it has taught me a lot about not only whether you embody those things but showing up.

That's what I always appreciated about Stokely and him showing up to a variety of Indigenous protests, because if you look at some of his earlier statements or even writings on whether Black people had a future in relationship to land, he was kind of hesitant early on, and then he explicitly stated, "This is Indigenous people's land, and therefore where do we go from there?"[19] Which I think still remains a profound piece of history that has been erased in many ways.

James

I want to echo something that I think is in alignment with what Professor Bogues was saying. It seems to me that even around abolition, critiques of capitalism and imperialism disappear. I'm wondering if [movements] have been mystified, or is there a new language now that veils material struggles? As you say, Kyle, people who went from one to another demonstration; we do it now, like multiples. There were connectors that were tangible, like relationality, as Professor Bogues says. When I read the materials and the text, often that relationality seems to disappear, along with a strong critique of capitalism.

Mays

What are the ways also that notions of tribal sovereignty uphold capitalism or do not critique capitalism enough? It's something that among my peers and so forth, and a variety of communities I'm connected with, I understand the trepidation, but we don't really leap to that. I mean, Indigenous nations are not immune to neoliberalism either.

Syedullah

It also links back to a question I had for Bogues. You were saying that you were thinking about freedom beyond domination – that distinguishes itself from both emancipation and liberation, and so I have a feeling that that might have something to do with this politics of recognition and sovereignty claims in tribal nations as well.

Bogues

I speak from a very limited experience, really very limited experience – where I think that there is a tribal sovereignty that may be problematic in relationship to the imperial state itself. At the same time, it is a necessary defense of the tribe. It might work both ways. In other words, recognition by the imperial, settler state, which means access to certain things and so on and so forth. It also is used for one's own self-defense, which I think is a certain understanding of sovereignty, which I think is absolutely necessary. But then what happens to the other tribes who are not recognized?

Then there is the other thing, we're not in an imagined world, so you are in the real world and you are in a world where people are, after 400 years of military conquest, of war and pacifications and genocide, are trying to find forms of organization and politic that will at least give them a certain sense of themselves and a certain sovereignty, which had been stolen from them. It is not that it works or doesn't work in the interest of the imperial state. It is much more complicated than that.

The relationship to the second question is this drawing on the African American and Caribbean experience, and Brazilian experiences, we know that emancipation is really a process that comes from above. You are emancipated, right? You are given what is called freedom. A dominant structure gives you, a slave master, a colonial, whoever gives you the tools. Gives you emancipation, and says you are emancipated. Even if you've fought wars and so on and so forth, it's like, "Okay, you are now free today." That, to me, is emancipation, but liberation to me is about, that you are liberated from something. You are liberated – whatever that form is, gender domination, racial oppression, et cetera, et cetera. Freedom for me, though, is another set of practices, is the other set of practices.

In other words, liberation for me becomes one ground from which you can begin to practice freedom. Emancipation becomes deeply problematic because the emancipation is the ground for a post-emancipation that is typically set by those who have dominated you. Whether it is in the United States, during the Reconstruction, after whose collapse saw the creation of Jim Crow. Or in the Caribbean in the post-1838, or in Brazil after the 1880s, wherever it is, in my view, this question that, the ex-slaves then fight for freedom, but that because the ground is already laid in a certain way, and the horizons of what you can do are already structured in a certain way, then you can't become full free. You can't begin to do practices of freedom.

One of the things that fascinates me is how in many emancipated societies, post-abolition societies, was how there were revolts that people, oftentimes led by women, asked the question, "What kind of free is this?" Because the conditions that are supposed to be there for freedom are not really there. From my work, I begin to think, "Okay, there's some distinctions here that we must begin to think about." I don't have that answer for you. But thinking about freedom is a much more complicated way and is a set of practices that does not have a kind of normative sense to it. It always, in my view, opens up a different horizon and tries to struggle against domination.

James

Considering what Barbara was saying about being haunted – what's our North Star? I understand and I agree that we cannot define freedom, but the haunting continues. Months ago, I was listening to *Democracy Now!*, and according to them the number of environmental protectors assassinated throughout the Americas was 1000. Disproportionately, [the casualties would be] Indigenous, Afro-Indigenous or Black. The people were protecting land, water, and forest, and under those conditions [of terror which] was the everyday mundane. The North Star exists, but there is also this hyper-aggression from the state, which will now intrude into the womb. With the attacks on abortion [exist reactionary attempts toward] total [state] control of reproduction so that abortion becomes a "homicide" if you even take a pill [Mifepristone]. There is criminalization of reproductive rights ... in some states [despite rape, incest, ectopic pregnancies, maternal mortality]. Is there a North Star? Even if we cannot define "freedom," how do we follow a North Star when we're haunted?

Krauthamer

It's a beautiful question. A harrowing question. Actually, I'm now at the point of thinking about what Professor Bogues just said about freedom as a practice. I'm not sure what the North Star is. When I think about being haunted and I think about some of the individuals that I wrote about, there's a story that always comes back to the mind of a man named Simon Harrison, who was enslaved in the Choctaw nation.[20] Missionaries purchase him and give him his freedom, as it were, and he then embarks on this colonization venture to go to West Africa and become a missionary himself. He writes these letters back to the States and he says, when he got to the coast – I can't quite remember where he disembarked, probably Liberia somewhere – and he says his heart just sank when he realized that he had to get on another boat and take another water journey.

He's really evocative about the Middle Passage. All I could think about is, here's somebody whose quest for emancipation was realized, though his life was so completely wrapped up in colonization ventures, and he becomes acutely aware of this as he is sent on another kind of Middle Passage back. For me, that's sort of the haunting, that there's no escape from this. I like what Jasmine said, thinking about being in solidarity with other generations, that there's no escape. I think we shouldn't even be trying to escape. It's only by embracing that haunting.

SOURCE NOTES

1. Glissant, Édouard. *Poetics of Relation*. East Lansing, MI: University of Michigan Press, 1997. Note that Glissant sees "imagination as the force that can change mentalities; Relation as the process of this change; and poetics as

a transformative mode of history," (xii) and discusses the Poetics of Relation, "in which each and every identity is extended through a relationship with the Other" (11).

2. *Cherokee v. Georgia* (1831) which defined Native Americans as belonging to a "domestic dependent nation," and *Williams v. Ranger American of The V.I. Inc. et al.* (1945), respectively.

3. Krauthamer, Barbara. *Black Slaves, Indian Masters: Slavery, Emancipation, and Citizenship in the Native American South.* University of North Carolina Press, 2015.

4. Mays, Kyle T. *City of Dispossessions: Indigenous Peoples, African Americans, and the Creation of Modern Detroit.* Pennsylvania: University of Pennsylvania Press, 2022, p. 140.

5. Ibid.

6. Five Civilized Tribes: Dawes Records. Accessed July 11, 2023. www.archives.gov/research/native-americans/dawes/background.html#:~:text=Cherokee,%20Chickasaw,%20Choctaw,%20Creek,%20and%20Seminole%20Tribes%20in%20Oklahoma

7. Wilkie, Laurie A. *Unburied Lives: The Historical Archaeology of Buffalo Soldiers at Fort Davis, Texas, 1869–1875.* New Mexico: University of New Mexico Press, 2021.

8. Deloria, Vine. *Behind the Trail of Broken Treaties an Indian Declaration of Independence.* Austin: University of Texas Press, 2000.

9. Carmichael, Stokely. *The Red and the Black*, 1975.

10. Lorde, Audre. "Learning from the 60s." 1982.

11. "The learning process is something you can incite, literally incite, like a riot" (Lorde, Audre, and Adrienne Rich. "An Interview with Audre Lorde." *Signs: Journal of Women in Culture and Society* 6, no. 4 (1981): 713–736. https://doi.org/10.1086/493842).

12. Moten, Fred, and Stefano Harney. "The University and the Undercommons." *Social Text* 22, no. 2 (2004): 101–101. https://doi.org/10.1215/01642472-22-2_79-101

13. Lorde, Audre. "Coal." In *The Collected Poems of Audre Lorde.* New York: W.W. Norton & Company, 1997.

14. Smith, Christen Anne. "'In Front of the World': Translating Beatriz Nascimento." *Antipode* 53, no. 1 (2021): 279–316.

15. Smith, Christen Anne. "Toward a Black Feminist Model of Black Atlantic Liberation: Remembering Beatriz Nascimento." *Meridians* 14, no. 2 (2016): 71–87. https://doi.org/10.2979/meridians.14.2.06

16. Audre Lorde, "Coal."

17. Lorde, A., and Rich, A. "An Interview with Audre Lorde," 1981.

18. McTell, Blind Willie. "I Got to Cross the River Jordan." *The Library of Congress.* Accessed July 11, 2023. www.loc.gov/item/afc9999005.12065

19. Carmichael, Stokely. *The Red and the Black.*
20. Krauthamer, Barbara. *Black Slaves, Indian Masters: Slavery, Emancipation, and Citizenship in the Native American South.* Raleigh, NC: University of North Carolina Press, 2013.

5

Abolition, Care, and Indigenous Liberation

Dian Million, Stephanie Lumsden, Joy James,
and moderator Margaux Kristjansson

July 1, 2022

Stephanie Lumsden

I wanted to begin by emphasizing and celebrating the long history of Indigenous resistance to the carceral logics of genocide, containment, removal, and surveillance, which have been deployed against us since the onset of invasion. Since I'm Hupa, and a California Indian, I feel compelled to begin with a couple of stories of personal heroes of mine and I know heroes to us here in California.

I want to begin with the story of Toypurina, a Tongva medicine woman who in 1784 helped to plan an attack on the Mission San Gabriel and the Spaniards who had invaded her homeland. Tongva territory, the Los Angeles basin, was seized and occupied by the Spanish who, being experienced colonizers, had developed a system of *reducciones*, or forced reductions and removals of Tongva people from their land. Tongva people, like so many California Indians throughout Central and southern California, were forced from their land to the site of the mission that they would be forced to build and maintain under threat of torture, or the torture of their children and loved ones. The mission was built in 1771. Once there, Tongva people were baptized and held captive and made to labor under a system of enslavement that made life for Spanish conquistadors possible.

Tongva prisoners at the mission labored to make bricks, build dwellings, and tend livestock, all of which reproduced the Spanish and their capacities to extend their imperialist invasion into Tongva territory. Toypurina no doubt witnessed and endured the horrifying violence of this genocidal invasion that wrought destruction for the Tongva people. During the

Spanish occupation, Toypurina had a vision of reclaiming stolen wealth from the mission and redistributing it to her people. This vision is perhaps what gave her the courage to act. She coordinated an attack on the mission with other Tongva warriors at great personal risk. Sadly, her vision would not come to pass, or at least not yet. The rebellion that she had been instrumental in planning with other Tongva outside of the mission was found out, and she was arrested along with her co-conspirators.

Toypurina was tried and banished from her home to another mission far north, where she was a prisoner until she married a Spanish soldier and lived at Mission San Juan Bautista until she died in 1799. I'm going to hold onto that "not yet" of her prophecy and bring it up again later. Far north and some years later in Humboldt County during the gold rush, Native peoples in the northern part of California experienced a different but similar apocalyptic era of violence. An 1859 newspaper article out of San Francisco reads, "a party of four soldiers recently abused a woman at Hupa and the woman resisted, stabbing one of the party fatally. An investigation was to take place." They don't use the word woman, but I'm over saying slurs, reproducing them.

This mention of a Hupa women's resistance to US military invasion stood out to me because it challenges patriarchal readings of history that erase Hupa women's role in defending their own lives and the lives of their people and non-human kin. This woman's act of survival is an example of the resistance of long-standing Indigenous resistance to the carceral state. When I read this excerpt about the woman at Hupa who fought back against the soldiers, I imagine her fear during this and the vindication she might have felt when she killed one of these men who had a hand in destroying the world she knew. Her act of resistance and the story that the settler archive erases, the story of why she's resisting, which is against the United States, against the formation of a carceral settler state. That act of resistance and her story that the settler archive erases are the lasting legacy of California Indian survival.

The Hupa woman was from the village of Tsewenaldin, where the water goes around the stone. Tsewenaldin the village of Tsewenaldin John, a Hupa leader who never forgave the attack on her and remembered it when other Hupa leaders wanted to make peace with the invading US. Tsewenaldin John took the attack against the Hupa woman as such an affront to the entire village, that he would not make peace with the United States. Hupa's resistance to the US goes on for five years. They fight the Bald Hills Wars, they fight the invasion of the United States that wants to remove them from the valley, our home forever. We're not going. And he says his resistance, his unwillingness to make peace with them, is in a sense premised on respect for Hupa women's bodily integrity and a recognition of their centrality to Hupa life and the future of Natinixwe, the Hoopa Valley.

I wanted to start with these two stories because I want us to remember them in our discussion of resistance against the carceral state. I want to begin with these stories for a couple of reasons, the first being that acts of resistance by Native women and queers are so often silenced in colonial archives. Even this is two lines in a collection, and I'm hanging onto those because there's so much more to say. But these ancestors and their fight for freedom must be included in our intellectual genealogies and what Dian, you call resistance families. Our resistance kin. They must be included. They are our ancestors. Another reason is that when we think about resistance to the carceral state, we're often thinking only in terms of very recent history and specifically about the prison itself. Which is good, we need that, but I want us to extend the scope of our consideration of Indigenous resistance. It's beneficial to our analysis of abolition if we think about the carceral state as having a much longer life: if we agree that presidios and missions were prisons, and that soldiers and padres were wardens and police, or that military forts and reservations were prisons and that soldiers or militia and everyday settlers who do the work of these soldiers, are police and wardens. Then we have to reckon with the simple truth that the settler state has always been a carceral state. Toypurina, and a Hupa woman from Tsewenaldin, I'll call her "Tsume-hsło:n Tsewenaldin," Hupa woman from Tsewenaldin, since I can't find her name; their acts of resistance against the invaders who destroyed their ways of life demonstrate the necessity of abolition for Indigenous Liberation.

They knew that to stop the destruction of their homelands, they would have to fight. They knew that in order to save the young people and those not yet born, they would have to fight. They knew that we would one day come looking for them, for ancestors who could show us what needed to be done and so they fought. In this political moment, the necessity of abolition is startlingly clear. As Audra Simpson has argued, settler state sovereignty is a death drive, hell-bent on realizing the completion of conquest through the murder of Native women and queer folks. The expansion of settler state, territorial, and jurisdictional sovereignty marginalizes the legitimate and ethical grounded sovereignty or nested sovereignty of Native nations that has made us vulnerable to environmental, spiritual and physical violence. All of which is gender violence.

Since it's the National Day of Awareness for Missing and Murdered Indigenous Persons, I want to pause for a moment to consider how violence against Native women and queers, and our collective grief for our family members, loved ones, and kin is weaponized against us to extend the reach of the carceral state and legitimize its violence. On May 4, 2022, Joe Biden's White House issued a press release naming today the National Day of Awareness for Missing and Murdered Indigenous Persons.[1] The press release says the usual things; that it's a national tragedy that Native people have been denied justice for far too long, and that Biden himself reauthorized the Violence Against Women Act in March[2] in order to address the crisis with more training for cops, pilot programs for collecting more data on missing and murdered Indigenous people, and expanding the special jurisdiction of tribal courts over non-Native perpetrators of sexual assault, child abuse, stalking, sex trafficking and assaults on tribal law enforcement officers on tribal lands.

That last protected class of person, tribal cops, is interesting. We should be very suspicious of how that gets used. Many Native people and organizations in the public eye celebrate the reauthorization of the Violence Against Women Act (VAWA) and applaud Joe Biden – of all people, Joe Biden – for making Native people and Native women, girls and queers in particular, a priority for his administration.[3] I am not among the people clapping for Joe Biden. In related news, in September 2020, California Governor Gavin Newsom signed Assembly Bill 3099 into law in order to address what is often perceived as a dearth of police presence on tribal lands.[4] The lack of police or culturally competent police, whatever that means, and under-resourced tribal cops are cited by the state mainstream carceral feminists, and many tribal governments as the cause for violence against Native people.

To alleviate that, this bill promises guidance for police, education for police, support for police, crime data, and recommendations for more laws, no doubt. These responses to colonial gender violence against Native people are what many scholars call reformist reforms, top-down approaches to the crisis of violence that expand the power of the carceral state. This state can only exist if violence against us continues unabated. It is foolish to think otherwise, so we must fight. We must resist these easy, cheap solutions that do such a disservice to the ancestors whose stories I shared with you. And we are fighting. I turn now to a couple of examples of the abolitionist and decolonial work that so many of our tribal communities and comrades are doing. First, I highlight the story of Maddesyn George, a member of the Colville Confederated Tribes, a mother and survivor who was criminalized for defending her own life against her attacker. Her story is much like the Hupa woman at Tsewenaldin, defending her own life against this colonial invasion and sexual violence.

Maddesyn was detained by tribal police on the reservation. Without an attorney present, she gave it a detailed and unequivocal account of her sexual assault and the events that led to her shooting her attacker. Instead of receiving support after suffering a major trauma, Maddesyn was jailed.[5] She was never given access to a rape kit. The US attorney's office for the Eastern District of Washington, whom I hold with a special energetic and vehement dislike, recommended that she serve 17 years incarcerated and a lifetime of state supervision after she took a plea deal. The campaign to free Maddesyn, a grassroots organization comprised of family, friends, and abolitionists, comrades, tribal members, and people who are just sick of it, came together and hosted letter-writing events to offer love and support to Maddesyn and power hours to put pressure on the prosecutor's office and demand Maddy's freedom.[6] In November of 2021, after a year in Spokane County jail during a pandemic, Maddesyn was sentenced to six and a half years in a federal facility. Not the win we were hoping for, but a significant victory over what she was facing.

The campaign to free Maddesyn George is not an isolated campaign. We're not done. The work we did and do for Maddesyn is directly related to the fight, we feel, the fight to free all prisoners on stolen land. Prisoners and people held in cages anywhere is an affront to our sovereignty everywhere and the campaign to free Maddesyn is firm in that belief. There are also other freedom campaigns with which I'm not closely tied, freedom campaigns and mutual aid funds, bail funds for all of our community members who put their bodies and lives on the line, the front lines to protect our land, to protect the drinking water for us, for our non-human kin, and for everybody who lives on our land, invited or not. That they're defending their land from pipelines and environmental degradation and resource extraction.

For that they're criminalized and incarcerated, perhaps most famously recently Red Fawn for defending Oceti Sakowin against the pipelines and for doing that, she served 57 months in prison until she was released in the fall of 2020. I also bring up Red Fawn's case because she was sentenced and served her time at the federal facility, FCI Dublin, which is here in California, but it's a federal prison where Maddesyn is also likely to be sent because if you are convicted of a crime on a reservation, you go to a federal facility. FCI Dublin is currently under investigation for multiple complaints of sexual assault by the COs, the corrections officers, the chaplain, people who offer services, health services, spiritual services, and the warden.

When we think about what it means to fight the carceral state; when defending our land will get you sent to a federal facility; when defending your life will get you sent to a federal facility that is rife with sexual violence and abuse. The colonial connect-the-dots game there is easy to play, and I wanted to emphasize that. I want to close by highlighting some of the cultural and spiritual work that is also abolitionist and decolonial even though it is often depoliticized. In Humboldt County, the Native Women's Collective is a small non-profit that puts on regalia-making workshops, volleyball camps, and awareness and outreach events for missing and murdered Indigenous women in our area. This area has seen an explosion of those numbers [of missing/murdered Indigenous women] due to the cannabis industry up here.[7]

Because this work is depicted as cultural with a lowercase "c," and even cute, like making necklaces and dresses is somehow hobby work; anyone who's ever stabbed their finger with a leather needle knows that it is not cute hobby work or just paper cut with maple or grass. It is not cute, de-politicized work. And people assume that maybe it's unrelated, that this work we do is unrelated to the crises of environmental, spiritual, and physical violence in our communities and because of that, it gets counted out of abolition. And then we think of ourselves as not doing abolitionist work, not doing political work; but the cultural work that brings us closer to one another and strengthens our relationships to place outside of relations of property and domination is inherently life-affirming, life-generating, and in opposition to the carceral state. Simply put, the fight is everywhere we take it to.

Dian Million

I'm from Alaska, and this a different kind of history in Alaska, that of the 577 nations and the many hundreds of thousands that are not so-called "recognized" by any state across Turtle Island; we are a great diversity when within ourselves and our places.

I want to honor that and talk about how that challenged me as a young woman coming out of Alaska and not knowing what other people had gone through. There were no reservations, or only one reservation set up in Alaska, but what had happened was the same thing that had happened everywhere – anywhere in which a carceral state, a racial capitalist state had been put into operation. Before I go to how I came to write about trauma in terms of capitalism and the state, I want to just to say that we, until the Alaska Native Claims and Settlement Act was established in the late 1960s, and early 1970s, were here a long period of time.[8]

We were still mostly self-governing villages. We didn't have reservations. We had villages and we did have an internal order in which policing was carried out by our own peoples and a council. I'm not going to lie or romanticize it. It was not un-police-like, but it was established by us and it was under our own order. I bring this up mainly because one of the effects of the Alaska Native Claims Act was to reorder it so that we then had no policing at all.[9] Our tribal governments, our village governments, then began to have to rely on the state of Alaska. It was a great vacuum, and lawless settlers and everybody else came through our country, just like they had for many hundreds of years.

Gold rushes and everything else wreaked havoc on us, and we had no protections. There was a huge vacuum in which the violence occurred in Alaska, which was somewhat different than the minute surveillance and intimate policing that had been established under colonization in what became the continental United States. Today when we are evoking the spirits of the women that were taken from us, I have to evoke the name of my sister, Karen. Karen disappeared in Anchorage, Alaska, between 1971 and 1972. She was supposed to meet my mother at a mall for lunch and never showed up. They tried to demonize the memory of my sister by saying that she had been involved in devious affairs, etc. But that is untrue and unrelated to the circumstances of her death, or her disappearance rather. We never found our sister, and she remains missing.

This kind of self-policing sometimes gets left out, go back to it to establish how I first came to begin to understand exactly how we have established a kind of intimate policing of our own selves under colonization, and the ways in which our resistance is in such a way as to actually be a struggle to reestablish our love and social relations. That we hold up every person because they fought, and they struggled. The aim was to take us apart at a very intimate level.

When you see this in many of the reservations over a 50-, 60-year period with people struggling and fighting and being moved around and pushed into each other, scrambled up here in Washington territory – they would shove 14 tribes together, ones that didn't even have close relations. Internal struggles occurred in which there was internal policing. In 1878, there was the inauguration of the first self-policing system.[10] That's when the tribal police themselves were first established. These today still have the legitimacy of the United States, these are the ones that are funded and cared for and educated, etc. But these have been a feature of different communities for a long time. A lot of my research has been about the Office of Indian Affairs, the bureaucracy that was established after the war department gave up direct management. First, we were under the management of Indian Country as they called it. And then it migrates to the Office of Indian Affairs, which does the rational thing, to establish this surveillance system over every aspect of Indigenous life even that far back, like the 1878s onward. It's a very rational system, it's a measurement of assimilation, cards are established for each family. Surveillance goes out, they interview the families. They mark them for whether or not they're wearing white clothes or whether or not they have white manners, et cetera. This is the same time they are establishing the racialization: instead of being Hupa, you then become an Indian. And the blood quantum, so-called rational measurement of our family relations and ableism, because they're trying to insert us in capitalism.

My interest has always been this kind of intimate policing, this absolute close surveillance of all of our means of reproduction, both social and biological. I know we're not the only groups of people that have actually endured the implementation of gender roles, sexuality, every single way that you can look at how we have been under absolutely tight control. At the same time, we have resisted this control meant to sever our ability to cohere as able, capable families and societies. There isn't any other answer to this. When they say we weren't supposed to survive, we really weren't supposed to survive, either not embodied, or in any form of our social relationships.

I've spent a long time looking at how is it that we did survive though, to continue to fight and struggle and cohere. I thought that some of the lessons from it had to do with other peoples who had endured this kind of absolute severing of the most intimate relations. I've brought my energies around over the last few years and back to basically what I had been interested in doing when I first got into this work, which was organizing. I had been organizing 30 years ago with United Indian Women, and we were all about being really supportive. All of us had these experiences of having been removed into urban areas, cut off from our family, our kin, our places, our senses of support, and in some cases, our identities – because we didn't really even know who we were.

There were lots of people who'd been released from boarding schools. There were some people who were not capable of taking care of themselves any longer; how do we establish care in this kind of a situation? I didn't even realize for a really long time what a beautiful job we did, at least in that moment. And these are the relations of activist families. Our activist families actually established really cohesive relations, which we took away with us as actually big lessons. We unbanded there and moved on.

I'd like to turn for a second and ask questions about: what is our role in establishing any relations of abolition? What does it mean to provide care under the conditions that I just named? They're not inert; they're still actively trying to break our relationship because we know that racial capitalism requires us to be atomized in order to become the subject of the nation-state, okay. The subject of capitalism is a consumer; an individual consumer. So how do we continue? To establish these relations that I'm calling acts of intentional kinship. Intentional means that you want to actually plan to open your relations up in order to learn, and also to establish responsibilities, to establish all those kinds of things. Intentional kinning, or intentional kinship, occurs in places, and these are not places that don't have history. These are not places that don't already have relations there. It's also an intentional responsibility to those relations as well.

An intentional effort to make lateral relations. And this is where I was very inspired by Ruth Wilson Gilmore into wanting to get into this conversation around what abolition is. Whether we had anything to bring to the table to give us food. I thought we did of course. I'm going to read just a little passage of this, and then I'll end my comments for the second.

I bring Indigeneity into this because Indigeneity is not our racialization. Indigeneity, I think, is a set of relations. I suggest that Indigeneity is foremost a practice of governance, ontologically, and epistemologically lived within places that are not imagined as static. Indigeneity is a global practice in living that liberal humanism and racial capitalism have tried to eradicate from the Earth for over 500 years. Indigeneity posits ways of living that create governances that are never the same across places at all times. Indigenous practices emerge specifically within a set of relations that are material, spiritual, and dynamic. Indigenous practices form governments, not nation-states. Our peoples have variously expressed their ontology, their premise for being as a set of relations, where all are sent in possessing agency.

Indigeneity strives to create relations of care and reciprocity, understanding the interdependence of all in a place with a shared goal of thriving in a place without destruction. This is a governance that seeks to continue the conditions for all life. This is the core of what became understood as Indigeneity globally. You often express caretaker relations of peoples with land denying a singular understanding of land as property. Land is not property as a part of relation. And land is not the entirety of any relations as they are understood in any place.[11]

I read an invitation to a conversation on what Indigeneity means to the abolitionist call for practices of freedom in places. It is to speak to the sometimes fraught and sometimes generous questions that are opposed between Black and Indigenous feminisms. That's how I've tried to enter into this conversation for the last few years. I'm still learning – I beg forgiveness and opened myself up, because I am intentionally trying to make kin and draw other people into speaking, how we might make relations, acknowledging that we are all in places and that we can be something here together that is not based on either exclusion or violence to each other in any form.

Joy James

My recognition of the spirit. There's so many sisters and children, brothers, fathers, mothers, aunts, and uncles we've lost, but we stay connected. I appreciate this call for deeper connections in order to ensure the longevity and health of our peoples, and all peoples. Thank you for teaching. The questions that you've posed are really powerful. We're all grappling with them in different ways, because I don't think we're quite comfortable with the answers, particularly the answers that come from sectors we don't fully trust. Sometimes, I think we don't fully trust ourselves.

When the answer tells us that we cannot go back inside the edifice, that we have to move beyond it, that can be pretty daunting if not downright scary. I appreciate the opening with the resistance of the women who understand the beauty of the land and water, and also the value of their own bodies as also being sacred. These intrusions – rapes, colonization – are acts of war in my understanding. To be a war resistor, what does that look like? I think of war resistors that will protest all wars: domestic and foreign, international. We can withhold our monies in terms of taxes [used for weaponry]; but of course, the state will come and take our stuff. I'm wondering how we could become more deeply organized as war resistors across various communities. What would that look like? We understand the war includes the child who is disappeared [from their communities and homes]. Even if the Pope gives apologies [for the abuse and killings of Indigenous children in Canada's Catholic residential schools], that is not the cessation of war, it's merely a *mea culpa* which is totally insufficient in a genocidal war.

Social workers understand or refuse to understand that Black families are no more violent or pathological than white families, but social workers continue child removal from Black families at a disproportionate rate – hence in Texas, they talk about "disproportionality" – rather than giving the families the support they need, or [just leaving them alone rather than have families] punished in a carceral system. The history of war is the dismemberment of family. It's a dismemberment of honor; it's the displacement of women and LGBTQ people. What we do is we stitch ourselves back together, which is what you've done. I come from people from Texas and Mississippi who quilt. You take … rags, and then you make art. And then the art can keep you warm at night or in the winter.

The traditions we have are really fierce. You both embody them. Thinking about the twenty-first century … our cultures … still distinct, I'm wondering about these alliances where we flow in the same direction. I was wondering, as you were speaking, what you might be able to say about our tolerance for both love and pain. The way we love kind of pushes us out to become very visible in our demands to reject a punitive carceral state, a genocidal policy accumulation, destruction of land, air, and water and communities. Do you see more about how we might find comfort in that love? Even when it gives us courage we might not want to have. Because that makes you more visible as a target of the state or the corporation or your university [and] its disciplinarian moves.

I was listening to a talk that Myisha Cherry did a year or so ago when their book came out focused on Black rage, titled *The Case for Rage*. This led me to wonder about how angry we are allowed to be and still maintain community? I think, all our emotions are legit, particularly if we've been dealing with genocide for centuries, which has probably mutated those emotions. They may not be even clearly evident to ourselves. Once you go to those schools [and are] taught to engage in self-loathing and to reject your cultures. I'm wondering how rage could be generative and not destructive. I was also thinking of the women that I organized with years ago in a dojo to give protections around anti-racism, marches for LGBTQ rights, or support for youth like the Central Park exonerated falsely targeted by the police. I'm wondering what is self-defense in this moment. From the women that I've been with in seminary or on the streets who assert that self-defense is not violent, I've begun to think how could we explain the use of force [as self-defense]? Psychological, or emotional, violence [are often not seen as] abuse; however, the use of force to defend yourself against abuse from the state, community members who've internalized the violence. Also, is there anything about security that's also sacred? We understand life is sacred not just because of our deities and our spirits. The sacredness of our own lives require force, which could be just what we say verbally or how we write a poem. Security is not solely a militaristic move, the state excels in warfare. Security is the force to preserve our lives, our lineage, our longevity, and our love.

Lumsden

I think we're flowing in the same direction now, thinking about these things, because they are the questions at hand. How are we to do all of this? All that is required of us to make life, to make freedom, to have the future we are getting to. How do we get there? These are the questions to consider. I'm going to think about just that first kind of opening question or query you have about, how to be an effective organizer against war, which I don't often think that way, but the military are cops and cops are militarized. Hupa people have never understood, or at least historically never understood, the militia or the police or the soldiers to be separate. To resist the state was to be an effective organizer against war. Hupa people were very reluctant to go to war, life is precious to us. We value and love one another in our own cosmological beliefs, and practices prevent us from being even cruel to our enemies or people we don't like. You would offer your enemy first, something to eat because it keeps peace and it keeps life in balance in Hoopa.

When I think about how to be an effective organizer against war, to me is what it has meant to be a Hupa person since they discovered gold on our river. Thinking about that now, as I was walking around my neighborhood the other day, we went around and just saw all these very pro-military messages around Ukraine, ones that kind of give permission to the United States war machine really to expand in the guise of kindness and brotherliness and solidarity and helpfulness. In actuality, it expands and gives more license to this war machine that got started by displacing us. I'm thinking about what it means to be Hupa as an effective organizer against war. That's an Indigenous epistemology and way of being and understanding justice as to be fundamentally against the state and violent states.

I want to just connect that to your question about love and what comfort love gives us, even if it's that love that gives us ... Courage that maybe we don't want. Or I see a lot of my friends now being like, "I don't want to be resilient anymore, actually. I would just like to live my life. I would just like freedom." We're kind of sick of being brave. We're kind of sick of being resilient. So how do we take comfort in this love even if it gives us a responsibility that we feel as though we cannot bear. Love is very closely related to rage.

The love I have for people, for our freedom, for the people I know we are going to be when we throw this state off. We get to return to ourselves and connect in a different way, that love is directly related to the rage and venom really that I have for the state. And all that they have done to us. And I just think about how to sit in productive rage and a student of feminist theory, of course, thinking about the uses of anger, of course, in Audre Lorde's piece. For me, it tells me that I'm still present. It tells me I'm still in connection and in responsible and ethical relation to others.

If I felt no rage for what the state did to us, continues to do to us, I wouldn't be able to have community, because I would know that would mean that I'm a step removed from my accountability to the people whose lives are on the line. Being Hupa is to be an organizer against war, at least historically that intellectual and activist genealogy exists, and we should all tap into it. We're all resistors and organizers historically, otherwise we wouldn't be here today. We all have those ancestors, those resistance families. And that we must take heart in the radical love we have for one another, even as it commands us to do rageful, maybe violent things against the state, because that rage of the state is an affirmation of the love and protection and sacredness of our relations and our own bodies and spirits, the waterways, more than human's can.

Million

I don't remember when I first became totally conscious that it couldn't be called anything but war, and fairly young, actually, took more or less an oath of sorts because I organized with the American Indian Movement for quite some time. Thus, as far as we were concerned, we were engaged in a war for our lives and these were for each of us. Also, just like Stephanie thinking in terms of our peoples, our families, and our places, even though we were displaced, that's our difference. In these places that we struggled, we didn't come in uninvited, we only came in by invitation of the community itself and then we went by their rules. So, there were rules of war.

I talk about it. I still talk about it that way, in terms of just actually as an actual war. There have been actual people who have organized to struggle, understanding it as a state of war in which somebody told me when I was young, "You can't do this work and not love, that this work is always done for love, not for hate." It's not about hating. It's for love and for building for a better time and better day for us, that, of course, like I keep referring to, it meant for our children to survive. You know what I'm saying? It meant for us to stop losing so many children to the state. It meant all the things, to stop losing so many family members to incarceration, to debt, to early deaths by alcohol or somebody else's hands or whatever. So, there's all kinds of different ways in which this war manifested, but it was a war. I still think of it as a war.

The other thing that I learned a little later on was that because of the generation that I came into this struggle with, I also envisioned that we would have a better day. We may reestablish good relations and good times and good places but cherish them very much because the system itself morphs when we actually establish or push back, that's why I don't blame it in reforming things, because to the extent that you reform it, then it reforms again because it's a constant kind of ongoing struggle with an organic system itself. It's an organic system of sorts that changes with the resistance that comes to it.

So, I get a little philosophical, but it has to do with what I feel about self-defense because I watch every generation now try to reestablish what it means by self-defense, and it's beautiful to watch the different strategies that people bring to this.

The second is one that is much closer to home and that is that one of my young relatives went up against the fascists in Portland as part of the affiliate groups with Black Lives Matter this past couple of years. Of course, a person came and attacked one of the Black Lives Matter organizers. She was organizing a march. She's like one of the last organizers there that is really active. Her support group was around her, some of them were responsible for traffic, and a fascist person came with a semiautomatic and killed at least two of them before our self-defense team could take them out.

For me it's not an academic question. It's a real question about the order that arises when we are at war or we are trying to protect. The Oceti, Standing Rock is a really good example of an Indigenous order coming into place that had to handle all these different peoples coming in, but the order held and they insisted that they were protectors, not protestors, which is really a different action. They insisted on particularly peaceful action, which is not what everybody always calls for in each situation. It really depends on who's in the the order or how people have organized the order in the situation.

Many of the times we have been with Black Lives Matter and other organizers in the last couple of years in which we listened and were with that order, and that the order that they had established there is really important around trying to take care of people in a place where violence is imminent to the situation. I'm just being very realistic about things that are happening right now.

It's just that I never rule out the fact that sometimes we have to physically protect ourselves. Especially at this point in time, I am very convinced at this point in time that fascism has always been a part of this country but is getting a real supercharged boost right now from a lot of different directions, which will mean that the question of self-defense is a real one, not a hypothetical one whatsoever. But underlying every single bit of it is love. It's love for what is life.

Lumsden

Can I add on to what you said, Dian, about self-defense? It's something I'm thinking about a lot as I struggle to write about struggle. What does a Native feminist practice of abolition look like? What is it? I think I start with cultural work, like gathering, making relations with the land, reintroducing ourselves to one another, sharing knowledge and holding space, the kind of talk that happens when we all sit around and grind pine nuts for two hours, right? That kind of stuff. That, to me, is abolitionist work because, like I said, it's life-affirming and life-generating. It is a defense. It is a defense of our relationship with this place and an affirmation and connection. But what then when that is interrupted? What then when we know that the park rangers or whatever are issuing tickets around people or counting pine nuts that we gather, or what then when the people who regularly come to those spaces, those cultural spaces are being detained, are facing attack in their everyday life, are endangered, imperiled by the presence and invasion of the US on our land. This is still an active invasion and occupation. So, then what constitutes self-defense? I think it's easy to stay or it's more palatable to a liberal audience, a wider audience that we talk about cultural work as a sort of self-defense. But also, that sometimes we need to be armed, that we need to physically fight and be prepared to do so. I'm going to pair that with a saying about cultural work, and gathering. There are magazine articles that we ourselves circulate and publish sharing us doing this very cheesy smile, gathering of our stuff.

Million

We used to print T-shirts. That's how we got money to travel around and pay for our stuff.

Lumsden

We make our own pamphlets, those things. But what we often leave out of those is that we have loaded guns in our cars when we go up the hill, that all of us have knives that are not just for scraping bark, that they're actually in case you face people, the illegal pot growers and others up in our high country, in our gathering space. I want to think about that. On the one hand, we have this reaffirmation, this reconnection to the land, to each other. It's like a nice way to spend a day. We have lunch; we gather. And there's a loaded gun in the car because we might actually have to defend violently our right to be in that place or defend our own bodily integrity or defend one another from being run off the road, being cornered, going missing. So, I don't think of those things as separate, I guess, the kind of everyday work that's unremarkable, or maybe doesn't sound political, but that work, that gathering pine nuts, the sitting around, that kind of atmosphere of the kitchen table, that that is protected by our willingness and preparedness to go back to war.

Million

That's it. And that's it in a pine nut. It always has been so, and every generation of us could articulate this in some different fashion.

I see a question: "I'm wondering if you can speak to the place of grief, grief practices in these conversations. Just as rage is love, grief is love."

I would talk about that just a little bit in that I just heard someone about a week ago speak from a specific practice that was going on in Toronto. I think that person's going to bring their own words out at some point.

I'm not going to try to go too deeply into it, other than I was just blown away by the actual practice there of understanding totally that grief is normal. We have a lot to grieve, and it's not just the specific grief of a lost one, a lost relation in a particular place in time. But again, that it is normal to bring it back into the range of our ability to feel that which is happening to us or has happened to us or that we're enduring or that we've experienced. There it was, again, those things I was saying. Indigeneity has things to bring to this conversation because it was very real, the use of local medicines, also the use of disabled and queer theory to create space, gorgeous spaces of kind of a wrap-around, allowing a space for a person to work through a process, which changes you. To understand that as an actual change thing, not something to fix, and that was my whole point about therapeutic nations.

I just thought it was a beautiful example to bring up and say, "Yes, grief is a process that is worked through your relations and you come out in a different place. It's not something you get over."

Lumsden

I've been thinking a lot about grief because it's so intimately related, as we all know, as you feel in your body how intimately tied it is to the deep love and longing that we have for these loved ones who are taken from us. But also, it's tied up in the rage we feel at the state because your grief tells you who is to blame if you're attuned to it, if you're not allowing it to manipulate it. I have found that at least in these instances that grief is a great teacher and telling me the state's to blame for what's happening here in the violence in our lives. Grief's very animating. Grief, it's a kind of North Star, guiding you to what justice could be if you listen to that feeling in your body. It will tell you there's an injustice here in that you should demand more. You should always demand more.

Also, I mentioned grief briefly in my talk about how the state really seeks to co-opt grief from us. It sees the swell of active organizing and campaigning and canvassing and looking for our own loved ones. It sees this great rise and resurgence in Native governance and collective capacities for defense and demanding justice, and it quakes in its boots, the state, because this is a war. This is a counterinsurgency. Violence against us is counterinsurgency still as it ever was. So I want us to be very, very careful about our grief and how the state might capitalize on it and turn it into an intimate investment in empire.

So, I am grieved. I'm bereft. I'm someone with a lot of loss, like all of us survivors are. The state, I think, sees that and dangles a carrot, and is like,

> Would you like love, belonging, safety, security, and a happy future for your tribe? All you have to do is say that we can help you stop the violence in your life. All you have to do is extend tribal cops and extend policing jurisdictions and extend the power and might of the state in its capacity to jail the most marginal of our people. All you have to do is sign off on the death and dying of the most marginal people, the dearest to us. And you can achieve that carrot of maybe this will end the violence against us.

I want us to be suspicious, angry, full of rage, venom, and maybe full of violence for the state that tries to cheapen our grief from our lost loved ones and turn it into a way to grow more cops. I just won't have it. So, I really want to highlight that point. It's my newest but long-standing and personal ax to grind. The state can't take our love, too. They can't take all they've taken and take the grief I feel for my loved ones. They can't have it. I'm not going to let them use it in the service of displacing and killing others.

Million

Yes. This is just exactly what I mean about the trauma. It's the point where the state itself wants to own our trauma and move it, wants to politicize it, or depoliticize it, or to own it, or to move us with it or what have you. This to me was one of the strongest lessons about it was is that for us to be the picture, well, that's what they're doing with missing and murdered women, too. We're making this, the poster children for the violence of the state, but it's a hidden violence. We're the subject of it in terms of our deaths, but there's no perpetrator. The perpetrator becomes faceless in that kind of postured event of our grief and our murders.

James

The state is so powerfully insightful in terms of what it sells back to us. It's like a package deal on an insurance policy. "You're afraid? Okay, come into the enclosure. Stay in the enclosure. Follow the rules. And we will give you some form of protection." Yet they don't tell you the real source of the violence. Most of it is structured and radiates out through the state and increasingly its laws. All of our movements were fierce and flawed, but they delivered. This is a historic moment. Proto-fascists get to come above ground, play with or shoot guns, intimidate [marginalized/racialized] communities, set abortion bounties, and ban same-sex marriages. It's [precarity] but they tell you as they increase the terror against us, that the safest place to be is inside their enclosure.

I love the way you laid it out. I've [heard] "Can you sign right here?" multiple times. I [will initially say] "Well, let me find a pen." [Then, I back off:] "Oh, no, I don't think so, not right now." But you just trashed it. You burned the contract with your words. There's no way [to go forward contractually] once we can communicate clearly ... as you're doing [by stating] that we care for ourselves and our progeny, ancestors and everybody who sacrifices. There's no way we can sign the contract [unless] they get us to forget [genocide]. If we remember [the genocides], we will never sign.

Margaux Kristjansson

There's a question that asks: "How do you think the increase in resource extraction and environmental justice increased carceral practices or even gender reproduction rights that go against Indigenous traditions of reproductive rights?"

Lumsden

Those two things that seem like they're at odds, but actually both kind of or make possible other carceral practices or that gender and reproductive rights go against reproductive justice that are more traditional, that these liberal substitutes or concessions that are offered as a way to diminish sovereignty, diminish bodily integrity, and to protect us, should protect us from the most violent machinations of the carceral settler state.

I think the "how" is the question. I would say, yes, that's true. How resource extraction and then environmental justice moves are more about conservation and reestablishing settler orders of property and the wilderness property binary.

To speak in Humboldt County, thinking about the huge increase in the cannabis industry since the decriminalization or legalization of marijuana in the state, which in abolitionist circles is positive. Decriminalization, decriminalize everything under the sun. The social problems associated with drug use won't be solved with criminalization. But the proliferation of the cannabis industry up here in the extractive economy has done huge amounts of environmental damage and has brought evermore policing into reservations and has brought something similar to man camps, which are traveling migrants. We call them trimmigrants, the people who come up to work pot farms. All of that has really exacerbated an already existing context of settler violence against Indian reservations. Where there are more Native people, there's more violence against Native people because whiteness feels threatened.

On the flip side of that point is the conservation movements that really seek to remove Native people from our lands, that my friend Cutch is obsessed with land trusts, non-Native land trusts, because they think of themselves as doing this really incredible freedom decolonial work because they're protecting land from this sort of extractive economy, except that they're keeping it in white hands. They're reaffirming white property ownership and they don't really get why Indians are mad that they too are stealing land. Even if you do it with a smile, settlers, that's still not your land. The right thing to do is to give it back.

We find ourselves kind of trapped in these multiple iterations of carceral logics of the settler state, but we must not confuse them. We must not think they're liberation just because this one seems nicer than the other. They work together. The cannabis industry and white property conservation kind of ethos and ethics or anti-ethics, those two things work together to create a carceral experience of living on occupied land.

And that's what we have. We have all of these different ways. And then thinking about even things like reproductive rights, and access, we should all be thinking about that very carefully right now. Because as Joe Biden is demonstrating in real time, it doesn't actually care about the bodily integrity and autonomy of anyone, least of all Native women.

Things that are offered in terms of individual rights, that get held up as radical freedom, the decolonial future, perhaps. I think we should really push back against that and be like, those individual rights, they aren't going to do a hell of a whole lot if we don't have water for the salmon to run. That's a very different discussion of reproduction and reproductive rights and one that really refutes the same carceral logics that silo these things from each other.

The way we live on our land is not separate from the empowerment we feel in our own bodies and the safety and security and sacredness of our own bodies. So, when we talk about those things, we have to talk about them more holistically. That's how I think, we're going to fight back against the state, because we won't be contained. There's a saying, "Be like the wind or be like the water." You can't be captured, really, if you're always fluid.

Million

In our own experiences, there is no dividing line between any of these things. They are emergent together. When you brought up the fish and the waters and the people's ability to live in place, I'm thinking right now in terms of livability. Livability because the extraction, of course, has gone on to the extent where we're experiencing 100-, 105-degree weather. We're experiencing fires nobody has ever seen before. We're living in smoke. There isn't any place that's not affected now.

Somebody just asked about healing. I can't even address that right now. The basic thing that we need to know at this point is: We talk about futurities, but the future is now. It's embedded in this moment. That's how all or most of our folks [view it]: ... all time is now, is what some people would say (probably not Natives). We're thinking, in terms of the Seventh Generations, at this moment in time. I cry because there's no healing on the Earth.

The Earth is not ill. The Earth is doing what the Earth will do. The Earth is all these systems. The Earth is not dependent upon us. The Earth is going to make the changes that it must make to put itself in balance and whether or not that still gives us actually the conditions to live in any particular place, which was what we knew from the beginning, which was the production of our society in places, dependent on our being absolutely totally listening, hearing, feeling, experiencing, knowing what was balance in those places.

We knew exactly what happens if you can't live there any longer because it won't support you any longer. That's reproduction in the most profound sense. I'm living in a time when I really worry about displacement. Our folks up north are being displaced. The ice is melting to the extent that many of us, in Washington state here too, must move away. We must move away. We must move higher or further or even away from our own lands.

This is not recent. This has been going on for some time. So, when we start talking about conservation, I would just say no. The reproduction of life on this planet, the reproduction of our peoples in these places, and the extraction have set some things in motion. You're either part of the solution right now or there's no stopping what the Earth is going to do. There's my rage.

How can there be more coalition- and alliance-building and awareness of the intertwined intersections between abolition and decolonization and the ways they're sometimes thought of separately? I just think we have to be brave enough to have the conversations and do more and act on them.

It can't just be talk. It has to be actual responsibilities, of undertaking the conversation and braving the out. Of hearing things, maybe you don't want to hear or actually contemplate what is being asked and how to go forward. I think that it's the most important time on Earth. I mean, there was a huge amount of energy that has been put into keeping these particular experiences separate. They are not the same experiences, but they have relations that are absolutely not just historical. They have relations in the flesh. Many of our families belong to both communities and we're already related, so we need to talk like we are.

Lumsden

I'm thinking about coalition- and alliance-building and awareness, intertwined and intersecting all these connections. As Dian said, a lot of that is being aware that doing organizing work is not the same as activist work. Activist means you show up to different events and you participate, maybe peripherally, in things. You would call yourself an activist. When the call goes out, I activate. That's a great thing to be.

That's a little bit different than being an organizer. I'm thinking right now of the work of Mariame Kaba in her book, *We Do This 'Til We Free Us*. In one of the chapters, she says something to the effect that to organize is a constant practice. It doesn't come with a paycheck. It's constant work. It needs to be part of our every day. It needs to be part of our social organization and part of our working networks. It needs to be part of the way we live our lives and organize ourselves, constitute ourselves as social and political beings. It means a lot of emails. It means a lot of figuring out how you're going to make those connections with others. It means always holding space to bring more people in.

A simple example I'll give to you, is from the California Coalition for Women Prisoners and the campaign to free Maddesyn George, Survived + Punished, all these different intersecting, interlocking and co-mingling co-conspirators against the state and state violence. What they do is they hold meetings. A part of those monthly meetings is open to everyone. It's a place where they welcome more people in. That's written into their agenda. It may seem like a small thing. But to me, that was a really important moment, to be a part of a group that actively did that.

You don't just show up at a meeting and sit around in a circle or now a Zoom room, and then be like, "Hi". You don't really know what to do because you're a newcomer to that space. Instead, as organizers, as planners of these events, as the people in charge of putting on these things and bringing everyone to order, like Diana was saying, what orders emerge in our defense of ourselves, we need to start organizing around these orders. How do we bring more people in? How do we feed and love and sustain, feed spiritually and with snacks, the people who are already in our groups? How do we just start inviting? How do we spread? How do we disseminate information? How do we reach out and ask for mutual aid organizing? How do we ask for help, and where our organization could use a partner like that organization?

It doesn't have to be as formal as an organization. This group of rabble-rousers could really use two more fighters. How do they find them? They maybe have those community events, where they're inviting more people in. It's not all that super militant. A lot of it's being really silly and really friendly. We're social. Part of that silliness and play, needs to be a part of the organizing work we do, to free us all, to free us all and deliver us to the future we deserve.

That's a long-winded answer, but on the other hand, we've got to be willing to sit in discomfort with each other and be mad at each other, even in our spaces of protection and love. Being in love is often about being mad at people, I have found. Then, we also need to do the kind of everyday social work of reconnecting, of being like, hey, this is what I'm about. Do you want to join me? That's political work. It challenges those of us who are very shy to be less so. It challenges those of us like me, who never shut up, to be quiet more and make space for others. It's that everydayness of making connections. You already do that work. You've already made friends in your life.

Million

I think that we should also be generous about forms. I think that there's all kinds of different groupings that accomplish different things. Find the form for what it is that is your mission, is your care, what it is that you wish to accomplish or what have you. It can be two people, four people, eight people, many people. It just depends.

I really think that we should pay attention to what order emerges because it matters. It matters, our own practices within these groups, many people who are veteran organizers. Which I don't necessarily include myself in. I have had my organizing history. But basically, those people that I know of, who have been dyed-in-the-wool organizers, are always very careful about what the relations are of their movement together. They really care, because how we treat each other inside these places is the measure of the change that we make.

I've learned a lot by being a part of groups I never thought I'd be part of before. I was absolutely shocked when I was with Food Not Bombs in San Francisco for a while because they had a much freer order than what I was used to. They had their own way of doing things, but it was really wonderful to learn from them. I think we could learn also from having different forms and paying attention to our relations and what they emerge as order.

James

I really like the idea of these meetings in the round, to build connections and also the difference, making the distinction between activists and organizers. I think that organizers actually build movements. But I'm wondering if the movements, at times, could also give birth to a kind of marronage or maroon sites.

The Seminoles [Indigenous peoples in Florida who embraced Black/ African people who escaped from slavery, and later defeated US military] keep coming into my brain. We have centuries of coalitions and intermingling and families converging. I'm still mindful of what we've said about the trajectory of the state. Its origin story is in enslavement and genocide. The first enslaved in the Americas would've been the Indigenous. Then they took Indigenous people from Africa and brought them into slavery in the Americas; colonialism kept the cycle going. How do we grapple with the need for sanctuary? If we find that schools are violent to our children, or laws in Texas [mandate that] parents are going to go to prison because they affirm their children [as nonbinary], then we have to rethink what schooling is [or should be]. We have to rethink what food systems, delivery of food would be. We have to rethink what housing is.

In New York City, we have a Black mayor [Eric Adams] who's a former cop and the first Black woman NYPD Commissioner [Keechant Sewell who resigned in 2023]. Things are going straight downhill in terms of civil and human rights. New York City government is not efficient ... it demolishes encampments for the unhoused and offers limited beds after displacing hundreds of people. Where are they to go? Into the subway to get hit by trains? The state has decided that our communities are disposable and should be targets for repression. We want sanctuaries. We want marronage.

Certain [movement] sectors got millions or tens and hundreds of millions of dollars and should tithe to the impoverished. Amazon Jeff Bezos gave $100 million [to CNN pundit Van Jones] for "abolition" work after George Floyd was murdered in 2020. Those funds should be put into autonomous food and housing support and also be used for education or freedom schools. I'm not calling for a shakedown. But it should be okay to issue a clear mandate: "You got that much money? Keep part of it ... but put the rest into an umbrella system that only [low-income] communities can access." Let under-resourced communities decide what their greatest needs are and address those material needs [with billionaire dollars].

Million

I think we're talking about scales. One of the things that I've wondered about or have been experiencing is, how do we sustain? I back away from trying to build. What happens is, of course, we know that sometimes what we create, in terms of care spaces, end up getting co-opted by their attempts to fund them, so that they endure. Of course, this is old news to most of the people that are in this conversation.

I worry about this. That's why I said, I think they should take different forms. I think you're right. I think that there is an absolute necessity because we have created these spaces before, where we've fed people and clothed them and housed them. This could be done again. But the idea, it's the endurance part for me. I think a lot of times in Indian Country, where I've seen us be successful is, we take over a space and we do what we're going to do quickly and with a lot of order. Our order emerges, whatever one we have decided on obeying in that space.

We get business done as much as we can, but we know we can't sustain it, and then we let go of it. We burn the teepees, basically, and move on. That's what I've experienced most of my life, our ability to organize moments with profound movement and learn from them and learn a lot from having established them, about establishing the order and helping people in that moment.

What I'm hearing you say, Joy, is that we should establish places of refuge, of this kind of care that we're talking about and find funding for them that is not dependent. Have it be more than having an open space in which we're just in community. In terms of who can be there, it's not specific, it's for the need and for those people that need it in that community, that would identify that need. So, I would be for something like that, if I was not afraid of what it takes to make anything like that endure very long. That's what we're trying to do in Portland.

James

I agree with you. When you were talking, I was thinking of the sanctuary movement, when the Reagan administration unleashed [US-funded] death squads in El Salvador and Guatemala. The US trained them at Fort Benning, Georgia, at the School of the Americas, also known as the "School of the Assassins." [which influences militarized "Cop Cities" today]. Radical organizers and a sanctuary movement got people out and housed them.

Maybe, I overthink the "war metaphor." This isn't what we individually, collectively do in academia. I think of contemporary coalitions within the "Underground Railroad" that create sanctuary. It's not something everybody can do. Maybe it will have a structure that is not healthy ... there's so much desperation out there. The autonomous zones ... maroons that coexist with "civil society" and the state, still have an unique role to play in liberation.

Million

I'm in total agreement. We need to have all kinds of different scales and levels of things established. I'd like to be part of a coalition that has established that.

Lumsden

I was thinking while you were both speaking about sanctuary, about getting our people where they can be safe. We protect us, because the state certainly won't and to step into that role. While you're talking, it just brought me back to Toypurina and her vision of ransacking the mission that her enslaved people built and then were incarcerated in. Leading that attack, after her vision, was very much about striking down their captors and taking back all the wealth they stole and then redistributing it among the survivors.

That's what I hear in this call for organized sanctuary, coalition, for keeping our people safe and housed in the face of what the cops do, that footage from New York, of all the sweeps they were doing of homeless encampments. We can invoke Toypurina's vision of organizing those of us who can organize, against our captors, so that we can take back what is stolen from us and redistribute it among ourselves, our comrades, our kin, our loved ones and the ones who aren't born yet. That day's coming. Big and small, that day's coming. Huge, romantic, organized, maybe small, every day, criminal, violent maybe. We're taking the fight wherever we go, in big and small.

SOURCE NOTES

1. "Proclamation on Missing and Murdered Indigenous Persons Awareness Day, 2021." *The White House*, May 4, 2021. www.whitehouse.gov/briefing-room/presidential-actions/2021/05/04/a-proclamation-on-missing-and-murdered-indigenous-persons-awareness-day-2021/
2. S.3623 – 117th Congress (2021–2022): Violence against Women Act Reauthorization Act of 2022. Accessed July 12, 2023. www.congress.gov/bill/117th-congress/senate-bill/3623
3. Biden, Joseph R. "Violence against Women: The Congressional Response." *American Psychologist* 48, no. 10 (1993): 1059–1061. https://doi.org/10.1037/0003-066x.48.10.1059
4. See also: "Assembly Bill 3099 (Ramos, 2020) – Tribal Assistance Program." *State of California – Department of Justice – Office of the Attorney General*, July 5, 2023. https://oag.ca.gov/nativeamerican/ab3099
5. "Assembly Bill 3099 (Ramos, 2020) – Tribal Assistance Program."
6. "Maddesyn's Story." *FREE MADDESYN GEORGE*. Accessed July 11, 2023. www.freemaddesyn.com/maddesyns-story
7. "Campaign." *FREE MADDESYN GEORGE*. Accessed July 11, 2023. www.freemaddesyn.com/campaign
8. "Staff." *Native Women's Collective*. Accessed July 11, 2023. www.nativewomenscollective.org/staff.html
9. Hirschfield, Martha. "The Alaska Native Claims Settlement Act: Tribal Sovereignty and the Corporate Form." *The Yale Law Journal* 101, no. 6 (1992): 1331. https://doi.org/10.2307/796926
10. Ibid.
11. Indian Law Enforcement History. Accessed July 12, 2023. www.tribal-institute.org/download/Indian%20Law%20Enforcement%20History.pdf

6

An Ontology of Betrayal

Frank Wilderson III, Selamawit D. Terrefe, Joy James,
and moderator Taija Mars-McDougall

November 15, 2022

Selamawit D. Terrefe

In thinking about how I wanted to open the discussion, of course, the term "work," rather than "labor," came to mind. I say, "of course," because I cannot but think of the work – rhetorical, corporeal, and psychic labor – that Blackness appears to do in relation to both ontology and betrayal. But is it betrayal or ontology, or perhaps even both ontology and betrayal, that presents the heuristic par excellence for an ontology? The article here, "an," is important for it unveils a singularity unto itself: the fiction of being. This singularity, absent and not denied to Blackness, betrays the performance of non-being as a supplement rather than any semiotic or action. Hence, betrayal, like the anticipatory mourning of a fictive end rendered to the debt that is *one* metaphor for time – its relationship to ontology, rather than ontology itself, presents Blackness as the curious case, at least in my estimation, of what occasions our discussion today. An ontology of betrayal, then, betrays the locus of what I interpret to be the cloak of a performance of reducibility – to language, to meaning, to a Symbolic that rests upon the guarantee of Black death and its dishonor – that is, like the inverse of the gerund form in "dying," Blackness retains its subject at the level of syntax, the noun "death," but without the facticity construed in the regimen of the verb "to die." When could or would this death appear when its performance of legibility is what maintains the Symbolic's anchor to its schemata with the Imaginary and the Real? Can *any* moniker of singularity provide a heuristic to describe the ontology of Blackness when Blackness itself is what is made to appear as being and negation's guarantee? In other words, the questions I begin with are what is the Black psyche's relationship to betrayal when the latter implies both trust and relationality? One can only abandon something with which a contract has been rendered or understood. Would violation's betrayal not mirror the deceit of a dialectic that promises transcendence at the end of its *Aufhebung*? And what, if anything, undergirds the Black psyche's continual investment in the assumption of being as a denouement to the vestiges of violence foundational to its instantiation? What is the Black psyche's investment in betrayal?

Frank Wilderson III

There's a way in which my remarks really echo what Selamawit has just said. A while ago I was interviewed by George Yancy, the Samuel Candler Dobbs Professor of Philosophy at Emory University, for *Truthout* magazine, and there was a certain portion of that which was edited out. It will appear later in his book of all the interviews that he's done – from Joy James to Robin Kelly to Noam Chomsky – but I wanted to actually share with you the portion that did not appear. Most of this did not appear in my exchange with George because it's my way of entering into the title of our topic today.

At one point, George asks this question about what it would be like if all Black people became Afropessimists – and I hadn't actually considered that. Then he says,

> There's a way in which our very desire for inclusion means that we desire to be part of a system from which we are structurally barred, and which would mean our continued social death. Hence, if Black people in the US collectively became Afropessimists, there would be no desire for inclusion, no desire to mimic the false category of the Human, no desire to comply with the parasitic logics of a world whose sense of its own coherence needs Blackness as the object. I think this would frighten the hell out of those who instantiate the category of the Human. I think it would also frighten the hell out of Black people.

And he says, "What do you think, Frank?"[1]
I said:

> Yes, and I want to make it clear that I think this is a beautiful dream that you've articulated here – all Black people becoming Afropessimists. I'm not sure what that would look like as a mass movement. As someone who's written extensively on Afropessimism as one of the so-called founders of it, I would say that if the first Kenyan and the first

Ugandan who were taken across the Gulf to enter Arabia understood that these other people are developing spirituality, family culture into Arabs and their development has a symbiosis to the destruction of my body.[2] Nuance, maybe even untheoretical understanding, has been in the literature, has been with Black people and their stories, and has been in the way we talk to our children for centuries and centuries. That's how old Afropessimism, intuition, and thinking are. But what has not been there and what Afropessimism has brought is a sense that it's okay to say that. It's okay to theorize that. It's okay to struggle for the rights of Indigenous people, struggle for the rights of Latinx people, struggle for the rights of the working class, *and* ridicule the puniness of their demand as we, Blacks, struggle with them.

All that is okay. But your question about how Afropessimism might frighten Black people and would frighten everyone else, this whole question takes me beyond where people like myself, Jared Sexton, Zakiyyah Jackson, Sora Han, Kihana Ross, Connie Wun, Camille Emefa Acey, and Amanda Lashaw started back in Berkeley.[3] I know I've left someone out, and that not everyone agrees on everything, but those are the names that stick most profoundly in my mind. We were critiquing, on one side, the multiracial coalition that had an unconscious symptomatic knee-jerk response to Black people in the political coalitions of San Francisco, the San Francisco Bay area, as those Black people articulated the singularity of their suffering. We were also critiquing that symptomatic response. We were also critiquing our graduate seminars on Marxism and psychoanalysis because we were seeing that these are really wonderful tools for understanding suffering, but they do not explain the fullness of Black suffering. And so, we were offering a critique, not a blueprint, for struggle.

We are now in the year 2022, almost 25 years later, and Black activists, artists, and intellectuals across the globe are thinking through and with Afropessimism. It informs their political activism and their art in ways that we couldn't have imagined in Berkeley at the end of the twentieth century. No one is more surprised by that than me. So, I'm new to the question you've posed. Afropessimism is new to the question, but I do believe that one of the reasons why the massification of Afropessimism into a movement would frighten everyone is because Afropessimism has a critique of the world writ large.

Marxism has a critique of the economic world. Psychoanalysis and feminism – which are informed by Marxism – have a critique of the filial, oedipal, patriarchal world. All those people suffer contingent violence. All those people suffer dishonor through transgression. Afropessimism is a global critique, one which includes the whitest white supremacists and the colored victims of white supremacy.

Another thing to consider is that the unconscious mind in everyone is a rather conservative entity. The unconscious mind desires pleasure at any cost. Anita Wilkins[4] and I were watching *Ryan's Daughter*[5] last night. In that film, you can see how unconscious desire ignores or sidesteps prohibitions set forth by preconscious interest. The preconscious's rules regarding marriage, worship, and civic order – and here, by civic order, I mean the Irish Republicans, not the civic order of the British colonialists. All these things collide with the unconscious mind's quest for gratification. Pleasure is to be conserved at all costs. The unconscious isn't going to just automatically put itself at risk.

Now, Black people have an unconscious too, but it is an unconscious that is garrisoned by non-Black desire, usurped, overridden by the anti-Black imperative to turn white or disappear. If we ever got to a Black unconscious informed by Afropessimism – wow. That would not mean the end of a political-economic order like capitalism, nor the end of an oedipal, filial order like patriarchy – that would mean the end of the order of order. We would be on the cusp not of a crisis, but of an epistemological catastrophe. What I'm trying to say is that on the other side of anti-Blackness, people could still live and breathe and have families, but no one in the world can tell you how that would look because Black people exist beyond semiotic logic.

Yancy asked,

Can you elaborate just a little bit on that, that Black people are beyond semiotic logic?

I responded,

Well, the way I do it with my students because I'm a rhetorician, is to explain that the way semiotics understands conflict cannot really apply to Black people. And if people are interested more about this, I've written about this with respect to the Black Liberation Army.

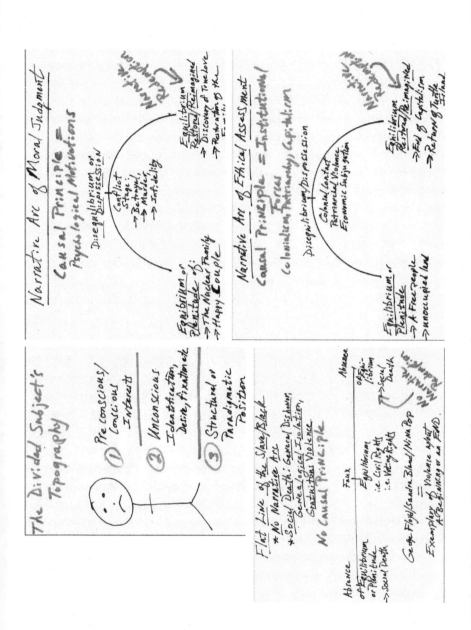

I'll move on in the interest of time for a theoretical explanation. For a theoretical explanation, I draw a triangle on the board, and at the top of the pyramid of the triangle, I put a question mark. And then on the two lower corners, if I'm doing humans, is that I say Native Americans on the lower corner, and the other lower corner, say, white settlers. The point is that they are in conflict, indeed genocidal conflict. The triangle helps students understand why this is not an antagonism. Because at the top of the triangle where there was a question mark, I erased the question mark, and I wrote, "Land," for example. In semiotics, in order to understand conflict, whether we're talking about colonialism, patriarchy, or class struggle, you have to apprehend the third-term mediator.[6]

The third-term mediator is the concept at the top of the triangle. Here, it's land, that little point at the top. That is what makes the genocide, the so-called Indian Wars, sensible – what I mean by this is that it gives it sense, so that Chief Justice Taney in the *Dred Scott decision* can say that Dred Scott goes back to slavery because he's not a subject of jurisprudence.[7] He's not a subject of jurisprudence because he is not a subject of community. He's not a subject of the community because Africa is a place outside of the community. Then the Chief Justice, John Marshall, makes the point that Native Americans have fought with white people over what to do with this land in their 1823 decision.[8] What kind of polity is apropos? He's saying when Native Americans whiten up, when they learn what settlers have been trying to teach them for over 200 years of genocide, they'll become full citizens.

He is unconsciously arguing that there's a semiotic relationship between whites and Indigenous people. A third-term mediator, land, makes genocide sensible and armed resistance to it sensible. So, he's unconsciously arguing that there's a semiotic relationship between whites and Native Americans. With Ulrike Meinhof and Andreas Baader, on the right side of the diagram here, in the Red Army Faction in Germany, they were in a struggle against the German state over temporality, which is to save the wage, economics, and the working day.[9] At the top of that triangle, there would be economics or the working day, a temporal rather than spatial third-term mediator.

The unconscious – and this is true for progressives as well as Trump supporters – does not give Black flesh the capacity for spatial or temporal creation. What it says to us is you have no time. You have no place. Because when there's Black on one point at the bottom of the triangle, and at the other point of the triangle there's white or another non-Black person, the question mark at the top of the triangle cannot be filled with a concept like land or the working day. There's never a semiotic entity that is allowed to articulate with Blackness. Obama found this out when he became president. In other words, you can become president, but you cannot be presidential. You can be a professor, but you cannot be professorial. You can be a tool of everyone else's hegemony, but you cannot be a contributor to hegemony or counter-hegemony. So then Yancy asks: "As you were talking, I was drawing your diagram, and I would extrapolate that with respect to anti-Blackness, there is no third term. There is no mediator." I write and I say:

> Yes, there's no third-term mediator for anti-Blackness. And this is what makes raising children so hard because you try to say, "Here's how to act so you don't get shot by the police." No, it is necessary for the police to shoot you. So that phrase doesn't work. Just like people who are suffering go to therapy, anti-Black violence is a form of therapy for the rest of the world. You can't act in a good way because you have been dishonored as a priority.

Joy James

I want to talk first about connections, how we know each other. I first met Frank Wilderson almost 20 years ago at Brown University when I was organizing around political prisoners and hosted a conference on "Imprisoned Intellectuals," which led to several anthologies.[10] Taija Mars-McDougall works on George Jackson, whose image is on the cover of *Imprisoned Intellectuals*.[11] Michel Foucault terms Jackson's death in prison as a "masked assassination." Staying with the concept of betrayal, perhaps emphasizing it, I note that I am not an Afropessimist, although I respect the work. I'm always learning more; I knew little about psychoanalytics in terms of political function until I started to look more closely at the research and the work of professors Terrefe, Wilderson, and Jared Sexton.[12]

At this conference some 20 years ago, Wilderson was on a panel with Jared Sexton. And in the middle, there is Safiya Bukhari, who has transitioned.[13] A former member of the Black Panther Party in New York, a former member of the Republic of New Afrika, which some describe as a self-defense unit forced underground by the FBI and COINTELPRO lethal and illegal attempts to eradicate Black rebels. The complexity of the thought that Wilderson was outlining with Sexton at one moment seemed to overwhelm the auditorium and the students who were present, but then entered Bukhari, who spent eight years in prison and captivity and the prison forced a hysterectomy upon her, another expression of the state's power, its capacity to inflict harm and torture, dishonor and sever natality.

What Bukhari said was to point to one scholar – actually, scholarly doctoral students – and to distill what they were saying in "everyday" language. It's the language of rebellion, the language of resistance, the language of love for community. For me, there was a stunning moment. Even though I don't recall all the words spoken at that time in the auditorium, I understood the intent and the capacity for theory to move through all these spaces in terms of Black liberation theory or liberation theory at large.

My connection to Wilderson and Terrefe [offers] an intellectual connection. I welcome their contributions. I believe what cements our bonds are our commitments to a certain kind of political ethics. Wilderson said before that it's not about personal morality per se, it's about ethics around the captive. That led me to think about the Captive Maternal. For decades, I wrote about and anthologized Black feminist thought. Yet, I found "Black feminism" to stumble in confrontations with the state as an imperial structure, born out of enslavement and genocide (against both the Indigenous and Africans).

This concept, "Ontology of Betrayal," came out of a collective community. Academia can isolate or polarize, it also can be a zone of connection. Wilderson mentioned George Yancy, a prominent philosopher at Emory University. Yancy bridges the academic world with the world of intellectuals who are more engaged in material struggle. [For example, Michelle Smith, co-director of Missourians to Abolish the Death Penalty.] He also mentioned *Truthout* as a platform that Yancy uses to interview people in order to make connections around ethics, liberation, Black freedom, and what democracy could be other than what we've inherited. *Truthout* will publish tomorrow an article and an interview with Kevin Johnson.[14] Kevin Johnson is in a Missouri prison. He is scheduled to be executed on November 29, exactly two weeks from today. The betrayal cited in the title of this talk and chat is very piercing, and it has to do with the formal captivity and the execution through two types of death penalties: the formal execution; or, holding people in prisons till they die of old age and/or disease. Medical fragility is heightened by zones of imprisonment and containment.[15]

I came into organizing and speaking about Kevin Johnson fairly late. Missourians for Alternatives to the Death Penalty, an organization based in Missouri, picked up Kevin's case; you can Google it; find it online; sign a petition; figure out what might be helpful.[16] The concept of death, of course, is theoretical, analytical, psychoanalytic. It is intellectual. It is emotional. The level of physical death that we face as a people in zones of disposability are stunning. This, for me, becomes the catalyst of a need to speak in clear terms about what the betrayal is in a political landscape, not just from democracy. The US is not a direct democracy. It is a representative democracy shaped by a three-fifths clause (where the Black enslaved were a fraction of a white person) that allowed Thomas Jefferson to be elected president in 1800, and defeat John Adams, who had no slaves. Slavery enabled the clout of plantation owners to be presidents as they "won" the electoral college which determines US presidents.

Such an inheritance entails a Trojan Horse in democracy baked in, along with the 13th Amendment, which legalizes slavery if you've been duly convicted of a crime, and the 14th Amendment, which redirected personhood for the emancipated Black to white corporations through the Supreme Court ruling of Citizens United in 2010.[17] These constant betrayals have an impact on our capacity to visualize and articulate what a liberation movement might look like. In "Maternal (In)coherence: Feminism Meets Fascism," in the first issue of the journal *Parapraxis*, titled "The Problem of the Family," I discuss the instability of the maternal. I will read a few paragraphs of the article.[18] I want to point back to the imperative to do something for, not just about, Kevin Johnson, and the imperative to do something against Death Row organized through formalities and informalities against people.

There are multiple types of death by state and by empire. Within US domestic and foreign policy, one finds the repetition of our dying and our dispossession as the norm, not as the aberration. Think about AFRICOM under Obama being accelerated among other things.[19] Here are a couple of paragraphs from "Maternal Incoherence: Feminism Meets Fascism":

> The maternal is not an inherently stable concept. Narratives constructed upon the maternal as bedrock cannot truly describe a shared experience. The emotional intellectual register of being maternal and its function are a political issue shaped by material conditions of captivity, exploitation, resistance, and child removal or disappearance. US democracy historically accumulated through racial capitalism and imperialism, genocide, and enslavement, as I said before, the concept of Captive Maternal was and remains a fulcrum for predatory accumulations until the Captive Maternal decides to depart from conflicting caretaking.

I think this goes back to George Yancy's question or imaginative query: What would happen if we agreed to the terms of sacrifice in order to resist?

That is, to move from the initial stage of conflicted or complicit caretaker through the stage of protest, beyond movement, into marronage and war resistance. Since we're hunted whenever we rebel, we move into the zone of war resistors. The Captive Maternal remains the fulcrum of democracy. In "The Womb of Western Theory: Trauma, Time Theft, and the Captive Maternal," I discuss how democracy merged with enslavement in order to shift burdens and feed rapacious desires through the consumption of enslaved caretakers:[20]

> Captive Maternals are those most vulnerable to violence, war, poverty, police, and captivity, those whose very existence enables the possessive empire that claims and dispossesses them. Global dominance in economics, military and cultural commodities allows the United States' imperial reach, despite the blowback of its devastating unwinnable wars alongside the genocidal violence the US unleashed abroad, its interventionist warfare resulted in the year 2016, at least 20 veteran suicides a day, trillions of dollars in military debt, and projected decades of warfare in the Middle East.

> There is AFRICOM, [in US-driven drone strikes in] Africa. [Yet,] the United States' longest legal war is with its domestic target; I argued in "The Womb of Western Theory" (2016) that the enslaved or captive Black woman is shaped by a 1658 narrative of war tied to the Commonwealth of Virginia's attempts to re-enslave Elizabeth Key, one of the first Captive Maternals to have her battles enter the public record."[21]

> I'm not sure about ... our "victories." Our first Black woman Vice President, Kamala Harris, was a prosecutor who targeted parents who could not maintain their children to attend school on a regular basis.[22] NYC has its first Black woman police commissioner of the NYPD, Keechant Sewell. Chicago elected a lesbian Black mayor, Lori Lightfoot ... The Black woman judge [Lucretia Clemons, Philadelphia County Court] decided that Mumia Abu-Jamal would not be allowed a new trial despite the corruption in the previous trials that condemned him to [over four decades] of incarceration. Our imagination ... would have to be so politicized that the way we saw the world – whatever terminology we use to describe it – would need a clear vision of what we face. [With an adequate] emotional register, we would agree to engage in resistance based on what we actually see, not what we hope to see in this democracy.

Terrefe

What resonates in the discussions that all three of us have posed relates to my question about our psychic investments in terms of Black people. There's an assumption in this conversation that we all share the same psychic investments, at least politically. I wonder if we're thinking Black internationally about betrayal and ontology, outside of some of the parochialism that has become Black Studies, especially with these graduate schools in Black Studies becoming more and more "finishing schools" as opposed to critical thinking programs. But *if* we're thinking politically, we have to be honest about psychic investment in betrayal, meaning a psychic investment in ontology and being attached to this idea that we are political subjects. If we were to destroy this notion that we are political subjects, that means there's absolutely nothing to risk. And if there's nothing to risk, what is it that we actually want? We can't think about betrayal unless we actually have, number one, an enemy in mind. What is the enemy of Blackness? Who is our target? Who are we investing ourselves in thinking that they have violated our trust? Betrayal itself is such a huge term to think about, thinking about it politically, and internationally. I wonder what can we actually say about Black psychic investments in political freedom if we're not all on the same page in terms of knowing ourselves. I was teaching Arthur Jafa's film, *Dreams Are Colder Than Death*, and the uncomfortable portion of that film is at the end when a prominent theorist said, "What I do know is that Africans were just as culpable in putting Africans on those ships as Europeans." But if we're thinking in Lacanian psychoanalytical terms, the subject who presumes to know or is assumed to know is the person who's transferring.[23] So, what is that transference? Where's the psychic investment in terms of who's been betrayed by whom? Are you betrayed by your ancestors on the continent? Or you have been betrayed by Europeans who followed your ancestors in the violation of your people? So, once again, what are these psychic investments that we're assuming unconsciously – *not* in our preconscious interests in terms of what we've been talking about thus far.

Wilderson

I'm not sure I have a direct answer. I would say that I agree with you if what you're saying is that we can't imagine how the massification of Blackness could come to share the same psychic investments. Yeah, I would be whole-heartedly in agreement with that.

Because we have those investments doesn't mean that we're subjects in whatever we're investing in, which is precisely what [President Barack]

Obama finds out and what we find out every day that we're teaching. So, I don't have an answer – it's a perplexing question. When you said that the students became uncomfortable with the notion that we were "just as culpable" – I hope I'm not going too far out on a limb, but I don't necessarily believe that phrase.

I mean, it's the Sonderkommandos in Auschwitz who beat and tortured other Jews, but there's no discourse of them being part and parcel of the Holocaust.[24] Everybody thinks of them as victims, but when it comes to us, a whole other calculus gets infused where we become responsible for our own enslavement, just because we were the implements of it. We weren't the agents of it.

Now I'm with you. I understand exactly. I want to say anecdotally, Joy, about our meeting [at Brown University at the conference on "Imprisoned Intellectuals"], it was exactly 20 years and about four months ago. What you didn't say is all the shit that you took from that. I won't put you on blast now, because you've got a good job and it's not there anymore.[25]

James

There are costs. This goes back to what Selamawit was saying about being housed in the academy and its performative nature. Twenty years ago, it wasn't "cool" to be engaged with political prisoners who challenged the state. As faculty in African American/Africana Studies I was called into the office of a Black woman president [and "spoken to"] after I used my research funds to create the conference "Imprisoned Intellectuals" at Brown. Twenty years later it is permissible to write about [imprisoned, slain revolutionary militarist] George Jackson. When I taught a political seminar, with all-white students, I assigned Jackson's *Soledad Brother: The Prison Letters of George Jackson* and Wilderson's essay "Gramsci's Black Marx Whither the Slave in Civil Society" which contrasted the white worker and the Black slave. The students staged a mute strike; they wouldn't talk to me for two hours during the seminar on political philosophy.[26]

What is betrayal? The same students helped organize the conferences and edit anthologies [*New Abolitionists*; *Imprisoned Intellectuals*; *Warfare in the American Homeland*] on political imprisonment (for which they were credited). But the students were disturbed by the agency that they found in the text. It's easier to be pitied or to be celebrated [as outsiders].

The [*Truthout* November 2022] article on Kevin Johnson notes that Kevin [is a poor, Black teen from a dysfunctional household.] In 2005, at age 19, he sees his twelve-year-old brother collapse while police are doing a raid on the house. Police step over the twelve-year-old's body while looking for Kevin who is hiding in an attic next door.[27] Johnson sees the ambulance come. Because of alleged parking/traffic tickets or domestic violence against the mother of his daughter, he remains hidden while watching his young brother "Bam Bam" lay on the floor reportedly without assistance until EMS places the child on a stretcher; watching his foot dangle off the stretcher, Kevin knows that his brother is dead.

According to Johnson, when his mother tried to enter the front door, the police pushed her out. The same treatment occurred when she tried to enter the kitchen door or window to reach the child on the floor while police were stepping over him to search for Kevin. Believing that police killed his brother (the hospital determined that he died from cardiac arrest), Kevin left the house where he sheltered after the police departed. He walked the streets until he found police supervisor, William McEntee, a white police officer. Johnson executed McEntee in the street, shooting him multiple times. Almost 20 years later, Kevin Johnson is waiting to be executed. The courts do not factor in his mental state. Kevin Johnson's remorse is not enough [the state wants his life].

… If it's only rebels that you can trust [to battle violence], what's your metric for a rebel? … Because people are Black [does not mean that they build] a stable foundation for a resistance movement.

Wilderson

I would agree.

Terrefe

I agree, but I also think that if we're talking about any political program that would upend the contemporary order, it cannot be done without Blackness. And that's what becomes threatening. It's not the idea about solidarity and that Afropessimists are presumed to say "Don't do coalitions." That's a ruse that they don't want to be authorized by Black violence, period. It's a tautology to use these two words together – Black violence – because Blackness, rage, and any Black political program that would want freedom would have to include violence. That is what's interrupting any critique of Black solidarity that gets leveled against Afropessimism. It has nothing to do with affect. It has everything to do with an investment in who actually wants to be free. I think on one level, it's always easy to level a critique about nationalism, that we want an all-Black formation, that Black this, Black that, Black everything is what's causing any sort of impediment upon progress. Black people's inability to work with other people is impeding progress. That is the discourse against Afropessimism. Frank and Afropessimism will cause gingivitis and erectile dysfunction. I mean, everything wrong happens …"because of Frank." But what will actually interrupt any bullshit critique like that is when I say, "But if you really want to talk about radical revolutionary politics, the only Black academic in the world right now theorizing is one who was actually part of an armed resistance movement, and that is Frank Wilderson." And then the conversation ends. We have a lot of people who want to talk about abolition, but nobody wants to talk about how to get to abolition. And the biggest critique against Afropessimism is there's no toolkit. How do you do this? How do you do that? Nobody asks that of a Marxist theorist: "Why don't we have a Marxist regime, what are you doing wrong?" The issue is violence. It's always violence, but nobody wants to talk about it. So that's why on one level, of course, we're not saying all Black people, all Black formations are what is required. What we're talking about is a Black consciousness or a Black movement or Black revolution. That is the problem.

Wilderson

Yeah, that is the problem. It is based on what you've just said – that the responses are not an engagement with anything that has been said. They're purely symptomatic. Going back to [the conference on Imprisoned Intellectuals] some 20 years ago that Joy started [at Brown University], Joy had read something [on Afropessimism written when] we [Wilderson and Jared Sexton] hadn't even started our qualifying exam [as doctoral students]. We came out there and you changed the lineup. And I want to say, I apologize for something that I did say. If you had told me that the Black woman sitting next to you in the front of the auditorium was the president, I would not have said all the shit that I said.

James

[The woman sitting next to me at the Brown conference was a dean of students, she] was not the president, but people reported back to the president what you said. That's okay. It's years past.

Wilderson

Anyway, someone asked, "How do we deal with administration?" And I [from the conference platform] said, "Well, you should probably ram a truck through their front door." It was real, but off the cuff. My point is that there was a certain point where Safiya Bukhari said, "I don't understand everything that these two have said, but I can feel it and I'm with it."[28]

And then Bukhari said, "It wasn't the Black Panther 10-point program." This aligns with what Selamawit has been saying. [Bukhari stated:] "It wasn't a Black Panther 10-point program that made me a revolutionary, a Black revolutionary. It was the NYPD." So, Bukhari brought it right back to violence and took it right out of [academic] discourse. And at that moment people were freaking out in the audience – and it was the people from Weather Underground. It was people like Ward Churchill, Henry Giroux, and others, whose struggles I support. I'm just going to say it because we took a lot of flack.

Everyone accused the panel of dividing the room. The audience accused me and Jared Sexton of being paternalistic toward Safiya Bukhari when she had said on her own steam, "I'm feeling everything that they're saying." And we hugged each other at the very end.

It was as though they were repeating the very same thing that I said in my response to George Yancy: You can be a professor, but you can't be professorial. You can be a revolutionary, but you cannot be a part of the thinking of what it means to have a revolution. She was always their widget, their implement, and they let it be known the moment she spoke her mind.

And at that point, there was no discussion about anything that we had said. It was just the accusation that we're trying to destroy solidarity. And there was also no recognition that all the people who were graduate students who were just thinking about this before Saidiya Hartman gave us the word "Afropessimism," all these people were involved in political struggles as we were going through grad school that was taking up so much of our time and was getting us penalized in very horrible ways.[29]

James

What do you think about the possibility of the distinction between violence and self-defense, or force and violence? The right to protect yourself would be a form of force. The people I knew from seminary … who started non-profits in New York City about domestic violence or intimate partner abuse. For example, Marissa Alexander gets to [point and fire a gun at a ceiling to stop a male partner from battering her], but is prosecuted and incarcerated.[30]

[We] should be able to analyze, theorize, and talk about violence without circling back into the democratic norm of decorum. Is it anti-Blackness … [or] fear [clouds] a clear discussion around self-defense?

Terrefe

I think the distinction is nominal. It's when people want to focus on the fact that Martin Luther King died – he was *murdered*. So does the distinction between force and self-defense matter when, in the end, he was assassinated? I think Black people can only be associated with force. We have no right to self-defense, if we're talking about ontology. Blackness has no right to defense whatsoever. It's a tool, it's wielded to show others that they actually do have bodily integrity. We don't. That's what I mean; there's nothing to risk. We're going to be seen as violent whether we're lying on the street, sleeping on our grandmother's couch at night like Aiyana Stanley-Jones.[31] There is no such thing as self-defense. If you want to use the rhetoric of self-defense, that's a smart political strategy. But I think it's a tactic. It can't be the strategy. We're at war.

Wilderson

Before 9/11, back in 1992, Edward Said would go to the Muslim community around Cape Town, and he's a person who is secular to the core. But he would say, "I support your use of Islam and Muslim identity as a strategic essentialism to move forward in a battle."[32]

I'm sure he wouldn't want to do that now, but he could do that then because that's available to them. As Selamawit is saying, that's not available to us. In other words, we have to come to grips – and I don't even know how to do this – with a certain level of equanimity about not having a discourse that justifies our actions and acting anyway.

Terrefe

Isn't this why Afropessimism is descriptive and not prescriptive?

Wilderson

Exactly. And it scares the shit out of me, okay? I'm telling you right now, I'm not saying this in a cavalier way.

James

I want to justify my position. To say that I'm *not* against Black feminism suggests that I'm justifying why I'm theorizing the Captive Maternal … Everything has to be fundamentally altered. But I would like to think that my need for justification has a rationale or logic to it and that it's not just my preference, but that it also constitutes a political strategy or a communal connection. Does that make sense?

Wilderson

This is a little difficult for me because I share the same kind of desire. As a theorist, I'm not sure it's possible, but it also doesn't mean I don't act in the world. This is what drives me crazy. What if we look back – you and I are in our 60s now, and if we look back over the past 45 years, what we have really been doing, you've been an activist all your adult life. I've been one also.

But we've been struggling for other people. I don't mean consciously not struggling for Black people, but what I mean is that what we need is so far in excess of what they need that even when it's just us working for better pay, for example, we're still working for them. So, what I haven't said is go home, shut the shutters, get a fifth of brandy, and do nothing. What I have said is I'm always problematizing that we could have an end goal.

That we could have an end goal that could be coherent beyond the end of the world.

Terrefe

Can you clarify the "coherent" part in "would be coherent"?

Wilderson

I hear myself wanting to adjust what I'm saying as I'm talking. Because I'm aware there's an audience out there and so I want to just talk to the two of you. But even that is captive.

Let me put it like this. When it becomes possible for us to think and speak beyond the confines of incarceration, then we will not be who we are. We'll be something else. There'll be something else.[33] I'm aware that there are young people out there. What I don't want to say is do nothing, because I think that through struggle you educate yourself and you educate others, but at the same time one could get caught up in thinking that what one is struggling for is really going to make one free. One could get caught up in thinking that one could actually write a sentence as to what Black freedom means. As opposed to writing a sentence that says that the conditions in which we can write that sentence are not here and cannot be here until the epistemological order that we exist doesn't exist anymore.

That's what I meant by the triangles. That makes us different, and this is what I mean by coherence, somehow. There's no third-term mediator that makes what we're trying to do. What we need is rather coherent. That doesn't mean doing nothing. Not at all. Because if you say to do nothing, then you'd also be saying that where we are is a function of divine intervention … I'm going back to arguments around my family. But the point is it is constructed, but I don't think we can think coherently outside of what is; we can only act against what is.

James

This discussion of "hope" versus "agape" keeps emerging. I don't even focus on the concept of freedom – I know it exists, though. I've met some Black feminist philosophers who are talking about hope on a regular basis. That's not my go-to either. But agape as political will, as a form of love, as a form of commitment, surely will not appear in my lifetime. But the commitment to do something that looks like resistance seems to be tied into our emotional landscape of care and kinship for each other.[34]

Terrefe

This is the reason why you state that you're not an Afropessimist in many ways. Because there's a commitment to an intramural that is shared, but there's also a desire for justification, like you said, that … what *is* the justification for violence? So perhaps that's the psychic investment in betrayal. Maybe that's what needs to be discarded in a way to *not* have to justify the use of violence as self-defense. I don't want to have to discuss love or affect or emotion or care in order to justify why we need to end the current order. And I share that sentiment with many; this is a violent world order. It's parasitic on Blackness. We have a body count that's piling up; it's parasitic on other people by extension. I don't want to have to say that I love my people, or I love anybody else in order to wage war against the current order. I don't want to have to say there's a justification for anything.[35] But that's the educative function of our jobs. When you have your educator hat on and then there's also the theorist's. And when you tell yourself you're a librarian. "I'm the librarian, I collect the bones, this is the evidence, this is what I do. Political philosopher." So, it's how do we negotiate the political parts of ourselves with the theoretical work that we do in the academy knowing that our checks are signed by the very systems that enslave and genocide and occupy and everything? That's why I tell my students, that you cannot trust anybody in the academy to give you a political program for liberation whatsoever. I taught a class on Black insurgencies and there's a moment in time when the

United States Department of Defense stopped publishing its own counter-insurgency manuals and the University of Chicago Press started publishing them.[36] There is a reason to not trust academics whatsoever.

James

I agree. When I talk about "20 years later," it seems to me that the Black revolutionary has become an iconic symbol for academics. I don't personally trust academics either: my self-acknowledgments include land, labor, and "don't trust me." Increasingly, I see this Panther-adjacent or rebel-adjacent figure becoming the focus.

As academics, we understand our job description and we follow it to keep a job and also not to end up imprisoned, or offshore, or, as in the case of some rebels, people shot up by police. I think the very definition of the "revolutionary" is being recrafted or re-engineered by academia and then distributed [through a] network of dissemination. What's repackaged as simulacra and sent out is much more comforting than the material and historical facts of what it means to be in rebellion against a predatory state.

Wilderson

This is why I was saying to George Yancy. I'm not sure that Afropessimism as a lens of understanding the world could be actually massified. It's a very difficult thing to hold. I've written three books informed by it, and it's not like every moment of the day I'm into it. In other words, I'm calling myself out in a certain way that I would call the people out in the conference you organized 20 years ago, Joy, as though we put forth an analysis of Black suffering. They took it as a demand for them to do something or an intervention in their joy or a disruption of their formations where we didn't even have that kind of power. I would also say that this new radical chic that you're talking about, it's missing something.

When I lived in Germany this new look at the Panthers was the accumulation of Black revolutionaries, not the engagement with them. In Germany, they were asking questions like what did we do wrong to produce a world in which Ulrike Meinhof picked up the gun and blew up their speaker?[37] How did our daughters come to this? There was even an art exhibit where there was an AK47 and a baby carriage. In other words, there was this weave of secular political thinking with theological thinking that went together seamlessly, which we are never a part of when they think about us in any way. I don't think there is, anyway. This new literature is often spectacularizing Blackness, not engaging it as a mode of thought. We just don't get that.

Terrefe

I also want to say that I appreciate Joy's work in maintaining fidelity to the truth, and the historical accuracy of our revolutionary movements.

That's why this librarian moniker that you don somewhat sarcastically is important. But unfortunately, it is true that we have to continue to make sure that our own academic departments and disciplines are not responsible for doing the revisionist work that colonizers and masters have done in the past.

Wilderson

I want to actually echo that as well. In 1990, I was in the Brooklyn Public Library and a young Black woman in high school was in front of me moving toward the reference desk – and this is just supporting what Selamawit has said about you, Joy. And the young woman said, "For my 11th-grade project, I'm going to do a study on the Black Panthers. Where would I look for information on that?" And the librarian said to her look under "Criminal." And I said to the woman, "If you don't mind, I know you don't know me, but I'd rather help you with this project as opposed to you dealing with this woman here. I actually met some Panthers when I was 13 and they educated me." So she goes, "Really? They're not criminals." I mean she really said that to me. And so yes, I'm just saying you're right we have to teach our own and maintain the integrity of our departments.

Mars-McDougall

First question: Could Dr. James and Dr. Wilderson speak about the Black political prisoner movement; Wilderson through the prism of Afropessimism; James through the Captive Maternal. The question continues: "Aren't all of the white American and Puerto Rican prisoners out? And what does it say for the Black political prisoners who remain, what does their continued imprisoned existence mean to Blacks and others?"

Wilderson

I just have a short anecdote. Right before I met Joy, Jared Sexton, myself, and Sora Han (Associate Professor, Criminology, Law & Society at the University of California, Irvine) were part of a group. Joy had a relationship with this group also in San Francisco, Claude Marx of Freedom Archives, and all of them who were trying to get all political prisoners pardoned before President Bill Clinton left office before the swearing-in of George W. Bush as president. I was going to see Marilyn Buck,[38] who would never have affiliated with the white underground – she's white and had always affiliated with the May 19 group, a communist organization which is an auxiliary of the Black Liberation. Buck was in prison in the same prison near UC Berkeley, where I was a student with Linda Evans of the Weather Underground Organization and the May 19th Communist Organization. I was a regular visitor out there to see them. People in these groups were going into the prisons and having people put makeup on, having their hair in a stylish way and she says, "Oh, I was a good young woman back in Iowa going to school, and I just fell in with the wrong people and got involved in violence." This information went to David Dellinger, pastors, and the Black Congressional Caucus. David Dellinger was vacationing with the Clintons in the Poconos, and Dellinger would send them these write-ups. And my point is that in this period – there are a lot of details I'm leaving out[39] – you could look at the gradations of conflict and the absolute otherness of antagonism by the symptomatic way in which he responded; first: Making Marilyn Buck and David Gilbert – to white people – "Black," because they didn't have a good enough association with white underground organizations. President Bill had given clemency [to over a dozen *Independistas* as political prisoners] and white people while also giving a public conditional [warning] statement to Puerto Ricans: "I will not support armed struggle." The FBI [issued a warning to the POTUS]: "If you do this [release political prisoners], your wife [Hillary Clinton] will not become a senator in New York." [In 2000, Hillary Clinton won the Puerto Rican vote and became New York's first female senator.] The FBI would [remind elected officials:] "Remember what we did to Frank Church in 1975 when he was [head of the Senate Select Committee to Study Governmental Operations with Respect to Intelligence Activities also known as]; the Church Committee [(https://www.senate.gov/about/powers-procedures/investigations/church-committee.ht)] tried to reform illegal and lethal policing and surveillance]. My point is that the narrative of a good little boy or good little girl who went to college at a tumultuous time, fell in with the wrong people, [and so became "revolutionary"] allowed some white radicals to have lesser sentences or prison terms].

... You can be a revolutionary, but you can't be...professorial. I don't mean this is preconscious or intentional, what I mean is that the *unconscious* didn't give them a political space and time in thinking out of which they operated against, to identify what has changed or what is the same; it was just a last lack of consideration. All Black prisoners – whether they're politically conscious, or what the IRA calls ODCs (ordinary decent criminals) – are considered in the same way [as a lethal threat or antagonist to the state]. I don't think that there's a way to make your political present or your political ideas part of your embodiment for someone else.

James

For people who are concerned about political prisoners, go to the Jericho website.[40] There's a list of the currently held political prisoners in the United States. The United States claims that there are no political prisoners in the US, that assertion is Kafkaesque.

I have written that I was introduced to politically imprisoned people because I knew some East Coast Panthers from Harlem. This would be how I met Dhoruba bin-Wahad [in 1990] after he was incarcerated for 19 years, framed by the NYPD and FBI. He received some monetary settlement for all those years.[41]

I was the first Black person hired to teach in an all-white women faculty Women's Studies program at UMass Amherst. When Dhoruba was just getting out, I was asked if I would host him at my house so that he could give a talk on campus the next day. That would've been my first encounter with a political prisoner [after I met and worked with Angela Davis]. Dhoruba bin-Wahad is the author of several texts, including *Still Black, Still Strong* co-authored with Mumia Abu-Jamal and Assata Shakur.[42] (He has critiqued the popularized creation of a "Black Madonna" surrounding Assata Shakur [that obscures] the material struggle that only rebels and revolutionaries waged.

What motivated me to do the anthologies on political prisoners was that Kim Kit Holder, Harlem Panther, introduced me to three other Panther vets. I invited all four to attend a conference that Angela Davis asked me to organize at the University of Colorado Boulder in March 1998 as a precursor to the Critical Resistance launch at UC Berkeley in September 1998. Holder, Safiya Bukhari, [Gabe Torres, Lee Lew-Lee] attended. I tried to invite Geronimo Pratt as the second keynote along with Davis. The faculty largely freaked out because he wasn't an academic. Framed by the LAPD/FBI, Pratt did 27 years in prison [as many years as Nelson Mandela; Pratt also received a financial settlement] from the federal government. Pratt did not receive or respond to the invitation to speak at CU-Boulder. With Davis[43]

When I mailed copies of the anthology [*States of Confinement*] developed from that 1998 academic conference to incarcerated Panther vets, Jalil Muntaqim wrote back that the anthology book did not reflect the reality of militant struggle or the lives of political prisoners. When I went to Brown

Univ., I then began to start edit anthologies only about US *political prisoners*: Leonard Peltier, Mutulu Shakur, Mumia Abu-Jamal, etc.[44]

There is surplus torture for political rebels. What the state has to do is kill your mind, and kill your principles, and your ethics. There's a certain terror that most academic texts cannot capture – so that was a rightful criticism [from Muntaqim] decades ago.

As noted earlier, Hillary Clinton ran for the US Senate after being the First Lady. Puerto Rican communities voted for her when she moved to New York, and her husband President Bill Clinton gave clemency to *Independentistas*.[45] No US presidents have negotiated political deals with Black revolutionaries.

Mars-McDougall

Another question asked: Does the rhetoric of "self-defense" move us away from revenge, both conceptually and materially?

Terrefe

My answer to the second question is absolutely, yes. It moves us away from revenge, but it also moves us away from attempting to adapt the subject position of white women, right? Because generally self-defense is used as a category for women and children, especially in justifying Black women's use of force. And the only people that would work for, and that *has* worked for, are white women. And I think that's another psychic investment that we can talk about, in terms of politically and ontologically, this investment in gender as if it's going to save us – a subject position itself. And I think more people need to read not just David Marriott's previous work, but Marriott's *Whither Fanon?* and study, and continue to study and study how he's interpreting Fanon's notion of invention and the leap. I'm not going to presume to be able to summarize accurately. That's why I say study. It is our job to study what he has studied of Fanon's work on invention. Arendt has done work in specifying distinctions between force and violence and strength, etc. And I don't think that's helpful for Black people. And in terms of justifying, I don't think we need to justify the use of force or violence or defense in any way, shape, or form when what we are in is a continual war without end.

Wilderson

The question solicits us on two levels. I want to echo what Selamawit has said about acknowledging and celebrating Joy's political work, her librarian work, and her teaching work, because I've certainly learned from that and continue to try to do that. When I'm answering these questions, I'm emphasizing more how to think about the thought and less about what to do when their boots are on the ground. The three of us did a workshop with 35 leaders from Black Lives Matter in Philly, New York City, and in Newark, NJ; and, it was at the Audubon Ballroom in Washington Heights of Manhattan, NY.

I certainly did not start that workshop with, "Here are the concepts of social death and why we don't exist ourselves." It's just not how you begin to do organizing; you begin where people are, and then you hope to broaden that out. And I think we need everyone's work on this Zoom screen here, but my work is actually weighted in failures. My work is not weighted in what could come about precisely, because, for me, that's the hardest part to deal with. I know that from my activism in South Africa as a Marxist, and then being up against the fact that the division between the haves and the have-nots was important but inessential to what was going on and having a crisis of faith when that became clear to me.[46] So, part of what Selamawit says about the concept of study would bring you to a point where you would understand that there are sentient beings with selves, and then there's me, without a self. That would have to be inculcated to the point where one could rather than answer the question of self-defense, but interrogate it as a category, which is what Selamawit has been saying for the past hour.

Now, that's not an easy thing to do. It's not easy in the classroom. Someone once asked me: how do we keep Afropessimism Black? The fact of the matter is it's not really, ultimately possible. Afropessimism is something that is – to quote Saidiya Hartman – an extension of the master's prerogative.[47] Hopefully, we can broaden Afropessimism quickly enough to the point where, while it's being accumulated and recalibrated by non-Black people, Black people are also inculcating it and spreading it for our own uses and terms. But it's a hell of a leap to get over; to even think that one is not a self and one cannot be a self because one's not being a self gives everyone else selfhood. To get to the next point, which is to not care about who doesn't understand our violent response, that's a journey. But as Selamawit has been saying, it is a journey.

James

Let's just assume that everybody on this platform has trained. For me, that's a form of preparation. Whether or not the predatory acid rain directly falls upon you – or you have an umbrella, or can dodge into the doorway – we have still trained. For me, that's strategic, and that has to be amplified and extended. Think about the mass killer of Black parishioners at a prayer circle in Mother Emmanuel African Methodist Episcopal (AME) church in Charleston, Dylann Roof – Obama can cry at a funeral, but he can't rage following the massacre. And, it's fine to cry. But if you can drone-strike people on another continent through AFRICOM, tell me you can deal with white supremacist killers in the US.[48]

In Buffalo, NY – shopping on a Sunday [May 22, 2022] for groceries at TOPS after church – becomes a sporadic terror moment. I know little of the manifesto of the white supremacist mass murderer in the Buffalo supermarket; [but his manifesto stated that the objective was] to trigger Black people into a rebellion so that police would just shoot them down. These white nationalist performative massacres seek to get a response [in which the state policing apparatus supports them].[49]

The function of training is not that we learn to tolerate terror, but that we learn ... to anticipate some of its moments. For me, this is really hard. Revenge, as much as I would like it, can become messy and a distraction. Training is something different. It's strategic, and it doesn't mean that we wouldn't feel all the painful loss. I work with mothers who've had their children murdered by the police. I listen to them and they'll curse me out, too. I'm not talking about the ones [the Black mothers] who ended up campaigning for Hillary Clinton in 2016, but the ones [who say that they stay] "outside of this ring of fire, ring of hell." And, will find a path.

There is a way that if I train, it is not just for myself, it is also for the kids and the elders. That becomes a commitment. Even if we can't deliver full protection, we work to have the capacity to do so. I'm not so dependent on calling it "self-defense" right now, although I'm going to keep doing that. I see the way we move, and the way we move goes beyond our individual care for ourselves. When I hear us talk about training, we are talking about something beyond the individual. Our motivations are not always clear to us, but our practical and intellectual capacity expands.

Terrefe

I think the Black poet would know more about meaning than any of us on this stage who isn't engaged in the art of poetry right now.

Mars-McDougall

Who do we understand to be a citizen, a sovereign citizen subject, and in that way a human? But I reject freedom as a goal.

Someone asks: Is there still space for meaningful imaginations despite the language of freedom not being available? And is there a way to give Black freedom meaningfulness? This person asks basically, what advice would you give to Black radical poets? The question is about there being space for meaningful imaginations despite the language not being available to give Black freedom meaning. If there's no meaning for Black freedom – if it is fundamentally incoherent – is there still space for imagining?

Wilderson

It's interesting and symptomatic that Selamawit has talked about violence for the better part of an hour, and we don't have any real engagements with it. It seems like the engagement from the audience about that is statically nervous. If she was Jewish, it'd be picked up immediately. Bomb the hell out of Dresden, assassinate Hitler. In 1991, I had a professor at Columbia University when I was talking in Marxist terms about George Bush Sr. putting 500,000 troops in Kuwait and getting ready to invade Iraq. Is this a fascist, imperialist intervention? And she says to me, "No, no, no. There's evil in the world and we have to stamp out evil by whatever means necessary." But when you get that same thing coming from a Black person, it's either a diffused avoidance around what she has said or just a non-engagement.

In regards to the meaningfulness of freedom: This is where I take my hat off to Afropessimism. It is not, as Selamawit has said, a program. It is an analysis, a lens of interpretation, which has only one kind of destination, which is: How do we understand the ways in which Black people suffer? And once you get to that, then I think that it does something for the imagination. I don't want to say *what* it does for the Black imagination, but it does something for the Black imagination because I think it does – if I can use the word freedom – free one from having to articulate the meaning of freedom in the ways that other people articulate that. Or even having to address it, that whole question, "I want to be free, I'm doing this to get my freedom," assumes a prior platitude of freedom that has been taken from one.

This is what I agree with her saying, the poet would know better. The arts have always explored that, but never consciously, I would say. And I would say that one of the things Selamawit would help me understand about *Song of Solomon*, which all through high school was my jam, is the redemptive sellout of Black struggle. I had to reread the book in a completely different way.

James

Art is what keeps us alive, and it is, for me, a foundation of culture. Selamawit recently introduced me to Alice Smith singing, "I Put a Spell On You"; there's a particular clip where she's performing in the Gagosian, walking through a gallery of Black art.[50] I thought of Screamin' Jay Hawkins who originally wrote the song in 1956. Love seems to be connected to culture and people and family, and that's real. There's a part of me that's just practical. I'm not thinking about freedom, just to be honest. I'm really grateful for this conversation because now I better understand what I'm trying to do. I'm interested in *efficiency*. I'm interested in protections. I don't believe that I can personally protect myself. I do believe that under certain conditions, I can work with others to offer more protections to communities and political prisoners.

If you look at Assata Shakur's autobiography, there's poetry throughout that memoir.[51] If you look at Mumia Abu-Jamal's writings,[52] it is the same. Political prisoners are courageous and vulnerable given the state's predatory powers. Political prisoners are also artists; [we] still need to get them out of prison. There is a practicality I think in the way in which I'm wired. I'm not saying the way I do politics is the way everybody else has to do it, but I do see this as a form of discipline that everybody on this platform shares, however they express it. I also believe that's part of the imagination. Can you technically free them all? Likely not, but the desire and the will to try and to keep reinventing strategies is what we do.

I do agree with Frank. I was giving a talk at Northwestern, I shared that I grew up on military bases, including Fort Benning, Georgia. So, I learned to play kickball on the same base with the School of Americas (SOA), also named the "School of the Assassins" because the US military trained torturers and death squads there. In these zones of violence, military and the police are practitioners who can look at violence. They call you/me "civilians" who cannot face imperial armies, cannon fodder, and other horrors. Civilians are talked down to dismissively because they/we reportedly "don't have the stomach to face violence, let alone talk about it, analyze it, and do anything to stop it." Police and military have contempt for the citizenry [as do] of course proto-fascists.

Mars-McDougall

Another question: Is there a way to talk about Black revolutionaries or Black violence without falling prey to the comfort, or the desire for comfort, that Professor James talked about? Is there a way around this or is there a way to talk about violence? Even me, publishing a book on George Jackson and Jon Jackson and Abbie Hoffman, is there a way to talk about violence in an academic space without this problem of comfort invading the question/conversation?

Terrefe

I think it depends on the person's comfort level with violence and familiarity with violence. I think it depends on who's in the room. That's it. I think there is no academic space that will not be hostile to Black discussions of violence, period. Unless it's a pathologizing discussion of Black violence; that's where Black culture comes in, which is why it's so easy for finishing schools to talk about Black culture as opposed to Black revolutionary politics. That's true. And I was talking to the brilliant Cecilio Cooper the other day, and they made a really important point that being anti-AP has become an industry. Dr. Cooper strikes again. To be anti-AP is an industry at this point. You don't have to know anything. You don't have to cite anything. You don't have to critique or analyze or study. You just have to take the position of no. And you will have jobs, you will have research accounts, you will have everything laid at your feet. So, I think there are various reasons why people have a discomfort with conversations about violence. I think a lot of graduate students are reticent because they have advisers who refuse to allow them to write about it and to study it. I think a lot of people are worried about having a job. They're worried about the messages of capital. I think perhaps I don't care enough, or I am crazy enough to discuss it. Frankly, I don't know. I think everybody has a choice in how far they're willing to go to be honest. And I think you can't actually have an honest conversation about war and violence and Black suffering unless you talk about violence. It's impossible.

Wilderson

Yeah. I just wanted to say Amen. And yes, I love the whole phrase of finishing school to talk about academia.

Terrefe

I must give credit to Mlondi Zondi for that one.

Wilderson

Okay. That just blew me away. But Joy, you said earlier that you are not an Afropessimist, and I did not respond by saying I'm not a practical person.

What I'm trying to say is that we've got two trainings running here, and they inform each other, and they work together. This is why this whole notion that Afropessimism is outside of the political sphere is just bullshit because most of what we do is informed by our work, the kind of work we did in the spaces that you make possible, Joy. It was the shock of all those people yelling at me. I wasn't even ABD (all but dissertation) yet after that conference of yours with Safiya Bukhari, where everyone's a revolutionary in the room – from AIM (American Indian Movement) to SDS (Students for a Democratic Society) to Canadian anti-capitalists – that we're just going to have this conversation. People yelled at us on the plane back from Providence to San Francisco. That's how bad it was. And the other thing I would say, so I can close and come on to the next question, is that I want us to remember what Joy and Selamawit have been saying, and I've been saying is that everything we do is incarcerated. So, whatever we get on the other side is allowed.

There are moments when there are eruptions that open up space for us to do more of what Selamawit is talking about. But that's not based upon the scholar, the integrity, or the rigor of our work. That's based upon what's happening with Black people in the streets at any given moment. Normally, someone has to die in such a spectacular fashion that embarrasses civil society. This is what Fanon says. It's not caring.[53] We're hiring all kinds of people. I'm not saying that the people who are doing this are lying consciously. It would be great if they were because that would be an analytic response as opposed to a symptomatic response. Black people in the streets are blowing up the world. Let's see how we can expand the capacity for Black thought to happen in the academy. That moment, which is where we are, is going to close down, just like it always closes down and comes up again. Emmett Till; it opens up and it closes down.

So, the other day Sekou Odinga (1944-2024) from the Black Liberation Army was here at UCI (University of California, Irvine) in an auditorium that held over a hundred people, and it was sponsored by a program that the chancellor put forward. That is how we know that we have become little dolls on a shelf, because when I brought him here almost ten years ago, I got hate emails. Bridget Cooks (Professor of Art History and African American Studies at UCI); there were people talking to her from the whole Orange County community about, "Why are you having this terrorist?" this, that, and the other. And we got a little dinky room that held about 70 people and we had to have 90 people in there. Okay, so now it's chic. He didn't change, I didn't change. Nothing changed. It's just that occasioned and allowed is what happened. At this meeting – this comes right back to Selamawit – a Black person says to him, "How do we deal with police violence now?" And here was this 70-some-year-old dude, Odinga, who very calmly said, "Well, you got to make it costly for them." You could feel the gasp in the whole room because no one misunderstood what he had just said. No one said, "What do you mean by that?" There was just silence. "You have to make it costly for them".

Mars-McDougall

One last question – this one, I think, is a nice one to wrap us up. I'm wondering if you all can talk a little bit more about the Black intramural, or a lack thereof, as it concerns this discourse of betrayal and ontology. In an anti-Black world, are all Black people not called to serve anti-Black interests and thus to be or to exceed the category of the traitor? I'm wondering if the call to mistrust Black academics might be carried over more broadly to discourses of community itself.

Wilderson

The best answer I heard to that question was given by Selamawit in late August of 2017 at the Tate Modern Museum in London when she asked the group, who were about 40 Black activists from Britain, "Are we in an intramural space?" And everybody nodded yes. And then she said, "No, we're not."

Mars-McDougall

I also have a similar story about Selamawit when she asked, "Do you really think we're alone right now?" to a group of Black academics.

Terrefe

I think the desire for intramural runs on the same train track as the desire for liberation. I think it is a loving desire, but I also think it is one that is bound to disappoint if you're waiting for that in order to act.

SOURCE NOTES

1. Yancy, George. "Afropessimism Forces Us to Rethink Our Most Basic Assumptions about Society." *Truthout*, September 15, 2022. https://truthout.org/articles/afropessimism-forces-us-to-rethink-our-most-basic-assumptions-about-society/

2. Schwegler, Marc. "Frank B. Wilderson III: Afropessimism." *Various Artists,* July 17, 2021. https://various-artists.com/afropessimism/

3. Zug, James. "The Italicized Life of Frank Wilderson '78." *Dartmouth Alumni Magazine,* October 2010. https://dartmouthalumnimagazine.com/articles/italicized-life-frank-wilderson-%E2%80%9978

4. Wilderson is married to Anita Wilkins, a noted poet and author.

5. "Set in the wake of the 1916 Easter Rising, a married woman in a small Irish village has an affair with a troubled British officer." See also: "Ryan's Daughter." *IMDb,* December 10, 1970. www.imdb.com/title/tt0066319/

6. Wilderson, Frank B. "The Black Liberation Army and the Paradox of Political Engagement," 2014. https://illwill.com/the-black-liberation-army-the-paradox-of-political-engagement

7. Bowers, Dana, Logan Cornell, Darcie Dreher, Jake Harder, and Jennifer Minnis. *Dred Scott v. Sanford,* 60 U.S. 393 1857. Accessed July 12, 2023. www.americanhistoryk12.com/wp-content/uploads/Court%20Trial%20Documents/dred_scott.pdf

8. Riley, Angela R. "The History of Native American Lands and the Supreme Court." *Journal of Supreme Court History* 38, no. 3 (2013): 369–385. https://doi.org/10.1111/j.1540-5818.2013.12024.x

9. Wilderson, Frank B. "The Black Liberation Army and the Paradox of Political Engagement."

10. James, Joy. *Imprisoned Intellectuals America's Political Prisoners Write on Life, Liberation, and Rebellion.* Lanham: Rowman & Littlefield Publishers, 2004.

11. McDougall, Taijia. "Left out: Notes on Absence, Nothingness and the Black Prisoner Theorist." *Anthurium A Caribbean Studies Journal* 15, no. 2 (2019). https://doi.org/10.33596/anth.391

12. James, Joy. *Imprisoned Intellectuals America's Political Prisoners Write on Life, Liberation, and Rebellion.* Lanham: Rowman & Littlefield Publishers, 2004.

13. Throughout her lifetime of activism, Bukhari was a member of the Black Panther Party in their Harlem office and co-founded several organizations, including the Jericho Movement for US Political Prisoners and Prisoners of War. Her works were published posthumously in 2010. Discussed in: Wilderson, Frank B. "The Black Liberation Army and the Paradox of Political Engagement." See also: Bukhari, Safiya. *The War Before: The True Life Story of Becoming a Black Panther, Keeping the Faith in Prison & Fighting for Those Left Behind.* New York City: Feminist Press at the City University of New York, 2010.

14. Changa, Kalonji, and Joy James. "Kevin Johnson Speaks from Death Row About His Impending Execution This Month." *Truthout,* December 14,

2022. https://truthout.org/articles/kevin-johnson-speaks-from-death-row-about-his-impending-execution-this-month/

15. Gunn, John. "Medical Powers in Prisons, the Prison Medical Service in England 1774–1989." *Criminal Behaviour and Mental Health* 3, no. 2 (1993): 119. https://doi.org/10.1002/cbm.1993.3.2.119

16. "Missourians to Abolish the Death Penalty (MADP) is a statewide organization working to repeal the death penalty in Missouri by educating citizens and legislators regarding the costs and consequences of capital punishment," according to the MADP website. See also: "Home: Missourians for Alternatives to the Death Penalty" (*MADP*, December 29, 1969. https://www.madpmo.org/).

17. James, Joy A. "Dishonored Citizenry: Black Women, Civic Virtue, and Electoral Powers." *Community as the Material Basis of Citizenship*, 2017, 49–60. https://doi.org/10.4324/9781315113159-5

18. James, Joy. "Maternal (In)Coherence." *Parapraxis*, November 21, 2022. www.parapraxismagazine.com/articles/maternal-incoherence#:~:text=When%20Feminism%20Meets%20Fascism&text=Whether%20they%20are%20biological%20females,of%20maternal%20lives%20and%20bodies

19. "Obama to Announce AFRICOM Joint Force Command HQ in Liberia." *US Department of Defense*. Accessed July 11, 2023. www.defense.gov/News/News-Stories/Article/Article/603259/obama-to-announce-africom-joint-force-command-hq-in-liberia/

20. James, Joy. "The Womb of Western Theory: Trauma, Time Theft, and the Captive Maternal." *Carceral Notebooks* 12, no. 1 (2016): 253–296.

21. Ibid.

22. "Contrary to Ms. Harris' claim that the penalties were an 'unintended consequence,' Senate Bill No. 1317 specifically *amended* both the state penal and education codes and included imprisonment as a punishment," The New York Times reported. Qiu, Linda. "Fact-Checking Kamala Harris on the Campaign Trail" (*The New York Times*, June 8, 2019. www.nytimes.com/2019/06/08/us/politics/fact-check-kamala-harris.html).

23. Lacan, Jacques. "Intervention on Transference." Translated by Juliet Mitchell and Jacqueline Rose. *Feminine Sexuality* (1982): 61–73. https://doi.org/10.1007/978-1-349-16861-3_4

24. "The Sonderkommandos were groups of Jewish prisoners forced to perform a variety of duties in the gas chambers and crematoria of the Nazi camp system," according to the United States Holocaust Memorial Museum. See also: "Sonderkommandos." *Holocaust Encyclopedia*. Accessed July 11, 2023. https://encyclopedia.ushmm.org/content/en/article/sonderkommandos

25. Wilderson is referring to the April 2002 conference "States of Confinement and Imprisoned Intellectuals," organized by Joy James and held at Brown

University. See also: James, Joy. "Academia, Activism, and Imprisoned Intellectuals." *Social Justice*, 92, 30, no. 2 (2003): 3–7.

26. Wilderson, Frank. "Gramsci's Black Marx: Whither the Slave in Civil Society?" *Social Identities* 9, no. 2 (2003): 225–240. https://doi.org/10.1080/13504630320001 01579

27. Changa, Kalonji, and Joy James. "Kevin Johnson Speaks from Death Row About His Impending Execution This Month." *Truthout*, December 14, 2022. https://truthout.org/articles/kevin-johnson-speaks-from-death-row-about-his-impending-execution-this-month/

28. Bukhari was not an academic; her activism included grassroots work, including a period of going "underground." This quote refers to the notion that radical intellectualism can transcend academia.

29. Hartman, Saidiya V., Keeanga-Yamahtta Taylor, Marisa J. Fuentes, Sarah Haley, and Cameron Rowland. *Scenes of Subjection: Terror, Slavery, and Self-making in Nineteenth-Century America*. New York, NY: W. W. Norton & Company, 2022.

30. Marissa Alexander was prosecuted for aggravated assault with a lethal weapon and sentenced to a mandatory minimum sentence of 20 years in prison. Alexander said she fired a warning shot after her estranged husband threatened to kill her. She was released in 2017 after three years of imprisonment. Discussed in Dionne, Brittany. "One Year Later, Marissa Alexander Speaks out on Her Release, Corrine Brown." *The Florida Times-Union*, January 27, 2018. www.jacksonville.com/story/news/2018/01/27/one-year-later-marissa-alexander-speaks-out-her-release-corrine-brown/15332075007/

31. Aiyana Mo'Nay Stanley-Jones was shot and killed by police officer Joseph Weekley at seven years old. See also: "7-Year-Old Girl Accidentally Shot by Swat Team." *American Civil Liberties Union*, March 5, 2013. www.aclu.org/documents/7-year-old-girl-accidentally-shot-swat-team

32. Burney, Shehla. "Edward Said and Postcolonial Theory: Disjunctured Identities and the Subaltern Voice." *Counterpoints* 417 (2012): 41–60.

33. Clifton, Lucille, Kevin Young, and Michael S. Glaser. "New Bones." In *The Collected Poems of Lucille Clifton 1965–2010*. Rochester, NY: BOA Editions, 2012.

34. James, Joy. *In Pursuit of Revolutionary Love*. S.l.: Divide Publishing, 2022.

35. Terrefe, Selamawit. "What Exceeds the Hold?: An Interview with Christina Sharpe." *Rhizomes: Cultural Studies in Emerging Knowledge*, no. 29 (2016): 1–10. https://doi.org/10.20415/rhiz/029.e06

36. See *The Counter, Counter-Insurgency Manual: Or, Notes on Demilitarizing American Society*, Chicago: University of Chicago Press, 2006.

37. Ulrike Meinhof was a founding member of Germany's Red Army Faction. Discussed in: Wilderson, Frank B. "The Black Liberation Army and the Paradox of Political Engagement."

38. Her role in the 1979 prison escape of Assata Shakur. See also: James, Joy. *Warfare in the American Homeland: Policing and Prison in a Penal Democracy*. Durham: Duke University Press, 2007.

39. James observes that "Dellinger added that as a married, older male, he had not participated in this comfort station approach to Civil Rights radicalism. His race politics reflected a feminism that years later refracted his antiracist narrative into a profeminist testimonial" (James, Joy. "Antiracist (Pro) Feminisms and Coalition Politics: 'No Justice, No Peace.'" Essay. In *Men Doing Feminism*, 238. London: Routledge, 2013).

40. "Home: Jericho Movement." Home | Jericho Movement. Accessed July 11, 2023. www.thejerichomovement.com/

41. Dhoruba bin-Wahad was released from prison after suing the FBI on the basis of failing to disclose evidence that would have aided his case. See also: Sullivan, Ronald. "Court Erupts as Judge Frees an Ex-Panther." *The New York Times*, March 23, 1990. www.nytimes.com/1990/03/23/nyregion/court-erupts-as-judge-frees-an-ex-panther.html

42. Wahad, Dhoruba Bin, Mumia Abu-Jamal, Assata Shakur, Jim Fletcher, Tanaquil Jones, and Sylvère Lotringer. *Still Black, Still Strong: Survivors of the U.S. War Against Black Revolutionaries*. New York: Semiotext(e), 1993.

43. Event details are archived on the University's website: "Angela Davis to Speak At CU-Boulder March 15." *CU-Boulder Today*. www.colorado.edu/today/1998/03/01/angela-davis-speak-cu-boulder-march-15

44. James discussed the 1998 conference entitled "Unfinished Liberation: Beyond the Prison Industrial Complex," which was held from March 15–18, in an article published by the African American Intellectual Society. According to James, "Some 2000 participated in Unfinished Liberation. The documentary was well received." In the article, she further discusses pressure from the university to omit revolutionary people and ideas from the presentation. "Essential for intellectual and political development, alliances between abolitionists and revolutionaries are destabilized by the airbrushing of revolutionary struggles," she writes. See: James, Joy. "Airbrushing Revolution for the Sake of Abolition." *AAIHS*, August 12, 2020. www.aaihs.org/airbrushing-revolution-for-the-sake-of-abolition/

45. Hilary Clinton won the 2000 Senate election in New York. James refers to the "Eleven Puerto Rican nationalists, among the longest-serving political prisoners in America, are to be released this week after agreeing to the terms of a clemency offer from President Clinton." Discussed in Gilson, Christopher. "Congress Strikes $1 Trillion Budget Deal, Democrats Clear

the Field for Hillary Clinton and Will Puerto Rico Default? – US National Blog Round up for 11–17 January." *LSE American Politics and Policy*, 2014.

46. The categories of "haves" and "have-nots" are popularly used to reference ideas of historical and geographic determinism, such as in Jared Diamond's landmark and controversial 1999 book entitled *Guns, Germs, and Steel*.

47. Wilderson clarifies in his 2022 interview in *Truthout* with Yancy that this "is where the violence is manifest even when no injury is visible." Yancy, George. "Afropessimism Forces Us to Rethink Our Most Basic Assumptions about Society." *Truthout*, September 15, 2022. https://truthout.org/articles/afropessimism-forces-us-to-rethink-our-most-basic-assumptions-about-society/

48. On June 15, 2015, Dylann Roof shot 14 people at the Emanuel African Methodist Episcopal (AME) Church in Charleston, SC. All victims were Black; nine were mortally wounded. See also "Charleston Church Shooter: 'I Would like to Make It Crystal Clear, I Do Not Regret What I Did.'" *The Washington Post*, May 24, 2023. www.washingtonpost.com/world/national-security/charleston-church-shooter-i-would-like-to-make-it-crystal-clear-i-do-not-regret-what-i-did/2017/01/04/05b0061e-d1da-11e6-a783-cd3fa950f2fd_story.html

49. On May 14, 2022, 18-year-old Payton S. Gendron shot ten people – all of whom were Black – at TOPS Friendly Supermarket in Buffalo, NY. See also "Complete Coverage: 10 Killed, 3 Wounded in Mass Shooting at Buffalo Supermarket." *The Buffalo News*, February 15, 2023. https://buffalonews.com/news/local/complete-coverage-10-killed-3-wounded-in-mass-shooting-at-buffalo-supermarket/collection_e8c7df32-d402-11ec-9ebc-e39ca6890844.html

50. Gagosian. Alice Smith: I Put a Spell on You | Sessions | Gagosian Premieres, December 9, 2021. www.youtube.com/watch?v=kz506sFHeJY

51. Shakur, Assata. *Assata: An Autobiography*. Chicago Review Press, 1999.

52. Mumia Abu-Jamal is an American journalist and political activist who was convicted of the 1981 murder of police officer Daniel Faulkner and subsequently sentenced to death. His death penalty was overturned, and in 2011, he was sentenced to life imprisonment without parole. See: Abu-Jamal, Mumia, and John Edgar Wideman. *Live from Death Row*. New York: Perennial, 2002.

53. Wilderson elaborates in his 2022 conversation with Yancy in *Truthout* that "Fanon can go off the rails when offering humanist prescriptions to stop simply exploring the antagonism and try to reconcile it."

7

Family, Freedom, and Security

Joyce McMillan, Samaria Rice, Amanda Wallace,
Dawn Wooten, and moderator Joy James

February 8, 2023

Joyce McMillan

First of all, I'd like to say that I'm an impacted parent [by state family disruption]. I've met other people who were former workers within the ["child protective" industrial] system transform their work the same way Amanda Wallace has. I want to shout Amanda out for having the inside information and sharing it with parents like myself that seek to make change. I would say that the system has not helped any of the families that I've worked with since I've been advocating [for family rights] about seven or eight years. The system is designed to make us fail. It is a place of surveillance and control. They lie to us and tell us that they're a benevolent system that cares about children.

In a conversation with someone from the state of New York just recently, I said "Why do you only care about children when they're at home with their parents and you don't utilize your money to support their family and make sure they have the things they need?" When most children come into the system, they don't even graduate from school. You can't even keep them in school, in the same school, for an entire school year. Children are changing homes and are given garbage bags to use as luggage while the CEOs of foster care agencies are making upward of $500,000 a year.

This system that has been created, after they claim to have abolished slavery, is the biggest farce that America has ever sold us. They've told a lot of lies, but this by far is the biggest because all of these systems are designed to capture Black and Brown bodies and white bodies that are poor, along with poor Black people. And the white people are collateral consequence, but they're the first ones to benefit when change happens from the work that people like myself and Amanda and others are doing on the ground.

What I seek is to be respected as a human being in America, which has not happened because this system is designed not to see us in any human form at all. And that is why almost anything we do becomes unsafe for us. Driving while Black, playing while Black, shopping while Black, walking while Black, bird-watching while Black, attending college while Black … I'm going to stop there because that's what we're going to discuss tonight during this conversation.

To me, "family" means people I love, care about, trust, and support. I don't think family is defined by blood alone. I think we can often choose our family members because I have some better relationships with people who are not blood-related, so I think family is really a determining factor for each individual to decide what family is to them and how they interact with their families.

What I seek is to have freedom, which is liberty, free from control, civil liberty, the absence of false narratives that endanger us, absent of government control via systems that claim to help us, but never help. Removal of systemic injustices that hamper our peace, and the ability to do normal activities without fear. Simple things like exercising our driving privilege without being afraid we're going to die if we get stopped by the police. I think we all seek, or I know I do, the security of what it would mean to be free. Being free would mean being safe from the harms created outside of decisions that we don't have control over as individuals.

Amanda Wallace

Tonight, I want to talk about the topic of family freedom and security from the inside out. As Joyce said, I come from this system, from the inside as being a child protective service investigator. And while working inside of this system, I think that I had a different definition of what these words meant. The definition of family is defined by the system. What is appropriate, and what is *inappropriate* for a family? What does a family look like? All of these definitions were taught to me by the very system that we seek to abolish.

In regard to freedom, I used to think that families could still be free inside of a system (while I was still working inside of the system). I thought that this family regulation system was there to ensure the security and safety of people and children. We now understand that family is not what this system defines it to be, but is how *we* define it. We now understand that freedom is something that we still have to fight for, and we have to ensure our security so that our families are free.

But what we also have to understand is that the very existence, the very existence of this system is a threat to our families, to our freedom and our security, so, we have to understand the root. And a lot of times we get caught up in the conversation of, "What will happen if we abolish the system?" And when we get to reparations and we talk about that and we reroute these funds to the community, we can deal with these problems. We first have to understand that this system does not serve us. A system that rips children out of their safe and loving homes and puts them in a foster care system where they are raped, murdered, and beaten is not what we need.

I want to show people the reality of this system. Take the example of Zephaniah and Ms. Sellers, a family in Kentucky. Ms. Sellers gave birth to Zephaniah and when he was two days old, two days old – she was accused at the hospital of being "impolite while Black."[1]

We can't talk about family or we can't talk about this system without getting to the root: this system was created to kidnap Black and Brown children. It's doing so well that there are states that can't even balance their budget without kidnapping children. To understand the root, a system is designed for certain formal and informal structures, functions and capacities assembled to prevent and respond to whatever it is that the system wants to respond to.

We have the criminal justice system, that prevents and responds to crime, so they say. Family regulation and policing systems, they say, are preventing and responding to abuse or neglect in children. In reality, we know that all of these systems come from colonialism, and capitalism, and they were only uprooted to be able to stop people from becoming free.

If we don't get that, if we don't understand that, we will look at this modern-day family regulation system and see the auction block, the sale of Black and Brown children. We won't see that. If we don't see it, we can't abolish it. And if we don't see the reality of this system, we'll see Tyre Nichols as another Black body murdered in the street by the slave catchers and not see the public lynching of our people each and every day in the United States of America.

When we talk about freedom, we got to understand that we are not free. Just because our houses might look nicer, our paychecks might have gotten bigger, they let us walk around what we believe is free, we are not free until we have enough political, and economic power to be able to demand everything that we want and we deserve, we are not free, and we have to accept that and understand that.

But I really want to take a minute to talk about security because we think about to what ends. We see how bad this is, we see the threat to our families. Again, I really want people to resonate with Ms. Sellers, this mother for whom it took 590 days to get her baby home after being snatched at two days old. "Well, what do we do with that? How do we get free?" We get organized, we get people power. I'm a part of the African National Women's Organization (ANWO) and there are other organizations, African-led organizations, that people can seek to understand the deeper political theory of what is happening so that we can [resist] systems in the United States government. It's not a fairytale. It's the United States government, that we are trying to abolish.

In order to do that, we have to get organized. So, the African People's Socialist Party,[2] the Independent Uhuru Democratic Movement,[3] all of these movements are fighting for freedom and the security of our people because security comes from the people. Of course, we got to talk about reparations... how do we do this? We do it through reparations and sending resources back to our community. A lot of times, we'll get the question, "Well, what are you going to replace it [capitalism] with? How are you going to do this?"

We've got to have the resources to be able to start to develop those plans. [The state is] able to print their money, keep the money, and continue to push up inflation and everything else to keep us oppressed. We can demand what is rightfully ours. Our labor that they have gotten off the backs of our people. It's time for us to be able to bring the question of reparations to every conversation. The African People's Socialist Party has already made reparations a household name in the question of when are we getting ours. I push that for us to be able to understand that security is tied to reparations.

Also, I invite everybody to the Black Mothers March on the White House.[4] because it is a mobilization to say to the United States government that enough is enough. Enough is enough. Family is what we define it as. Freedom is what we are going to fight for. And security is in our hands. It's in each and every one of us. You can go to the blackmothersmarch.com and register, and we hope to see each and every one of you in Washington DC, as we take this question right to the doorsteps of the White House and tell them that our babies are our babies, and that they're going to stop kidnapping them.

Get involved. Follow us on social media at Operation Stop CPS, so we can continue to do this work.

Dawn Wooten

I agree 100 percent when Joyce and Amanda talk about family and the definition of family. I'm coming from a medical position to where I was a nurse inside of an ICE detention immigrant facility for about four to five years working on the inside. Family is defined as what we make it as. It's defined as how we create it. Inside the facility, they have families with guards, and then they have families with the detainees or the ICE immigrants who were inside the facility. We were never taught to break code, to break rank. We were never supposed to develop families with the ICE immigrant women or men who were inside the facility.

I live down South where it is still developing and still undergoing white supremacy suppression. My counterpart or my supervisor was a Caucasian male who told me, when I brought my complaints and concerns to him, that because I thought I was Black enough and thought that I was woman enough and female enough to challenge his authority, that my position now will be made PRN (*pro re nata*, or "as needed").

So, I have not had employment in that place for two years. I would still be employed if these women had not developed family on the inside, to a point where they trust each other with their secrets and situations and circumstances years on end. It happened to come across my ears one day and I became part of the family, as a sick call nurse. I developed a relationship with different nationalities on the inside and upon the hearing of the things that were going on inside the facility as a family member who had a voice as a family member, that they trusted to talk about those things that were taking place with them on the inside of the facility.

I was cast out of a family that I was supposed to be structured into, which was supposed to be a family of officers and nurses. We were not to intermingle. So, family is what we make it. Yes, we do need to hear each other's voices. Yes, we do need to take the time out to hear each other. Also, in the confines of this place, I'm going to define freedom inside of a place where they were supposed to possess a right for their situations, and their circumstances and their concerns to go unhindered. But who hears you inside of a place that's already confined? Who's your voice on the inside of a place where you're already locked up and that you're policed and that you're secured on the inside of a place? There are not enough voices on the Earth to make the noise that it needs to be made against the voices that are suppressing the noise.

So, I am so loving and I'm so hearing and enjoying the movements that are being made in areas and places. Amanda was correct. I was the only one punished on the inside of this facility because I came outside of the box and

I became the scrutiny outside of the box. There should have been a way and a voice for them to express their freedom and those liberties. Whenever the women came against those officers on the inside, they were punished and water was shut off or food was denied to them. Or, a form of control was going on inside of this place where I'm seeing that we're *supposed* to be free here in these United States of America, the home of the brave and the land of the free.

A lot of the different migrant, immigrant people were on the inside not because they had committed mass murders. Some of them were women who had a credit to a local store and got insulin syringes, and the local store owner got upset, and turned them over to ICE. Or they were taking food without paying in order to feed their children. What they did was not so atrocious that they deserved to be treated the way they were treated on the inside.

We talk about security inside of a place that you're supposed to be secure, supposed to be taken care of, you're supposed to be watched, and you're supposed to be governed over with rights, even though they were on the inside of this facility. So, it's hard watching, and it was hard standing by as a nurse not to have that voice to stand up and say that these things [violations of rights] are coming across my desk. I'm doing this research and I'm looking up these things that I'm bringing to you that I know you had to have known that was transpiring on the inside of this place, but the detainees are secured and you're reassuring them that they're safe.

You're reassuring these women that they're safe, but their uteruses are being taken without their permission. You're reassuring these women that they're safe, but their tubes are being taken without consent. You're reassuring these men that they are being taken care of, but because they stand up for their rights on the inside and they're not the same color as you, then you're depriving them of a shower. You're depriving them of food. Or you're depriving these women, if they don't go out to see the gynecologist at the time, that they don't get to eat or they don't get treated at court, or they don't get to talk to their family, they don't get to talk to their loved ones. We're speaking in a sense of security inside of a place being secure.

I do not change my mind at any point for speaking out for injustice. I will not change my mind about speaking out. But listening across the panel and listening across the things that I've heard and the place that I've been in, racism and slavery has not stopped. It's just come to a place where people have come to another level of covering and sheltering and threatening.

There was a lot of threatening going on, on the inside. My life was threatened if I continued to speak out. We had to be up on the security for several months. Somebody threatened my life and my children. So, it's still going back to that form of control. So, I'm like Amanda, I'm interested to hear where we're going with this conversation. I'm excited to be a part of a move and the capacity that I'm in with this move.

Samaria Rice

I am the mother of Tamir Rice.[5] I am the founder and CEO of the Tamir Rice Foundation located in Cleveland, Ohio where we offer afterschool free programming. My way of giving back to the community is by offering tutoring and mentoring, expression arts, music, pan-African history, classic civic classes and much more, including performing arts studio and things like that. When I think about being free in this country, there's no freedom for us. People should understand that. I agree wholly with Amanda and Joyce and Dawn, that we have to have a conversation and develop some type of code of conduct with the people foremost, and teach them what Black liberation should look like and should be like: How to love one another because we are so broken from being, in this country, we don't trust one another.

We have to build up that love and that trust toward one another because we're the only race that does not stick together. We have to wake up and understand how it's important for us to obtain our reparations and get our security in place. As Amanda said, this is not designed for us, it has never been designed for us. We have to get with like-minded people, and have these conversations, and filter through the people that want to be there and don't want to be there. It's very crucial to understand that we are at war, and we've been at war for over 400 years now.

I went to the State of a Union address last night with the Tyre Nichols[6] family and the George Floyd family. I was invited by my councilwoman Shontel Brown. Let me just tell you, it was so sickening and pathetic and pitiful to see all of those politicians and homeland security and police officers in the Capitol, it was just sickening to see a lot of that stuff to me because of what I have endured in this country. It looked like a bunch of puppets and they are cheering on their master. And what we were able to do is just have a conversation. I'm tired of having conversations. Something needs to be done.

They talk about getting [the members of the] Senate out of there and some of the House of Representatives. These people have been in office for years and they're not going to change. The system is not designed for them to change. It is designed to keep us oppressed. They are white supremacy, and that's just what it is. This country is built on white supremacy, off of the blood of Black and Brown people, people of color in this country. It is time that we unite. It is time that we wake up and come together, but the universe set up the chosen ones to be leaders, and that's going on right here. I was chosen for this position. My son was a sacrifice for this position.

My experience with implementing superior oversight and just being a part of a political arena because of my child is quite sickening and I had to get woken up in a most horrific way. The most horrific way is to lose a child. I realized I was living in the bubble. I could say that because when you're not raised in the culture of Black liberation or you're not raised that way, you don't know. Sometimes our parents forget where we come from, they try to give us a better life and the things that they had.

I really thought that I was free in America, but I'm not. Look at the color of my skin, look at the color of your skin. The way they treat us, the constitution does not work for anybody. It is time to unite and come together. We have to have a code of conduct in order to make this work for everybody because a lot of people want to learn, they're going to be learning and it's a learning process for everybody. But we need the people. We need the people's government because this government does not serve us. We need a people's government that serves the people.

When it comes to security, we have to have those conversations and figure out what that looks like on top of getting reparations, getting land that's owed to us, that is much needed for us because a lot of people that were born in this country, people of color, they don't want to go anywhere else. I have had those conversations where people said, "I'm not going nowhere. I'm staying here. They should leave." At this point, we are entitled to security; and that looks like reparations, it looks like resources, it looks like land. We have to teach our people how to love one another, how to build up that trust between one another and how to continue to support one another.

It is time that we come together. When you talk about recognizing who you are in this country, we are Black kings and queens in this country, you understand that? [despite] white supremacy is designed to be that way. I believe God created all of this. I'm very spiritual. I believe He put bad people down here for us to deal with different obstacles. White supremacy is very much real and it's part of the history of this country. We have to come together, whether it is voting, getting these people out of office, maybe put the right people in. What I saw last night during the State of the Union Address was a dog and pony show.

I'm going to be honest with you, the State of the Union Address was very educational. I was able to see a lot of things. I was able to connect with a lot of families. But again, they keep adding to this group [of impacted families], with no accountability [from the state]. And it's not normal for any person in this country, especially people of color, to wake up to see another Black or Brown person murdered at the hands of law enforcement. That is not normal. That is sickening on top of trying to build our community, for we don't continue to have community violence, and to teach our brothers and sisters how to love one another, and how to care for one another. Through my journey and the death of my son, I tell everybody my DNA changed up.

I'm not who I used to be. I'm different teachers like Malcolm X and Marcus Garvey and Khalid Muhammad, and these are the people that help me stay focused on who I am as a Black woman in this country. I have to fight continuously to get whatever I may need from the white people, the oppressor, and sometimes our own, people, right? So again, we have to get a code of conduct because everybody is not going to be able to ride on this ride with us. We have to make sure that we have like-minded peoples like ourselves. Harriet Tubman could have freed more people if they knew that they were free. And, some of them were trying to go back. What did she do? She took them up out of here. We can't afford to mess up.

It's already messed up. We are already behind. This is so crucial; this is serious when it comes to this white supremacy. I'm not going to sugarcoat nothing for them. I don't have time. I have got plenty of death threats and I have got plenty of people telling me to be quiet and calling me out and stuff like that. But I don't have to be quiet. Y'all made it possible for me to have this platform, so I'm going to do what I need to do and wake up the masses of the people if that's what it takes. Keep waking them up, keep waking them up, keep being there supporting and being diligent to this movement and this work that I'm in. It is very crucial that y'all listening to these women on this line because they have the facts.

I just want to put some key points out, key things to awaken y'all minds. This country is crumbling and if we don't get us together as a whole, as people of color as a whole, we are going to have a lot of casualties.

That's something that I do not want to see. We can continue to wake up the masses and come together as one and form a people's government for us, to serve us, not the elites of the world, you know what I'm saying? Why we don't have no people's government?

It's just mind-boggling to me that they can actually serve a different master than the master who brought them here. And understand that it is designed this way, it's designed for our children, for them to be entertainers. This country is so messed up. We have to come together.

Joy James

There is a question asking about abolishment over radical reform when it comes to Black liberation. We've been talking specifically about the Black/ African experience. We know that the boarding schools, and the disappearance of Indigenous women and girls are also a reality and an expression of genocide according to the UN definition.[7] Black Americans have used *We Charge Genocide*, the 1951 document, [to support civil and human rights].[8] How do you see Black liberation, abolition and radical reform.

The audience who raised that question also writes: "I'm mainly thinking about what Amanda said because of foster care activists in the UK; this is international, and a friend involved in foster care activism does not want to be in their household due to violence, but they really want radical foster care reform." What are your strategies to move away from federal, state, and city legal systems that do expropriation of babies. That was a very chilling video that Amanda showed.

Another person asks: "How do you as organizers handle disagreements with others that you organize with and how do you work to confront or cope or develop strategies with people who disagree with your analyses or who might even co-opt part of your analyses?"

Another question: What do you think of a "political" family? Your contributions are shaped by vulnerability to the state: violence, lost jobs, death threats, "dismembered families", and dismemberment of families with police violence. How do you see the relationship between spiritual families and political families?

McMillan

First, I'd like to say that I don't believe it's a point that we don't stick together. I think it is a point that they make direct efforts to ensure our separation via systems. I'll give you an example. A mom that I was working with who lived in a housing project in New York City had a baby with a young man who was in prison. He was incarcerated for reasons unrelated to anything that happened in the building where he and his child's mother lived at, which happened to be the same housing project where his mom lived at.

When he was released from prison, he had to go live in a shelter because the housing project said he could not have a felony conviction for a drug sale and live in a housing project. His mom who was approaching her 70s and his child's mother, who had two other children, were both afraid of being evicted, for allowing him to stay the night with them or visit them in that complex. Their unwillingness to let him live there or visit there was not because we don't stick together, it was because the system was designed to keep us apart. There's a lot happening ... many things that the system does [are] invisible to the naked eye, and that's what creates the systemic ... systemic things are not seen.

I would like to say there is no "white supremacy." I wish we would stop saying that. I think there are only an extreme amount of white people with severe mental health issues that lead them to believe that they are "supreme." I say that because white people historically have been unable to do anything for themselves. We built this country with sweat and our bare hands, the teachers erase our history, our memory from this history. This is not the land of the free, it's not the home of the brave as they say. There's nothing brave about the things they do, it's very cowardly. This is a place that's plagued with systemic racism and it's the home of the slave, which is why we have incarceration, which is why we have the foster care system that prepares people to be incarcerated.

There are so many parallels between mass incarceration and foster care, where we created a system that we said was there to protect and care for children. But 87 percent of the children in the system across this nation are there for reasons related to poverty that was framed as neglect. But once they yanked these children out of their homes, they're strip-searched like prisoners. They're separated from everyone and everything they know and love like prisoners, they change homes as regularly as prisoners change cells, if not more often.

They use garbage bags and pillowcases to change locations just like prisoners do. They eat what they are served, like prisoners do. They have set visit times on set visit days like prisoners. They have oversight during a visit, like prisoners. If they get to go home, their parole, utilizing the same language as the Prison Industrial Complex. They have oversight during that parole period and can be re-separated for any minute infraction. The majority of children who spend time in foster care are more apt to be incarcerated and are mostly incarcerated as a next step.

It is not the "pipeline" that we call it. We must correct our language. It is a prerequisite, it is a training, it is a preparation. It is intentional, it is not by accident. And I ask you, why would you ask me if should we abolish something that's causing great harm and destruction to families purposefully and that don't care for the kids even when they do need help? To abolish only means to end, and why would you question and say maybe we should radically reform something that we know is causing harm. Should I cut you nine times instead of ten? Is reducing the pain what we are looking for? Or are we looking to stop the bleeding altogether?

Wallace

Exactly. How do we radically reform this system? It's trying to make the slave master or the slave catcher better people. And that's not what the goal is, the goal is to ensure that this system is not a threat to us. Like Samaria was saying, I watched the address that Biden gave last night in disgust. It was just a whole bunch of professional clappers that just kept getting up and down every time he spoke. But the one thing that really stuck out to me is he said that the United States is the only nation built off an idea. Which is true, if you think about it, this idea that people are supreme and that another class of people are inferior is the idea that these people have continued to put into, from generation to generation and then they've been able to keep it going through violence, right?

The police, the only thing they did was get better cars. They got uniforms, but the original slave catchers were not, they didn't have uniforms on, they just did the job. But now they're able to do the job and get a paycheck from it. And so every time you try to reform that, or you try to give them some type of training to help them see past what is deeply rooted into the very system that they take an oath to protect, how do we expect anything to change if we keep trying to just change it? We have to change ourselves. We have to change our mindset that we want anything from this system. The system has to be completely abolished and we need community control. We need community control just of our children, of the police, of every other system that is taking our people down. I do not believe in radical reform; it is all abolishment.

And then the other question was regarding organizing or how do we agree to disagree in movement space. But I think that it's definitely more ways to skin a cat. You got to be able to approach this thing from different angles. If we all agree to unity under certain principles, I understand that this system needs to be taken down. Just because we might not agree on the way to get to that, if we are all doing the work to get to that same goal, then the mission still gets accomplished.

The mission still gets accomplished, and so I think that that is what we need in this movement space is an understanding and respect for each other. That our purpose, our purpose is given to us. Like Samaria said, she said that she came to this work because this was given to her. This is in her. And so when we wake up in the morning, I know just like J-Mac, Samaria, we know what have to do to take this system down because it's our purpose and that's just what we are going to have to do.

Rice

Black liberation has to be first, [it] trumps everything. If there's no Black liberation, nobody can be liberated. I definitely agree with you, Joyce. And Amanda, everything you said is exactly right. But what I was saying – I wish my mother and father were Black Panthers and I was raised that way. That means sometimes it's a strong bond, although it's designed to still break us apart and stuff like that. But it's the strong bond with the teaching of your mom and your daddy, I just wish I was raised that way.

This came to my front door. So, I have to start from where I'm at. When I say we don't stick together, that's what I have been experiencing and on top of everything else, of course. But that's just what I see in certain cities, especially when I'm thinking I'm trying to make a change in my community. I'm going to these council meetings and they are all Black. I got my foundation, [but] it was all Black women that turned me down for capital funding. And I'm just trying to get back to the community and build the building. So that's what I mean, those types of people, what I'm saying. And they may not be "woke," they may never get woke, but it's okay. But we still have to keep it moving.

So even when they turn me down, I just keep it moving. I try not to deal with folks like that in my spirits because I'm very spiritual. I get sick. When I'm just doing what I'm supposed to do with somebody who just come and mess up my vibe. We're spiritual people and I like to excuse myself, if you are not going to come in here liberal with an open mind, how am I going to be able to work with you? I can't stress myself out. I can't kill myself because you don't want to wake up. But it's a lot of people that do want to wake up, so we give them the teaching of how to love one another and things like that.

When it comes to mass incarceration, I'm still trying to understand that just a little bit. I mean, I do understand this design and they took people out of their homes and broke families up. But I can't understand how you said don't say white supremacy, the powers to be, I'm going to say powers to be.

How do they still take our lives and take our precious men's and women's lives and just disregard them. I'm still having a hard time understanding that part of the system, which I haven't got too deep in, I'm sure Amanda could probably educate me a little bit more. Maybe you, Joyce, because it's a lot of positive good brothers and sisters that's in there in prison that don't need to be there. They don't need to be there. The country, it's just totally messed up.

James

A previous question corrected me on elevating the United Nations without pointing out the betrayal of Haiti and its right to autonomy or self-governance. UN "Peacekeepers" stationed in Haiti have raped Haitian women and girls and left babies behind; essentially none of the men from other nations are held accountable.[9]

So, how do you see [shared] causes and campaigns within the US and international working? We have a question from the UK: "How do you see your organizing within the US linked to outside of the US?"

McMillan

I think Black Americans or Black people have a lot of problems, not just in America but outside of America. I think that has come from the influence of Americans.

Part of the problem is that [US racial] hate has spread widely [with] it's hatred for Black people. They're given needles/shots [or are medically neglected; see *Medical Apartheid* by Harriet A. Washington and [https://www.mcgill.ca/oss/article/history/40-years-human-experimentation-america-tuskegee-study]. There [are] medical experiments falsely claiming to help children. Haitians are calling America out now for claiming to help when the US is causing confusion.[10] It's impacting us when we leave the US because America has had a great influence.

Hate is not going to continue to reign because the movement for change is growing. I am as sickened as you are, Ms. Rice, when we talk about our politicians, because our politicians are not our politicians. They are people we've elected to represent the voice of the community, but they don't even take the time to hear from the community. They represent only their own interests. Until we can begin to get a handle on that, hold them accountable, don't be afraid to call them out, don't take pictures with them. They are not celebrities. They are here to serve. We have boosted their ego to the point where they think that they are special. It is up to advocates, organizers to hold them responsible. They have [to] do their jobs so the resources can come to the community so that we can better organize the community and provide them with the things they need.

Rice

Absolutely. When I was at the State of the Union Address and I was talking to the Black caucus and some of the council people, councilmen and councilwomen, it really just felt really fake. Yeah, we vote them out … we have to demand and do it in a way where we still have dignity. But we need the power to do that. What does that look like? We may look like a rainbow of all colors being oppressed in this country, especially Black folks being oppressed. [The State of the Union] gave me very little hope. I was very angry. These are the people that were elected and they don't value our lives. They know the powers that be don't value our lives.

We had a example [of not being valued]: Tyre Nichols. How do we continue to have those conversations with these elected people? Sometimes I think it's useless because I'm not going to go back and forth with somebody who has not lost anything in this. These are celebrities. They are pretenders. Al Sharpton's been around for years and he's still having steak dinners up in the White House. What are you doing? What are you doing for us? I'm not going to play these games with these folks.

I'm to a point where I'm like: "This is what it's going be. Split it down the line. We stand over here, y'all stay over here. Don't come over here with all of that." That's where I'm at.

James

Impacted families petitioned international bodies by using *We Charge Genocide*, the 1951 document written by Black leaders in the CPUSA's Civil Rights Congress which included William Patterson, W.E.B. DuBois and Paul Robeson who delivered the text to the UN. It was circulated around the globe, and embarrassed the US, by exposing the white nationalist and police lynchings and murders of Black people, as well as labor exploitation, beatings, theft of property and salaries, rapes, etc. If 21st century activism continues the work of 20th century organizers and appealing to the international ethical order, one questioner asks: "How well does the UN work for us?"

The 2022 "We Charge Genocide" International Tribunal, hosted by In the Spirit of Mandela, was held in the NYC Audubon Ballroom where Malcolm X (El-Hajj Malik El-Shabazz) was assassinated in 1965.

Rice

Let me just say something about my going to the United Nations. I really thought that they were going to come in and help us in the United States. They are *not* going to help us, okay? It's just documentation. Watch *Hotel Rwanda*[11] – [and see] how important Americans are. But watch how during a genocide the Clinton administration didn't even send help [https://digitalcommons. trinity.edu/cgi/viewcontent.cgi?article=1062&context=infolit_usra].

Americans are known to be bullies. A lot of people are disgusted with Americans. It makes me a little skeptical when I go out of the country to talk to different people. My son has a memorial in Palestine; they may accept me, some people may not. So again, it's a tricky conversation because you don't know who could be our allies or who not. I don't know. But I do know that Biden has sent a lot of money overseas when he should have been keeping that money here in the United States. I don't know how we [can] build with any other country when they are laughing at us, they don't respect us. We are dying in different ways.

James

Any other thoughts about international alliances? Also, a student asked if you imagine that your work could restart another Civil Rights movement?

McMillan

I'd say Yes to the Civil Rights movement, but it would look a lot different than what it looked like in the past because I think there's a greater under-standing of what it is we need. I think Martin Luther King, with all of his good intentions and all the respect and love that I have for him, pushed for us to be integrated into white communities. I think that was one of the worst things that happened to us. We need to be separate and apart. We need to educate our own children, care for our own children, and run and control our own communities. We don't need to be integrated.

I went to Switzerland twice in 2022 to visit the United Nations to discuss the plight of Black Americans or Black people in this country. I went once to the Committee on the Elimination of Racial Discrimination here in America, and that group actually did release some recommendations to the United States of America regarding foster care and prison, which is what I went and spoke about. They released some other recommendations too based on things that other groups spoke about. Poisoning the community through air quality and other things. Like in Harlem, they just put a truck stop for 18-wheeler trucks in a very condensed Black neighborhood. This of course is going to up respiratory problems and other health issues.

We did talk about how America strategically does things. They use a formula. I was blessed enough to have a conversation with Angela Davis. I asked her, did she think going to the UN, staying in communication with the UN was something that could save us? I didn't believe it was when I asked her, but her being who she is, I wanted to get that question in. She said it will not save us, but it is a part of something that needs to occur. So, I'm going to continue to do my work with the UN regarding the things that's happening to Black Americans and Black people in general in America, but I'm also going to continue to do my work here on the ground.[12]

Wallace

I definitely think that we have an opportunity to partner with colonized people all across this world. We weren't just brought to the Americas. We were spread out all over. Yes, definitely there is unity; but I think for us, we have to first divorce America before we could begin to have a blueprint across the world. Even the fact that we still call ourselves African Americans. Again, we hyphenate that name as if we are married to this country, as if they have ownership of us. I know I'm an African. But that is something that we have to remember in our mindset when we're thinking about abolishing this system, we can't keep that name.

In regard to the Civil Rights movement, we have to also remember that the reason why the Civil Rights movement did not take us where we needed to go is because they killed our leaders. COINTELPRO [and the FBI and police] came in and wiped out [a lot of people] speaking about Black liberation. When we're thinking about how we are going to forward the revolution and finish this out. We have to understand that that is what is going to happen when we begin to fight for power.

The chairman, Omami Yeshitela, of the African People's Socialist Party, the FBI raided his home along with seven other locations in July of 2022 because of the programs of the African People's Socialist Party.[13] They are building basketball courts in St. Louis, community centers, fighting for true Black liberation and are not asking America or our oppressor for those resources.

I very much know that this freedom, we're going to get it in our lifetime. But I think it starts with having some really hard conversations about what we are willing to do, the stance that we are willing to take against American repression, or even being in America, right? We are currently colonized in this territory. What are we willing to do to get ourselves out and to get control of our own territory?

McMillan

I agree, Amanda.

Wooten

I also believe that alliances can be made internationally. I worked inside an ICE immigration detention camp, so I'm an American alliance for them. When the case was first brought with me, things traveled all the way to Australia and Quebec and Africa and different places to where people were wondering where one individual, single mom of five, a nurse, the only job that I had that, that stood up and risked everything for what was right. I came from a small background where my grandma taught me to treat people how you want to be treated. That grew up in me systemically.

Working against systemic racism took respecting all colors. I encountered all nationalities, all colors inside this facility. But what we have to first do is build trust. Because that's just what you are looking at here. If I'm mistreated and I go tell the next person, "This is how I was treated at X, Y, Z," then everybody's going to think that you were treated at this facility and everybody that works inside that facility or that place or inside of that entity is a bad person. If I take that back across international waters and I was treated this way in America, then everybody coming this way is going to think that this is the way that every American person treats every person.

Civil rights and civil liberties. I'm learning a lot from you ladies tonight. I've been in nursing for 14 years. But our civil rights? Do I think it can happen coming from the area that I'm in? Yes, I agree with Joyce. It's going to look different. I agree with Amanda, it's going to look different. I'm a different generation seeing things in a different light. I'm also being led to learn differently to where the person that was before me medically, not stepping on anybody's toes, but the medical person before me set a tone for me. Every person now is going to think that I'm coming in because I was afraid to lose my job or I was afraid to speak out or because I needed this job to work with my counterparts who were afraid to speak out that did need their job, and they were coercing along with this individual because they were in fear. Then they're going to look at me the same way.

There are barriers that have to be broken. It's going to take some time. It's got to be chiseled away at. But it can be done and trust can be rebuilt.

James

Sometimes when we say we're not united, we have different concepts, ideas and debates about the role of electoral politics. Do you see leverage in electoral politics and favorable changes in the law? Amanda, you're speaking as an African socialist, [you are not] trying to integrate into capitalism birthed in genocide and enslavement. Do you see the political family as reaching an agreement around electoral politics? Organizations mobilize against genocide: environmental pollution, health inequities, mass and incarceration.

Amanda raised the issue of COINTELPRO [the infamous FBI program to disrupt and destroy civil/human rights and liberation movements]. One of the byproducts of COINTELPRO is political prisoners: Jamil Al-Amin, Kamau Sadiki, Mumia Abu-Jamal, [Leonard Peltier, Joy Powell] and the disparities of how you're treated in prisons because of your politics. When they target you as a progressive person speaking for the people, your healthcare becomes more limited.

Wooten

As a nurse, there's control. I hear these ladies talk about the different controls that you're either policed or you're imprisoned or your kids are taken from you. There's some form of reprimand for utilizing your voice and utilizing the concerns that you have inside of the prison. Like I said, whenever women inside did not comply, their water was shut off. When they did not comply, they were denied food, phone calls, and visitation rights.

It's a form of control inside of a place where you're already being policed and controlled. Speaking out and speaking against that control cost me my job. Being unemployed for two years, as a single mom taking care of five kids, one child in college, now I'm having to rebuild and restructure a whole life.

But when people in power want [more] power, they get it by any means necessary. Even if that means that they're going to control the individuals that they already have. It's just another silent term that I agree to for enslavement, entrapment. I'm going to train you how to conduct yourself, and if you don't conduct yourself or respond the way that I want, you won't get your tooth seen by a dentist today. You won't go to the ear doctor. You're going to be deaf in that ear at some point. You won't go see the cardiologist. Your heart will continue to skip a beat. We are reaching a point where we find that the incarcerated are dying at the hands of security because they're not being given proper care.

The employees that I work with were scared. I'm having everybody telling me, "Oh, we see this. We know this is going on, but we can't do this." They're scared from the top, and my supervisor, the same color, same ethnicity, female, was watching me going back reporting to a higher authority, different colors, different gender. I was being policed, not knowing I was being policed.

McMillan

I'd just like to readdress the reform issue by giving an example, because I think people really get confused as to why we want to end a system of harm versus reform it. Reform is doing the same thing utilizing a different avenue. In New York, there's a piece of legislation called Informed Consent. It's advising people in the healthcare setting if they will be drug tested and getting their permission to be drug tested during the birthing process. So that's prenatal appointments and postpartum. Because when we test mothers and children at hospitals, we don't test them to give them a treatment plan if we believe that they are abusing a substance. We test them simply to refer them to the child welfare industrial complex.

That's not what doctors are supposed to do. You're not testing for anything related to a medical reason, then you should be asking this person for their consent to be tested. That's the idea of the bill. Health and Human Services, Health and Human Corporation, whatever the hell it is, HHC came out and said they were no longer going to test parents during the birthing process, prenatal or postpartum. People said, "Yay!" And people began to call me and congratulate me on that achievement.

Well, it's not an achievement because they [the state/hospitals] never committed to not testing the baby. That's reform. They were creating reform. They were doing something different, but still getting the same outcome of separating families during the birthing process because when they test the baby, more than likely, even if it's not in the baby's bloodstream, it will be in the umbilical cord. So, therefore, we are not here for reform. We don't want to do the same thing under a different name. We're not trying to change the face of. We are trying to change the reality.

That's really important for people to understand. What I don't understand is [why] aren't they helping more families? The minuscule number of families that are being helped is not worth having a system in place because more children would be helped if family members and other loved ones could step in and support them.

Joy, Dawn, Amanda, Sarah, Maxine, whatever your name is, as a woman, should have autonomy over trusting and believing who gets to care for your child. And it should have nothing to do with the government. It is the idea that they have utilized that word "protection" to cause great harm, because they don't protect people in my community. They protect white people's property that's in my community. And they don't protect us when we go places outside of our community and get attacked. They protect the people of that community to ensure that we're deterred from coming to that community, because they want to keep us rounded up like a bunch of cattle in a small, condensed area that's much easier to control.

Wallace

When I was inside the system and there was something that happened that forced some type of reform effort or the laws to change or policy to change, realistically though, that really didn't make it down to the front lines or what people were actually doing, because the culture of an agency is what runs the agency. It's the people at the agency and what they believe, what they believe is appropriate, and what they believe is not appropriate. Even at the state level, people might believe that they are, it's changing. But then what do actual families experience on the front lines?

Thinking about the money, understanding that children, even inmates, are a mode of production for the system. When we think about these children, for me, for ten years I did what's called day sheets. Every child that comes into the system has a number, a 200 number in North Carolina. Every minute, 480 minutes of the day is coded for a child. That's how my salary got paid. That's how the money comes down from the federal government. The more children that you have [in the system], the easier it is to pay the salaries of the people. It's not just about salaries, it's also about the paper, that is the ink that you print on, the cars that go out into the community to take children or go do home visits. All of these things are attached to the system and then they employ corporate loyalty in the people. Even when you think about politics, politicians are loyal to America because they believe that the system is what needs to continue. Again, I don't believe in politics that are attached to American [policies].

Now, if it comes to like us as a people coming together, self-governing ourselves, coming up with things, that's something completely different. But again, I think first we have to really abolish anything that looks like policing. We don't want to start policing each other. If we just abolish these people [as police forces] and the idea that we need this government agency or system to be able to live, we could also unlock our ancestral roots and be able to do what we need to be able to do.

James

There are different definitions for "reparations." Please describe what that would mean to you..... What would freedom and security look like? I'm still deeply disturbed by what happened to Ms. Sellers and her child. Amanda, what would it mean to give that mother reparations for 590 days?

Wallace

You start with US$590 million.

James

Thank you for being precise. I appreciate your courage. I see you all in different ways as healers or sharing comfort with other people who are traumatized by systemic violence. What would repair and reparations look like as a political, spiritual, familial endeavor?

Wooten

Repair, it would be different. It would be very, very different for me, because sterilization, how do you repair taking away my uterus? How do you repair taking away my ovaries? How do you repair taking away my fallopian tubes? How do you repair taking away my reproductive organs? Basically, telling me that you've thrown my legacy in the trash without my consent. Repair for me would be really tricky because you've taken something from me that I can never get back. I can never get back the ability to reproduce. I can never get back the harm that you did to my body. I can never get back the right to my body.

There's going to be years of healing that these women are going to have to go through, because they have to live with being dismembered or mangled beyond what they could control. Because they made one decision to go in and take a loaf of light bread to feed their kids; or they had a child that is diabetic and sought store credit with the owner, but because now the owner is upset or has a bad day, they can't credit insulin. Now I'm being told that I cannot bear forth or put forth. I can't leave a legacy. I can't leave heirs. A lot of reform for me is futile because you can't give me a new body. You can't give me a new mind. I've got to go through extensive years of healing to repair. I got to repair the mind. I've got to repair the spirit. With a broken spirit, it's hard for the body to function. I'm like, Samaria, very spiritual, a contract spirit.

What do I do now? For me, no money is going to pay for that. Time, that's something that I have to live with. So, I mean, Amanda mentioned 590 million. You going to have to grovel, a lot of groveling, a lot of begging, a lot of all the money in the world can't make me birth. For example, a 23-year-old female desired to birth. But when she got home, her life was in shambles, because there was a choice made for her. I don't think that there would be reform in this case. There's no replacing or healing or making it better. It's a done deal. It's hard to say, but you decided that I was not going to leave a legacy and it goes back. You just decided that my genocide – genocide was what it is – that my legacy was going to be wiped out because of the color of my skin.

Rice

Reparations, yeah. We have to continue to wake up the masses, because if we don't, there's going to be a lot of casualties. We need to demand what we want. I'm not in the business of negotiating. I hear Joyce when she says we have to strategize. We have to strategize with like-minded people, who will go in there with demands:

Look, y'all giving us half of this. Don't come over here with that. We going to have our own people's government. We got our own security over here. We don't need no help from y'all. We got our own electricians, our own plumbers, we got our own everything. We built the country. We could build another one.

They have taken, destroyed my life, destroyed my children's life. Many other families live across the nation. Just the law enforcement, the government itself, they don't solve many crimes. They got everybody in jail. I'm not in the business of trying to be their friend. Black liberation going to always be first, because if Black people can't be liberated, nobody's going to be liberated. Just like in the Malcolm X movie, the white allies, they will just be our allies, because they cannot help us.

They will never be able to understand what it is to be us. My mind is kind of on a militant side sometimes. But I know I have to wear the white hat, because I also service the youth and I try to service our brothers and sisters, the ones that want to be served. There is so much of a difference between wanting it and being in it. You got to have to want this. By my tragedy and what I have been through, I want this and I'll die for this. I work for the people and that's just it. I work for the people and the people, the ones that want to come on, we going to love on you, we going teach you.

We have to comb through with the fine-tooth hair comb and get the ones that don't mean us no good. That will sabotage us. I'm thinking for the future … they need to give us the land. Give us the money. They owe us. Because there's no money in the world that they could give me for the death of my son. I took a settlement [because] I wanted to go on with my life, and I did not want to continue to be bothered with these people. I still have three other children I'm raising.

If I would've known any better, I probably wouldn't have taken the settlement. This don't come with no book. I had to fire three attorneys to even get to the attorney that I had, because all my attorneys were trying to blackball me. They did not want me to speak. They said an *angry woman* will get nothing. I'm like, nothing? I want justice. I don't want money. I need justice for my son. A 12-year-old child. Where's the justice? I shouldn't have to wait no 80 years like Emmett Till's mother [Mamie Till Mobley who held an open-casket funeral for the teen]. And that lady [Carolyn Bryant who accused the 14-year-old of whistling at her and told her husband and brother-in-law who tortured him to death]; they gone damn near dead and they want to go arrest her. You might as well let her die [Bryant died in April 2023]. I don't want to wait 80 years for justice for my son. I'm in the business of taking what I want by any means necessary. It is what it is. They [killers] should not be able to go home and sleep peacefully at night.

If we start doing what they do to us, I bet you some things will change … that's my radical thinking. And again, sometimes I'm not a good strategist. I act on emotions. A lot of the time, and I'm a revolutionary. I don't have time to be politically correct. I don't have to be. They murdered my son, and he's a baby. Not only murder of my son but the genocide that has been committed in this country. They can't say nothing to me. I will tell them what to do at the end of the day. They will never tell me what to do. I will only comply, when necessary, because I want my life. And I will always think of myself as a Black queen in this country. It is what it is.

That's what I will be teaching at the Tamir Rice Foundation Afro Central Cultural Center. Yes, we will be teaching African learning over there. We will not, I will not, tell a child a lie, because they lied to me in this country. I [will] plant the seed [of knowledge] while young. You have to plant it [among the] young. You have to invest in your children and you will see the fruitfulness of them if you do it the correct way. I have four high school graduates. They gave Tamir an honorary diploma. I had three high school graduates, and two kids still in school when Tamir was murdered. It was not easy. I have a total of four high school graduates and I come out of the ghetto. It was very important that I made sure my kids had a high school diploma, because I wanted them to go to the next level.

Children should be having free healthcare and free learning in this country.

James

Thank you. Repair and reparations, Joyce?

McMillan

A lot of what Ms. Rice just stated resonates with me. For me, the repair is the healing, and you cannot heal when the same thing is happening. If I have a cut and it's starting to heal and you cut it open again, it never heals. And that's what we experience as Black people. We talk about PTSD. There's nothing posted about the stress disorder that we deal with in this country. So, we need space to heal. Space means, again, back to the same thing, getting rid of systems that can find us, that judge us, that create false narratives, that treat us inappropriately, that bully us, that threaten us, that take our lives away, that take our loved ones away, that traumatize, that do all of the things that only a sick person would do.

So again, with that white supremacy, there's nothing supreme about being evil. That's a mental illness. And the only reason we have some mental health problems is because they were never treated for theirs. We talk about generational harm for us. Imagine a little kid that grew up eating watermelon at a picnic as they hung, and I'm going to say it, niggers from trees. There's a lot to deal with and unpack there in the white bloodline as to how that has impacted their generations and why they continue to still feel so inferior to us.

I was at a college one day giving a lecture about systemic problems. One of the brave little white kids said to me, Ms. McMillan, please don't blame white people for Black people's failures. You're always blaming white people.

It's Black people who don't want to pick up a book and read. It's Black people who don't want to go to college so they can get a job. It's Black people who have a bunch of baby daddies. It's Black people, Black fathers that leave their children at home with the mamas and don't care for them or pay child support. I let him talk. When he finished the entire class was looking at me, all-white kids, and maybe two Black kids, I think.

I was looking at the expressions on all their faces and they were looking at me like what is she going to say? Did he throw her off her game. I'm like, it's not a game. So, I simply asked them, what is a historical house? What does it take for a house to be listed as historical? I said, entertain me. One of the students would tell me that it was a house that was built over a hundred years ago that had this landmark status where you couldn't change anything in it.

I had to remind them that it wasn't because of our inability that this house has landmark status. It was because we've been smarter than you from the beginning. We didn't need to read books. You tried to stop us from being successful by telling us we couldn't learn to read. But it didn't take us reading books to build the house that now has landmark status, the house that is still standing. Remember the houses that you built after going to school and getting your Ivy League education? I was at an Ivy League school. The houses falling down [are] made of materials that can't hold up to the weather, the ones that you can hear what's happening in your neighborhood homes. It's not the ones that we built with our bare hands [as enslaved people]. So never think that you're smarter. Never think that these situations that we find ourselves in because of evil doings are because of our inability.

We've been smarter than you from day one, from day one. Because even without reading, even without getting a high school diploma, even without going to college, you only put college in the play to try to stop us and slow us down. Listen, you cannot compare yourself to us. We have greatness. When will we be able to step into our own and live who we actually are and who we were born to be, is going to depend on our healing. How do we achieve that individually and collectively until we can become completely separate and apart from systems? There's not enough money to pay us reparations, but there is space for us to live in peace without having to interact with racists. That would be enough reparations for me. I'd feel like I've received reparations.

James
Amanda, last words.

Wallace

I would just say again, repair is just like everybody has said, healing. And that could look like so many different things for different people. Yoga, journaling, getting our chakras in line. You just making sure that we are good with ourselves so that we can get out of just kind of the system and into our minds and our bodies and our souls. And then when we think about reparations, yes, it looks like money. It could look like every white person in this country donating and investing in movements that are freeing us. We don't wait for somebody to tell you to invest in community. Just do it, right. If you have an understanding, it might not have been you, and it might not have been your granddaddy, but if you go back in your lineage, somebody owned a slave, and you need to pay for it.

Understanding that it is time to pay reparations; reparations doesn't just look like money. Just like Samaria said, it is also land and it is also our people. When we think about our political prisoners that are currently locked down, if we freed our political prisoners, we would have the army that we needed to take this thing forward. But the United States government knows that if they keep our people locked up, then we can't push this thing forward. So again, reparations look like money. It looks like land and also looks like freeing our political prisoners so that we can all unite on the front lines of this to push forward to freedom.

James

I am thinking of courage, candor, and care. I appreciate you for being teachers. Most of all, I appreciate – even as Dawn notes some things cannot be repaired, particularly in a context in which we are not free – your commitments to pushing us forward and to think critically and to work collectively.

SOURCE NOTES

1. "Operation Bring Zephaniah." *Operation Stop CPS*. Accessed July 11, 2023. www.operationstopcps.com/Operation-Bring-Zephaniah
2. *The African People's Socialist Party*. Accessed July 11, 2023. https://apspuhuru.org/.
3. "The Uhuru Movement." *The African People's Socialist Party*. Accessed July 11, 2023. https://apspuhuru.org/about/the-uhuru-movement/
4. "Home." *Black Mothers March*. Accessed July 11, 2023. www.blackmothersmarch.com/

5. "Tamir Rice Shooting: Justice Department Investigation Ends without Charges." *Guardian*, December 30, 2020. https://www.theguardian.com/us-news/2020/dec/30/tamir-rice-shooting-justice-department-investigation-ends-without-charges

6. Rios, Edwin. "Families of Tyre Nichols and George Floyd to Attend State of the Union." *Guardian*, February 7, 2023. www.theguardian.com/us-news/2023/feb/07/families-black-people-killed-by-police-state-of-the-union

7. "UN Permanent Forum on Indigenous Issues Calls for an Expert Group Meeting on Missing and Murdered Indigenous Women." *Indian Law Resource Center*, 2019. https://indianlaw.org/swsn/unpfii-calls-expert-meeting-mmiw

8. The Civil Rights Congress submitted a petition to the United Nations to hold the United States accountable for the genocide against African Americans, titled "We Charge Genocide." *BlackPast*. "(1951) We Charge Genocide." *BlackPast*, August 30, 2019. www.blackpast.org/global-african-history/primary-documents-global-african-history/we-charge-genocide-historic-petition-united-nations-relief-crime-united-states-government-against/

9. Elks, Sonia. "Haiti Government Demands Justice for Women and Girls Abused by U.N. Peacekeepers." *Reuters*, December 19, 2019. www.reuters.com/article/us-haiti-women-peacekeepers-idUSKBN1YN2HH

10. Ojewale, Oluwole. "Is Cameroon Becoming Central Africa's Baby Trading Hub?" *ENACT Africa*, July 14, 2021. https://enactafrica.org/enact-observer/is-cameroon-becoming-central-africas-baby-trading-hub

11. *Hotel Rwanda*. United Artists, 2004.

12. Santana, Sandy. "UN Calls for US Action to Address Racial Injustice in Child Welfare System." *Children's Rights*, March 3, 2023. www.childrensrights.org/news-voices/un-calls-for-us-action-to-address-racial-injustice-in-child-welfare-system

13. Goodman, Amy, and Omali Yeshitela. "'Bogus Charge': FBI Raids African People's Socialist Party; Group Dismisses Russian Influence Claims." *Democracy Now!*, August 10, 2022. www.democracynow.org/2022/8/10/black_socialist_chairman_fbi_raid_response

III

Liberation Education

8

Indigenous Pedagogies

Chadwick Allen, Sandra Barton, Américo Mendoza-Mori,
endawnis Spears, Tesia Zientek, and moderator
Christine DeLucia

April 18, 2023

Chadwick Allen

I decided to title my remarks "Centering Indigenous Methodologies."
I want to focus on a particular program that we've run since 2016 at the
University of Washington that we call the Summer Institute on Global Indi-
geneities (SIGI). SIGI is a week-long intensive summer program for Ph.D.
students – students pursuing their doctorate degree in any discipline, but
working within Indigenous Studies, broadly defined. It's team-taught by four
American Indian and Indigenous Studies faculty from three institutions. I'm
part of the teaching team, along with my colleague, Tony Lucero, and two
colleagues who are Pacific Scholars , Hokulani Aikau and Vince Diaz.

Each summer we've had a cohort of twelve Ph.D. students. They come
from our own university but also from other institutions. Part of what we're
trying to do is not only introduce our Ph.D. students to their local cohorts
in Indigenous Studies but to help them start building a more national and
even international cohort of Indigenous Studies colleagues. Our consortium
thus far has included the University of Washington, University of Oregon,
UCLA, University of Hawaii at Mānoa, University of British Columbia, University of Utah, University of Minnesota, and University of Victoria, up in
Canada, along with UBC.

SIGI is meant to be a space for articulating Indigenous Studies, and it's
not based on a specific curriculum. We don't have assigned readings necessarily. But it's a space for students who are working in Indigenous Studies to
professionalize, to think about how to articulate their projects in Indigenous
Studies for multiple audiences. Our key mission in articulating Indigenous
Studies is to help provide a set of epistemological, methodological, and pro-

fessional strategies for students' successful completion and dissemination of creative research projects in Indigenous Studies; and to help students make their Indigenous Studies projects legible to multiple audiences. This is really a response to hearing graduate students talk about the difficulty sometimes of trying to do Indigenous Studies work in various disciplines.

How could they articulate their projects in ways that will be legible to colleagues in their specific disciplines, while also being legible to the inter-disciplinary of Indigenous Studies, and how will it be legible as well in their Indigenous communities, either the ones they're working in or the ones they might be from? We have some specific outcomes that we're hoping students will leave our week-long intensive experience with. We're hoping that they'll leave with a strong understanding of various strategies for conducting Indig-enous-focused research toward formal presentation and publication. We're hoping they'll be able to describe their projects in concise and provocative ways.

We're hoping that they'll be able to make the case for their work in the context of Native American Studies, Indigenous Studies, and Native Pacific studies, and their respective disciplines. Finally, we're hoping that they'll be able to articulate the relationships between the local and global in the work of Indigenous Studies, and that they'll be able to describe the importance of their relationships to their research sites, to their archives, and to the com-munities they work with.

How do we do that? I want to talk about the specific methodologies we use in our SIGI program. I've highlighted five key methodologies that we use, that I think are portable, although I think that you would need to localize them in your specific space. That would make sense for the students you're working with, and the lands and waters that you're working on. One of our methodologies is to begin with formal introductions and then continue to introduce ourselves to each other throughout the whole week. We always send our students a prompt for preparing to introduce themselves to each other, to the teaching team, and to others on our campus when they visit us. Part of that is for them to think about whose lands and waters do they live and work on, and what their relationship is to that place.

Do they know the name of who they are in the local language? Can they use that local language to describe their relationship? Are they a member of that community? Are they a guest? Are they a settler? Are they a visitor? What type of relationship do they have with those particular lands and waters?

Another part we ask them to think about is, what ancestors do they carry with them when they come to do this work? I find this is a particularly powerful part of their formal introduction, thinking that they don't come to the work alone, and that part of doing things through Indigenous methodologies is thinking about the ancestors we carry with us into all of our research situations.

We practice this. We have them prepare for the first day, and then they find themselves in various situations where they need to introduce themselves across the entire week, and so they use similar types of prompts. Another practice that we use is what we call the Aloha Circle and the Mahalo Circle. This comes from Hawaiian practice, our colleague Hokulani Aikau, introduced this to us our first year, and it's a way, really, of opening and closing our week together, as well as opening and closing each day that we spend together in the SIGI week. The Aloha Circle, we began, we make a circle. Typically, we hold hands.

Everyone goes around and reintroduces themselves every morning, and says which ancestors they're bringing that particular day, and if they want to say why they've chosen those particular ancestors for that particular day of the SIGI experience. At the end of the day, then we have a Mahalo Circle, or a circle of gratitude, and everyone expresses something they're grateful for that happened that day. Sometimes this gets quite emotional, but it's really important for students to process what's happening in this intense professionalization experience. We do that each day, and then we, of course, have a final closing Mahalo Circle at the end of the week. That's turned out to also be an important methodology for centering Indigenous ways of knowing.

A couple of other things that we do that have been really effective, one is we have a visualizing research exercise, what we call Indigenous Collage. We started this because of one of our first students, in the first year we ran the SIGI program. An Indigenous student from Canada was using collage as a methodology in her Ph.D. work in Indigenous governance and introduced it to her adviser and introduced it to the rest of us. And for us, we think of it as a way for students to move out of the typical ways they're used to thinking about their research projects in their particular disciplines.

We have them think about, "How would you use the materials that are in front of you, the way you work with making a collage, and how would you work with the fragmented realities that are often the result of colonialism in Indigenous communities?" And so we break people up into groups with the materials, and we have them actually make a collage of their dissertation project. A lot of people are a little wary of this at the beginning, and then people get very excited about it as people are passing around magazines and other visual material, cutting things up, and gluing things together. Then, after about a half day of working on the collages, we do a sort of round of show and tell, and everyone explains what they've made. This, too, is often a very powerful way of people thinking about, "Well, how would you take the fragments of what's available and turn them into this major research project?" That has been a really powerful Indigenous methodology for our SIGI week.

One thing we do every year we've done this is to make sure we go into an Indigenous community and have the experience of we're introducing ourselves and introducing the work we're doing to community members. We're fortunate here, at the University of Washington in Seattle, that we're close to a number of local communities. We've mostly been going to the Suquamish Nation, which is just across the water from Seattle. It's a nice sort of day trip. They have a beautiful museum. They have a lovely longhouse, and they also have a canoe house.

We never know who's going to show up exactly. And that's part of the experience of going into the community. Sometimes we meet with elders. Sometimes we meet with multiple generations of the local community. Sometimes we've had a real focus on local children and young people. Sometimes we spent the day in the longhouse, hearing stories and learning about the local history, and sometimes we've gotten out on the water in canoes and had a lesson and sort of embodied learning. Part of the project for students, though, is gaining the confidence to explain who they are and what their work is in Indigenous community in ways that will be legible to elders, and to multi-generations of the local community.

The final strategy I wanted to point to is that we end the week with a more formal presentation of work, a more typical research symposium, but in the context of a supportive community. Unlike in the dominant academy, where we think of presentations and Q&A, which can be sometimes overly formal and somewhat hostile, we try to create this sort of supportive Indigenous community for presenting work. We give really clear parameters for the students on how they're going to present their work to that particular audience, and then we end with a sort of feast and bring our whole community together to close out the week. What I want to leave you with is thinking about how to stage a sort of professionalization in Indigenous Studies in ways that really draw on Indigenous ways of knowing and really creating Indigenous community at multiple levels for our students.

Sandra Barton

My English name is Sandee. My mother is Claudette Miller Weiterman. My grandparents are Arnold and Lydia Miller, who attended the Indian Mission Boarding School. [Showing photograph] This is my grandmother here in yellow and her sister, my great-aunt in Orange, and a bunch of my cousins in the background. This was a reunion of the boarding school children. My great-grandparents are Cassie and Wellington Miller. Wellington is a survivor of the Hampton Institute Boarding School in Virginia. I am a first-generation college graduate who experienced slow-downs and one stop-out to work in the oil fields.

I would like to read something before we start, and this is by Henry Real Bird. It's called "This Day."

> The spring rains, we've reached. The blue-green grass grows each day, and so will your thoughts. Fantasy does not belong to you. It belongs to all of us. That's what learning is all about. Theories and concepts are taught, but a feeling cannot be bought. We ask for the feeling of learning from sacred talk.

I really love this because it reminds me that, while I am talking, that my breath is sacred, my words are sacred, and so I need to have good intentions and good thoughts while I share with you.

As a little background, this is my dissertation title ["Web Walkers: A Phenomenological Study of Adult Native American Distance Learning Experiences: Toward a Standard Model of Indigenous Learning"], and you'll see that it was published in 2013, although I started my graduate work in the early 2000s. I pouted for a few years. As an elder – let me tell you young ones, don't pout, okay? Just keep putting one foot in front of the other and get yourself finished. Anyways, in the late 1990s, there was a big push for DL, distanced learning, and I was concerned that that might be the final step in the assimilation of our people.

I was also concerned about the digital divide and the construction of additional barriers being erected to keep people of the global majority from education, even though DL was being touted as this panacea to reach all people. I just thought, "Yeah. We've seen how well Eurocentric education has been for the Indigenous world." So I started with that, and I ended up toward a Standard Model of Indigenous Learning (SMIL), because I really didn't know what I had, what I had done, or how it was going to be used.

Let's go back to the beginning. One of my very first classes, I had to write two ten-page papers on a dissertation topic, and I had no clue what I was going to write about. I said, "Okay. Tribal colleges, I want to know about them." Very quick, easy paper, all historical, how they started, their journey, and what their future plans were. I had been learning in my courses about educational philosophies, learning theories, and instructional design models, and I thought, "Ooh. I'm going to go find and write about an Indigenous learning model." I was kind of naive. All of the stuff, the academic stuff that I'd been learning, was all Eurocentric based back in the early 2000s. I learned something very important, though: there were no set definitions for Indigenous education or learning, seriously. This is why I have a picture of those dream catchers up there. You could have a non-Indigenous person telling an Indigenous group to make a dream catcher, and that would be considered Indigenous education. The checkbox would be made for diversity and inclusion. I'm cringing because even today, this is still happening. "Oh. Let's have this group make a set of teepees." Well, *my* people didn't live in teepees. We had longhouses. This Indigenous learning and education, the words were mixed together, and there was just no proper definition.

So being a scientist, I really needed to figure this out. I spent a lot of time reading and talking, digesting it, and coming up with a definition for Indigenous learning. You see, Eurocentric learning, which most of us have experienced all of our life, it's basically to check the box, and reach a specific goal. With that, you've got an accomplishment and you have that power acquisition, or not power acquisition, but the knowledge acquisition, which is often used for power, because we always hear, "Knowledge is power."

The dominant culture has a tendency to use that to erect, maintain, and reinforce barriers. I mean, not so long ago, it was illegal to teach African Americans to read and write. Women were not allowed in higher institutions of learning at all. But on the other hand, Indigenous learning is not like that. What I've found through all my research is that learning is life, and life is learning. We learn. We pass it on to ensure the survival of our communities. I mean, if you didn't learn, you'd die.

It's true. There's some information related to ceremonies and medicines that's not openly shared. But generally, we get information, we share it. This is the definition that I came up with. It's the process of Native Americans receiving and internalizing information in order to solidify their place and interconnectedness with all others, seen and unseen, and then the knowledge can be shared. As I had mentioned, as I was going through the research, I couldn't find Indigenous learning theory in educational philosophies or instructional design models. No theoretical frameworks. There were some general guidelines, suggestions, or there would be very specific guidelines that were developed for a tribe, just a specific tribe that related to their teachings.

While I was going through all of this, reading the literature, the scholarly literature, the not-so-scholarly literature, and interviewing and discussions with a lot of people, I came up with five threads that seemed to go through all of the material. It was just hiding in plain sight. It was amazing. These threads are all, I think, Indigenous learning pre-contact, and that's why I think it's so important and why it resonates.

When I have a group of Indigenous people, I will start with place, but I'm going to start with storytelling right now, because it is a part of us. We have an oral tradition. We share our stories in the classroom. Every lecture is a story, and as you speak with someone else, you are weaving a story with your sacred breath and creating a memory or an experience. Intergenerational interaction, this is so very, very important. Our elders are our wisdom keepers and share their knowledge. Our children teach us as well. They teach us to stay curious, and they teach us to stay young at heart. The next one is experience. We can hear. We can see. We can witness. We can smell, but it's not the same, and someone can tell us, we can read about it. When you experience that event, it becomes part of you; it becomes part of your place. It's very important.

Interconnectedness. This is the belief that everything is connected physically, mentally, emotionally, spiritually. How are we connected and why is it important? Learning is all about relationships and connection. If you don't have it, why are you learning?

This last one is place. Some people think of their house, and then some people think of where they are in relation to other people. But some people, they understand that it's everything. It's in us and it changes constantly, but it doesn't change. Place is hard to define using Anglo words, but I'll try. It is more than a physical location. It is the emotional and spiritual connection of oneself to the universe and all that it contains at a specific instant in space and time. So, your place has changed from an hour ago, and will continue to change. But it really doesn't change because it's you.

To wrap it up here, after I finished my dissertation, I just let it go not knowing what would happen, and out of the blue in the fall of 2021, Katie Archer Olson contacted me asking permission to use the Standard Model of Indigenous Learning (SMIL) as part of a theoretical framework for her dissertation. She also told me that Laura Moore had used my SMIL as a case study of a TCU (Tribal Collage University) in Northern Wisconsin – that's a Tribal College. She validated that the threads were being used unconsciously by the instructors. It was in the curricula, the syllabi, the lectures that she attended, and in the handbooks. That was nice to know.

Katie also told me that she took those threads and developed a rubric and she calls it an Instructional Design Framework. Since implementing, she's had significant results in the passing rates of her students. She works for a small Alaska college that has the highest enrollment of Alaska Natives, and Native Americans, representing 23 villages. So, she takes and she puts all of the threads across the top, and then vertically she runs her weeks with the assignments, and then she just makes sure that they match together.

The one last thought I want to leave you with is that most curriculum is built around white comfort. So even if we Indigenize curricula, we still need to have a robust framework to hold what's been developed. If the framework for supporting that curriculum isn't there, or if it is Eurocentric, then that curriculum is just going to fall through. It's like putting berries in a basket that has holes. It's just not retained. Anushiik/Oneewe, thank you for listening to my story about the SMIL.

Américo Mendoza-Mori

I want to talk about "Indigeneity and Latinidad: Educational Planning and the Future of Latinx Studies in the United States." What do we imagine when we think of Indigeneity in connection to Latinidad? We tend to think of archeological places, very famous, like Machu Picchu, Teotihuacan, and Chichen Itza; they're part of the national narrative of many countries. Or for folklorical or traditional celebrations that have been part of the national narratives. However, sometimes we tend to focus on the past tense, like the Incas were great, the Mayans were great – always in the past tense. But we fail to see the ongoing demands of many Indigenous populations, but also the creativity of the youth. Now there are generations of musicians, artists, diplomats, who are fighting to create more spaces, within Indigeneity and Latinidad in Latin America.

But this conversation is more about what happens in the United States. As we know, there are many migrant communities in the US diaspora. And sometimes just by the name, Latinidad, or Hispanidad, the emphasis in the definition is on the European heritage. But I wanted to share these pictures from New York, for example, and from the southern United States of Latin celebrations, of Hispanic celebrations, that we can see that they're clearly carrying Indigenous heritage and presence. And many, hundreds, thousands of these migrant communities also count with Indigenous migrants, Indigenous language speakers, that could be Quechua, Zapotec, and Maya.

If we expand that into the conversation, into the public conversation, Latine websites in the US have highlighted that even among the youth, second and third generations of Latin American descent, US-born Americans, they want to expand or make more complex the definitions of Latinidad. And they realize that the lack of this conversation, it's also detrimental to the diversity of the community.

From the university, then, when we look at this reality, what are we, what are universities or schools doing then to support Indigenous languages and cultures, and how can we change the narrative of promoting open discussions at large about the coloniality, about anti-Blackness and anti-Indigeneity? In particular in connection to Latinidad, if we go through, let's say, the curricular aspect, as Professor Anne Fountain mentions, there are few texts used in even Spanish or Hispanic studies that attempt to focus on the contemporary presence of Indigenous communities. But then, if we have a wider look at Latinidad on campuses, we then see that there are celebrations like *Día de los Muertos*, Day of the Death, celebrations of Taíno heritage, and Quechua-inspired dances. It is there. It's just that we don't talk much about that or the way it should be.

Why? I mean, not just in the US, but usually the narrative around Latinidad is that there is a claim that everyone of Latine heritage is mixed, is *mestizo, mestiza*, and therefore that kind of makes it easier to dismiss Indigenous or Afro heritage within the community.[1] So talking about Indigeneity and Latinidad, we should see it as an opportunity to expand the notions of this discipline, and how can we expand those notions in a cultural but also in a curricular way. As scholars, curricular presence and methodologies are very important. One aspect that is gaining momentum, even of course Indigenous communities have been doing that for a while, is the discussion of Indigenous knowledge systems, a series of practices and wisdoms developed within Indigenous societies from across the world.

Being aware of that within the curricular platforms and across disciplines, is a way to consider that there is a tradition of knowledge, not just to know, let's say, more in a topic, but also to know in a different way. What I mean by learning in a different way, is to actually understand that storytelling, practices, dances that Indigenous communities bring, also should get the same status as science and philosophy. And that's why we as educators have the challenge to facilitate that bridging and to provide examples – because sometimes people might say, "Well, I don't do Indigenous Studies, so why should I care?" But maybe we do care about food security, technology, philosophy, healthcare, entrepreneurship, or the idea of reparations. For each of these topics, we can make connections with Indigenous knowledge systems. And once we do that, then, of course, we need to bring voices and to put out particular examples.

For example, I think in the case of the word *Pachamama*, which is a word in Quechua, that talks about the relationship with the Earth not only as a commodity, but as we belonging to the Earth. And then of course, we need the same way as when we learn French or Greek philosophy, we need Plato or Foucault; well, we need to find voices and learn from those voices. I'm thinking of my dear colleague Tarcila Rivera, who's a Quechuan activist, and very present in global platforms and practices like Andenes, which are concrete examples of care of the Pachamama, but also in connection to environmental studies. As we can see, and probably it's very obvious for people who are connected to these topics, the abstraction that is very praised in academia is also very attached to practice in the case of Indigenous communities and knowledges. Therefore, we need to talk about the need to move from research in Indigenous cultures to fostering collaborations.

Of course, making these Indigenous studies or Indigenous language programs is also a way to acknowledge the colonial legacy on where we are standing, institutions of higher ed, but also to send a message, hopefully, that things are changing. I would say that there are many opportunities to do community outreach to recognize the contemporary Indigenous heritage, to foster dialogues north-south, to enrich the curricula, specifically in the case of Latinidad, to enrich Latin American, Hispanic, or Latine studies, including the offering of Indigenous languages or courses on particular topics, to invite speakers, to then make a center recentering Latinidad around Indigenous issues, around Afro-diasporic issues. These are pictures, for example, with Quechuan writers, with a Zapotec poet, Dr. Felipe Lopez, with Quechuan musicians and students here at Harvard. These language projects also facilitate identity-oriented experiences among the participants, particularly in this case, US Latinx youth, who are affirming their voices while navigating the challenges of a racialized society.

This picture, and the next picture as well, belongs to the Quechua Alliance, which is an annual gathering that happens in the United States, which is intergenerational, multilingual, to celebrate the relevance of Quechua, but also recognize that universities now have more diverse bodies, and therefore universities are where the youth are receiving their education. And we need to make sure that those spaces don't just continue the acculturation. This image is from just a couple of weeks ago here at Harvard, the seventh Quechua Alliance annual meeting.

As I mentioned, universities are becoming more diverse, and hopefully, that could be a way to express also to the administration these diversity initiatives – and I'm thinking more of universities that are not tribal colleges, of course, because those other institutions have different needs. But in this case, it is to say that it's not that they're making us a favor, but actually is a way to keep up and to be at the forefront of conversations, to not only, let's say, shoot for being global, which is usually the usual narrative we get in academia, or in society, or in corporate spaces, but the value of being intercultural and therefore make sure that Indigenous voices are present.

Once again, I just want to go after the list that I shared in case you find it interesting, or if you are ever considering these topics on how we could connect them with Indigenous curricula, and therefore then include more Indigenous voices and acknowledgments into these disciplines, particularly, in the case of Latino and Latin American Studies. My final thought is to say that all of these strategies are aiming to recenter Indigeneity into contemporary issues, and also to global issues.

endawnis Spears

I'm endawnis Spears, and I am Yucca Fruit Strung Out In A Line clan. I'm an enrolled citizen of the Navajo Nation. I'm born for the White Earth Ojibwe people in White Earth, Minnesota. My maternal grandfather is from the Tangled clan, and my paternal grandfather is from the Choctaw and Chickasaw Nations in Oklahoma. It is an honor to join you from the homelands and the home-waters of the Narragansett people, the People of the Small Point, in South County, Rhode Island.

I wear several different hats at the time being. I co-founded a small consulting organization about four years ago. I also am the tribal community member in residence at Brown University, but this evening I am wearing my Upstander Academy co-director hat, and I'm talking a little bit about the work that we're doing at the Upstander Academy and sharing with you a little bit about hopefully some of the transformative work we do with K-12 classroom educators.

To share a bit about the academy itself, I have been the co-director for several years now, the Upstander Academy, which is also part of the Upstander Project. The Upstander Project was founded in 2009 by Dr.

Mishy Lesser and Adam Mazo, and it is a Boston-based educational organization that uses film as a means to educate about genocide. Their original
film focused on post-genocide Rwanda. With that particular focus, there was
also a suite of educational teaching resources that Dr. Mishy Lesser developed to be a companion piece to that documentary. What became apparent
and clear after that particular documentary was produced by the Upstander
Project, was the need to teach about genocide education in the United States.
The Upstander Academy was formed to give classroom educators the tools
that they need to teach about genocide in the United States, which is a completely different cultural and historical context than teaching about genocide
across oceans, or genocides that happen on different continents.[2]

The requirements that classroom educators in our K-12 public school
systems need to teach about genocide in the United States where they live
and learn, is a completely different set of tools. In partnership with my dear
colleagues at the Upstander Academy, we have assembled a faculty of Native
and non-Native teachers and educators who come from multiple roles in
their own tribal communities, and within their academic communities to
convene with classroom educators, and also with museum educators, once a
year in the summertime, and provide them with a professional development
that really centers an understanding and a deep understanding of the history
of this continent, and particularly the United States.

In the process of developing a curriculum for the Upstander Academy,
there are several things that have emerged as important guiding principles,
or some of the basis of what our teachers need who are primarily non-
Native, although our participants are oftentimes Native and non-Native, but
primarily a participant pool that is white. We have to recenter the way that
we understand educational work for them in their own classrooms. And so
we do our very best to embody and model some of these ethical practices of
truth-telling and truth-teaching in classrooms across the United States. One
of which has already been referenced several times here tonight, which is
the importance of expressing positionality to knowledge. Our teachers come
and bring with them ancestors and systems of knowledge that are of great
import and are reflected back in the way that they do instruction in their
classrooms. We want to foster that and encourage our classroom teachers
to understand what it means to have positionality in the subject matter that
you are teaching.

Also, fostering a sense of intellectual humility, by acknowledging that there
are thousands of Indigenous knowledge systems that predate newer knowledge systems that were introduced in the process of settler colonialism. We

understand that acknowledgment in and of itself is a process of humbling and understanding the methods that are used by the current public school education system and understanding where those are rooted and why, and how Indigenous methodologies and ways of knowing and epistemologies have a very deep history to the place where they do their education work. We do our best to foster those kinds of conversations and to illustrate that for our classroom educators, so they can begin to understand the homelands where they do their teaching and living.

We also encourage understanding, as Sandra mentioned earlier, that there is no finality in the process of education. There is no end point, this is a lifelong journey of learning, and in the United States public school system, a journey of unlearning as well – and that those are counterparts to one another. The learning requires unlearning the master narrative that is presented within our K-12 public school systems. We also do our best to model the mechanism through which our classroom teachers can unlearn their own educational experiences, as they went through the K-12 system here as well. Part of that is understanding the steps toward acknowledging the denial of Indigenous histories and contemporary continued existence across Turtle Island and specifically across the United States. And fostering, again, that conversation and that more dialogic nature of learning with our classroom educators, and making sure that we implement the time, the space, and the self-care to allow our educators to engage in understanding the very depths of the denial that is sometimes required to do education in our public school systems.

Of course, we always acknowledge the fact that the Earth is our teacher, that Mother Earth, the place, the geographic space upon which we live and learn is our original teacher. And that wherever our classroom teachers are living and learning and teaching, also requires a sense of accountability to that particular geographic space and to telling a comprehensive history.

We talk about the purposes of settler education. It was already mentioned by some here, that comfort is not the point. That we acknowledge the need for discomfort. We acknowledge the importance of engaging with material as human beings, engaging with the material of how we develop, not just history lessons, but any curricular lessons that our students, our non-Native students are doing in the United States. It requires discomfort. And so again, much of the academy is really focused on honoring the humanity of our classroom educators. They are entrenched in an education system that oftentimes does not acknowledge or honor the humanity of the educators, the administrators, and also the students themselves. It's of utmost importance to us as faculty in the academy to make sure that we honor the humanity of our classroom educators in this process as well.

Of course, we want to create communities of co-conspirators that can lean on one another in their approaches and the very specific challenges that they receive in their respective school districts, and in their respective classrooms. We really look to ensure that teachers engage in an active community of learning and practice, and that is always at the forefront of the work that we try to do, not just during our time together, but also after our sessions together as well.

Something that has become readily apparent to us who are on faculty, those of us who are also on this panel, and the participants who are watching from home, is that our K-12 system in the United States is an incredibly powerful one, and it has the power to shape the way that Supreme Court justices determine policy and make decisions. And we really feel that this early intervention in our public school classrooms is of great importance to our future generations. So in the spirit of acknowledging my own positionality to this work, as a mother, as a mother of four, it's of great importance to me to, I think, as Dr. Allen mentioned earlier, help to cultivate worlds that are literate in Indigenous knowledge and ways of knowing, which are the worlds that we are trying to create for our own children. And so that is really the motivating factor and acknowledging that is part of our modeling of practice.

I would love to be in touch with any of our viewers this evening, and I encourage you to visit the Upstander Project as they have ongoing documentary films that are being produced that focus on the Indigenous ways of knowing and epistemologies that are so important for our classroom educators to have access to, but also the public as well.

Tesia Zientek

My name is Tesia Zientek. My Potawatomi name is [*Native language*], which means like a crane. I'm originally from Shawnee, Oklahoma, but I live in Oklahoma City now. My family is Bear Clan and I am enrolled with the Citizen Potawatomi Nation. I am excited to share with you some of the work that's been happening at our tribal nation, the Citizen Potawatomi Nation. They're going to kind of focus on one tribal nation and what we've done to help our citizens feel connected to their identity. I also want to acknowledge that this land that is now known as Oklahoma is the homeland of the Wichita, Caddo, Apache, Comanche, Kiowa, and Osage, as well as several other than human relations that were negatively affected by settler colonials.

For those who may not be familiar with the Citizen Potawatomi Nation, I wanted to give you a bit of context that will help situate some of the programs that I'm going to share with you about today. Pre-contact our ancestors were located in the northeast of what is now the US and to what is now Canada. And based on a prophecy, we migrated to the Great Lakes where food grew on water, where there was Manoomin or wild rice. Then in the 1830s were the biggest of several removals for our people, which was known as the Trail of Death. We were moved down to the Kansas area and then ultimately became citizens and landowners in Indian territory or what is now Oklahoma. And then, of course, in the late 1880s there was the Dawes Act, which split our land into our allotments. Now the Citizen Potawatomi Nation has over 38,000 tribal citizens living all over the globe.[3]

Understanding that context, there are a lot of consequences. The aftermath of that removal is very severe. We have a disconnection from our homelands that I mentioned that where food grows on water, where our prophecies told us that we were to live. We are here in Oklahoma. We're so far from that environment. We have distance from our northern relatives. There are several bands of Potawatomi throughout the US and Canada, and we are geographically distanced and the most southern of those bands of Potawatomi. Our citizenship is hugely dispersed. About two-thirds live outside of Oklahoma where our tribe is headquartered. The language has been devastated by this history, taking into account also the atrocities of boarding schools and now not just within the Citizen Potawatomi Nation, but with all the Potawatomi communities as a whole, the average age of our eight remaining first-language speakers is 80.

Of course, there's this isolation from community because people are so dispersed. I often talk to tribal citizens for whom the only other Potawatomi people they know are within their immediate sphere. There's an insecurity, or an uncertainty, in relation to their tribal identity. Over the years, our tribe has tried to work to repair some of these consequences.

One of the programs I'd like to tell you about is known as the Potawatomi Leadership Program. It was started in 2003. At that time, the tribe was giving out the most scholarships it had ever given, which was a moment of pride. But tribal leaders recognized that despite that, a lot of those college students didn't know anything about their tribal nation. As is true now, the majority of our tribal leaders are in their elder years. When it came to thinking about who's going to assume that mantle as the next generation of leaders, they need tribal citizens who are connected to their identity, who have an understanding of our tribal cultural ways, of our governance structure, and of our operations. So, this program was an attempt to try to respond to that.

You'll notice recurring this similar image of a corn tassel. And the idea is that if every year you have a corn harvest, that you eat all of your corn, you don't have any seed corn to plant for the next generation. So, the Potawatomi Leadership is an attempt to plant that seed corn to prepare for that next generation of leadership and for the next seven generations of our tribal nation.

This program started in 2003, when I was in high school. In 2013, I had the opportunity to begin working with that program as the adviser and was able to work through some of the curriculum revamps. So, it's gone through a lot of changes over the years, but I'm really honored to work with the program. I'm proud of the progress that we've had. We invite ten tribal citizens. It's a competitive application process where we invite ten Potawatomi citizen students to live in Shawnee, Oklahoma where our tribe is headquartered, for six weeks essentially for six weeks, we immerse them in their tribe. They interact with tribal leaders – and when I say tribal leaders, that's elected officials, that's tribal program directors, that's elders. They get to ask them questions and find out about how all the pieces of the puzzle of the Citizen Potawatomi Nation fit together to run as it does.

Here, you see a picture of one of our weekly talking circles. As some others shared, it's important for the students to process what they're learning. They are sometimes, perhaps overwhelmed with the amount of information they're learning, but this is a moment to pause, to hear from their fellow peers, to tackle complex issues such as identity or what leadership looks like and means to them, what ideas they have or how the tribe should move. And then also they are required while they're with us to do some assignments to help apply the new knowledge that they're learning. The first assignment that they do is an elder interview, which is an opportunity either for them to connect to a tribal elder here in Oklahoma or another elder somewhere else.

Or sometimes it's just an opportunity to have a conversation with their grandparents who they've never talked to about what it means to be Potawatomi. They know they're Potawatomi, they just haven't had that conversation about what that means. So, we ask them to have that dialogue and then to capture that into a short paper that becomes part of a final portfolio. And again, we talk about leaving that record, leaving that behind for the next generations to come. They also work on a project. We pair them and we ask them to think about how they can leave an impact on the tribe. This is meant to be a mutually beneficial opportunity. It's not that they're coming in and we're dumping all of this knowledge or banking all this knowledge into them. They're coming with their own experiences and their own ideas, and they're seeing ways that the tribe could be better, could be more inclusive or more accessible.

So, they are encouraged and required to put together a project with their partner that they eventually present to tribal leadership. Last year, there was a TikTok cooking channel with Potawatomi recipes. There has been one group, one pair decided to write a drum song to be used for one of our ceremonies. There have been folks that have worked with specific tribal programs to address a need. So they're wide-ranging and it is wide open, but we want them to feel as if they're making an impact. And then finally, they present final reflections on their time. All of that goes into a final portfolio. Since 2003, we have had over 200 students participate in this program. Several of those students are now working here at the nation or they've gone back to their own universities where they've started to Native American student associations or been instrumental in that.

They've bolstered their sense of identity and now they're participating as leaders in the sense that that makes sense to them – not just we expect you to run for tribal office, although we do hope that that is an outcome. It's also: we hope that you will be someone in your family who can share this knowledge. We hope that you pass on this information to your children. We hope that you are an engaged voter in our tribal elections. If you come back and work for the nation in some way. So that's a program that's very close to my heart. And because that program has been so successful for years and years and years, I would hear from students' parents as they drop them off for that program in Oklahoma, "Man, I wish there was that program for me when I was that age," since those students are aged 18 to 20.

Out of that program grew the Mdamen Leadership Program. It's a seven-week virtual program, this is about intergenerational community-building. It is available to anyone 18 years of age or older. Because we have such dispersed citizenship, it is virtual. So that's accessible. And then Mdamen in our language, is how we refer to corn. But what it really means is that miraculous seed. And so again, it's that idea of planting that seed corn. But also we know that corn is one of our Three Sisters, corn, beans, and squash. Corn, that miraculous seed, it grows in connection. The intention behind the Mdamen Program is that these folks are not only learning together, but they're doing it in community.

We just wrapped up our second year of that program. As I mentioned, it's a seven-week program via Zoom. And for the first half of the Zoom, we invite tribal leaders, different programs, and different teachers in our tribe to give information about the tribe so that everyone kind of is on the same level playing field as far as their understanding of the Citizen Potawatomi Nation, which ranges from history, presentations to specific departments, service presentations to tribal leadership. The second half of that program, that growing and community part, is the small talking circles. We split them up into breakout rooms on Zoom and they have their talking circles. They now do a monthly reunion. These folks are really keyed in with each other, even though maybe before this program they didn't feel comfortable talking about their identity or didn't know anybody else, but now they're growing together.

We also invited them to do a final project and left it wide open. I have pictured for you here a cookbook that one of the students or one of the participants made. They gathered a lot of Potawatomi recipes and pulled this cookbook together. They shared with the other participants and a little story of where it came from. We talked about how learning about this made her want to kind of gather this knowledge that she had into something tangible.

Then the final effort I want to talk about is our Mokiwek Program. And Mokiwek in our language means, essentially, they are emerging, they are rising. And that is an opportunity to address that language loss. In our nation, in addition to the other Potawatomi communities, there are a lot of great initiatives happening to reconnect us to our language. But this is an opportunity to meet our college students where they are at the top universities, the universities where we have the highest population of Citizen Potawatomi students.

We've partnered with six universities throughout Oklahoma and Kansas. It is Potawatomi-centered. We have the Potawatomi language one that we offered once last fall, we'll resume again this fall. And we'll begin offering Potawatomi language two this coming spring. And Potawatomi language one is split seasonally is meant to be, again, from this Potawatomi perspective. And their final project, which you're seeing here on the screen, is one of our students' examples, they have to write a children's book. Again, it's that idea that you are gaining this information and now you're going to give back, you're going to add to the body yourself. One of the students who had never spoken Potawatomi before, took this class. As part of her project, wrote this children's book and we had it printed. With her permission, we are now using that book as part of our language learning efforts at our child development centers here in the nation. But again, the idea is we are getting this information and we're also giving them.

To close, why does this matter, especially talking to other higher education professionals or other universities, why does this specifically Potawatomi concept matter? Hopefully, it's very clear that we're not monolithic. Neither Indigenous people as a whole, Native American people, nor individual tribes are monolithic. Sometimes we're asked about, "What is it like to be? What does a Native American think about this?" I couldn't answer that much less could I answer what all Citizen Potawatomi think about a certain topic.

Many Indigenous students have complicated relationships with their identities depending on where they were raised, depending on what that tribal history was largely and within their family. It's extremely complicated and we'll all likely encounter students who are on some part of that spectrum, that are still wrestling with their identity and what it means to be Potawatomi or whatever tribe and whether or not they are Native or Potawatomi or whatever tribe enough. In-person tribal programming, which is ideal, is often inaccessible for dispersed citizenship. So, thinking about how we can use technology or other opportunities to help bring folks together and then really drawing upon tribes.

DeLucia

If I might offer one point of invitation to reflect, because I wrote this word down about 20 times as I was listening to everyone – "intergenerational." All of the ways that the work you are doing in community, with community, sometimes in different kinds of relation is connecting across generations and building to the future. One of the core goals of this grant, the Just Futures Initiative, is exactly that emphasis on futures and the work that it takes to build different and stronger futures. Do you have thoughts about experiences or challenges in attaining the resources, the structures, and the spaces to do that – to think with ancestors, elders, youth, children, and those yet to come?

Allen

At the University of Washington, when we applied for our first Mellon Mays Foundation grant in 2018, one of the things we asked for that we thought was pretty standard, was an elders in residence program. Many universities have them, many communities have them; all kinds of school systems. And Mellon said "No." Mellon said, "We don't fund elders" and "What would the CV look like?" and "How would you vet these people?" And we thought it was the oddest response and so the way we responded though, we said, well, "we want to host Native knowledge on campus. Our goal is to bring community-based Native knowledge to campus."

What if we had something called Native knowledge in residence instead of an elder in residence? Mellon bought that, which I thought was really interesting. It was about the packaging for the funder who didn't quite understand what Indigenous-focused education might look like. But coming up with that concept was actually very useful for us because it made us focus on, well, what is it we really want to bring to campus?

Now we have a position we fund as a halftime position for a community member who brings Native knowledge to campus. We call them our Native knowledge coordinator. The first Native knowledge we hosted on campus was the *Lushootseed* language. So our local Indigenous language spoken by Coast Salish people is Southern Lushootseed. And we had never had a full-time Southern Lushootseed language speaker and teacher on campus. Our American Indian Studies department felt like we were not a legitimate American Indian Studies department if we do not teach the local Indigenous language, we're not serving our local Native communities.

We had started with a language table, then we had a part-time course sequence. This allowed us to bring our Lushootseed language teacher, Tami Hohn, who's Puyallup from Spokane, up to full-time. She was able to offer them a sequence, a three-quarter sequence of the language, but also to work with more advanced students who took the sequence in doing research projects. We teamed her up with our library system, special collections, and the ethnomusicology library archives. She's working to create the first Southern Lushootseed dictionary. A dictionary doesn't exist of Southern Lushootseed, and she's training students, that next generation, how to work with settler documents to pull out Indigenous language, put it into International Phonetic Alphabet, put it into a database, cross-reference it, and create the beginnings of a dictionary that will then serve local communities and future students.

That was exciting, and we used it as leverage. Now she's a full-time teaching professor at our university. We were able to get Arts and Sciences to make her a full-time faculty member, which has been really exciting. Because we've increased the number of faculty, increased the number of Native faculty, as well as now we have sort of permanent Indigenous language instruction in Lushootseed.

Our new Indigenous knowledge coordinator is Philip Red Eagle, who happens to be a member of our local community. Some of you will know him. He's a fairly well-known writer and artist with local connections, and he's

creating a canoe family on our campus. Canoe journeys are a really important part of local communities in the summer. It got revived in the 1980s and
then really went strong in the 1990s and early 2000s. Every summer there
are large gatherings of canoe families up and down the coast in the US and
Canada. And the university has never had its own canoe. We're working
to build our own canoe family. Phil's been training our students on how to
carve canoe paddles and then learn all the traditions that go with that. That
will make it possible then for them to participate in canoe journeys in the
summer.

Spears

That's such an important model and so helpful for other campuses to
consider. If I could just take off my Upstander hat and put on my Brown University hat for a moment, in my position as a tribal community member in
residence, there's also an acknowledgment on behalf of Brown that there are
other forms of knowledge capital that our particularly Native American and
Indigenous students need to have access to during their time. And this goes
back to what's at the heart of many of the presentations here this evening,
that in order to learn, you have to feel supported; that human beings require
support to do their best at any kind of educational endeavor. In my role
as TCMR at Brown, I work with a complimentary second TCMR, also at
Brown, Sonksq of the Hassanamisco band of Nipmucs, Cheryll Toney Holley
also provides these opportunities for our Native and Indigenous students
to, during their time living in Providence, Rhode Island, make connections
with Wampanoag, Nipmuc, and Narragansett communities.

And that really undergirds the work that they're doing in a variety of disciplines. So, all the disciplines that our students are engaged in have these
opportunities for engagement with the tribal communities as well. I think
that it's such an important model. Every department on a campus should
have a knowledge keeper in residence or someone who is there to support
the spiritual and mental well-being of our students as they navigate predominantly white institutions.

Mendoza-Mori

A key aspect is validation. In this sense, unfortunately, traditional education may assume that if a person does not have a Ph.D., then that person has
nothing to contribute. And we need to work a lot with the wording and navigating those aspects, as silly as it might sound. But that's important. And

not just to the institutional level as it was mentioned by both of you, but also to the new generations as well that maybe don't see the value because of this acculturation process. And I have had many students who said, "I worked really hard to get into college. I don't want to take a class on Native Studies."

We need to be patient with that process as well and build up this validation also so it can benefit the community and therefore the youth, little by little. Sometimes, I don't know about you, but usually, let's say in academic spaces if we're going to do this project, we need to have an outcome on day one. Often the first meeting when inviting people from the communities, is just making sure that they feel welcome; and that they understand the potential ways of communicating and engaging, raising their hands, and participating. That would be enough. But sometimes it's important to phase that out into the process. So whoever is evaluating the efficacy of the program understands that's also part of the timeline. And then we can move into facilitating, sharing, etc. I was just thinking that for this Quechua Alliance gathering we did two weeks ago, we had many elders come in and then we got messages from them saying, "Oh, we came now after that we saw you all and we met you, now you can call us for workshops and activities," which makes sense, and I feel honored that that was a reaction. But those steps that, let's say, the typical scholar would be just, "Here is the event, here is the honorarium, here's what you are invited to talk to." It's like, "No, wait a second. We need to add these layers." But also, of course, mediate on how to express the complexity of the process, but of course, in the long term, there's a bigger winning for everyone.

Barton

I loved what you said about the elders. One of the things – because of the Eurocentric mindset in academia and then our Indigenous mindset – is that we don't go out, at least I was taught, you don't really go out and push yourself. You need to be invited. Once the elders met you, then they feel comfortable enough to say, "Okay, I know you now. I've made the connection, the relationship. I will help." But sometimes it's very hard in academia, especially if you're Indigenous, to walk that fine line between putting yourself out there or not putting yourself out there.

But I will say I am so encouraged by all of the research that I've caught up on in the last 20 years. Because, like I said, when I put my dissertation out there, I went back to my geology world of dinosaurs and microfossils, so getting that phone call in 2019 was just kind of a shock. Katie wanted me to do professional development with her group, and then I wrote a paper – and oh my goodness, there's so much good work out there that everybody is doing. I am just so pleased that within 20 years, or actually ten years, so much is happening and that it's continuing to happen because of the universities starting to open up.[4]

Zientek

I just want to add that thinking about intergenerational components, if I think back to our language, and I'm a language learner myself, I have a lot more to learn, but we have a word, [*Native language*], which means simultaneously my great-grandparents and also my great-grandchild. They're not root words. It's not this thing is like this thing. It is the same word. In our language, it is built in that those generations are not here and here. They are the same. They are collapsed together. When we're doing intergenerational work, that's why they're affected. That's why you hear what's happening now is affecting seven generations from now was planned for seven generations ago because it is kind of a collapse in time. Our great-grandparents are our great-grandchildren, and that's built-in in one word in our Potawatomi and our Anishinaabemowin language.

Audience Member 1

How do we approach the dilemma of getting our community partners to even consider Indigenous knowledge as legitimate and valuable? We get a lot of resistance in our community.

Barton

Indigenous ways of knowing – it's hard to explain and there's so much there. For me, when I was teaching geology and my other science classes, I would bring in the storytelling and then I would bring in your relationship to the Earth or whatever. But you can sneak it in. I call it my subversive teaching. I would sneak that in. Because that's all part of it, isn't it? You can bring it into an instructional design model of ADDIE (Analysis, Design, Development, Implementation, Evaluation) that the workplace uses. You can bring it in, but to have someone respect that is something else. I think maybe that might be part of that question is that: how do you get other people to acknowledge and respect that Indigenous way of knowing?

Mendoza-Mori

I do also work with language and sometimes when we think of Indigenous languages, we tend to imagine even, what is the perception around the language? For example, when we even see a flier of, for example, learning a European language, we know that it's not just the communication skills, but oral, knowledge, literature, and philosophy attached to that, is an access to all of that. Sometimes with Indigenous languages, that is not very clear, and therefore it's very important to code it in this context. In my experience, we have had the opportunity to partner with Fulbright to host Fulbrighters in Quechua, for example, which first it gives a specific slot for an Indigenous Quechua scholar.

We understand that Fulbright is seen as a prestigious scholarship, so we were very honored to be able to facilitate that and partner with that and offer mentoring in this case to young Indigenous scholars. But at the same time, understanding the calling of the perception that this fellowship has within academia. Some of you also mentioned the term global Indigeneity. Sometimes still for many people, "global" and "Indigenous" feel like contradictions. But then many in the US K-12 system is very common that students engage with Model UN, and Indigenous issues are usually not present during that conversation of representing countries. But at least they are familiar with the sense of the UN as a platform for global issues. Actually, we're going next week with a group of students to the UN for the forum on Indigenous issues.

That's another way on how students, we have students who are Lakota, who are Yaqui, Quechua, that of course they are going there because they have particular issues close to their heart and to their communities. But at the same time, they can indicate that that's part of our programming in terms of diplomacy, public policy, and the UN. All of these constant manifestations that I've seen that each of the panelists has shared trying to answer that question is a factor that I think we're always trying to navigate. But it's not a minor aspect, especially when a person is young and there's peer pressure or again, as I mentioned, they just felt so much to go into college that they feel like they can't afford to – don't deviate from the expected curricula. But that's why we need to work on that.

Spears

My own orientation to this, my answer to this question, is very unsatisfying, but really it is about the long game, and it is about instilling within

our K-12 systems an understanding of intellectual humility and that Indigenous epistemologies are older and more sustainable and regenerative to this
continent. That kind of legitimacy or that kind of understanding of what
is legitimate knowledge on Turtle Island or in the United States needs to
happen en masse. It needs to happen in our public school systems. That's
my orientation. What is a long time for Indigenous people is different from
what is a long time for non-Indigenous people. I sit in complete comfort of
the fact that it may be seven generations down the road, but that's fine by me.
That's a blink of an eye.

Zientek

I love the way you put that because I think often, especially if you're talking
about the school context, the question is: Why would we spend time on
this ethnic or this cultural programming? When really it *is* all ethnic, it's
all cultural programming. It's just naming that that's what's happening. It's
naming whose culture it is that we are teaching in the schools and recognizing that we can be broader, we can be more inclusive. Indigenous or Native
American Studies do not have to live only in social studies or history. They
are by nature part of all of the types of classes and all of the course areas, so
really just naming that already, our schools are cultural environments so to
pretend like Indigenous or Native American is some other is just false.

Audience Member 2

As I listen, I am thinking about a powerful learning environment as it
relates to Indigenous pedagogies. I am concluding that the environment
emphasizes intergenerational teaching and learning, the value of building
relationships, the importance of ensuring all communities feel welcome,
place-based learning, and intellectual humility. None of those attributes
seem to describe the settler colonial higher education institutions that I am
familiar with. What institutions out there do you feel are getting this right,
if any?

Barton

Your tribal colleges and universities are using the Indigenous ways of
knowing. They are using intergenerational work. They incorporate storytelling. They talk about following the Red Road.[5] They incorporate it
throughout. That's why they were established; to try to give equal, I hate to
say equal opportunity, but to have a place where Indigenous people could be

in charge of their education to a certain extent. There are still federal rules and things like that that are followed. We're very fortunate here in Wisconsin. We've got two of them, one in the north and then one right over on Menominee about 15 miles away from me.

Very small classes, language classes. Elders come in. Kids come in. It's a fun time. They are working on that. But again, you still have the assessments, and a lot of those assessments of the students are done on a Eurocentric assessment basis when they're coming into school or when they're leaving school. Those are not culturally relevant. They need to be revised as well, but that's work for the future, as endawnis said – she is very good with that. I love what you said. I love this new generation. They've got the fire and they're going to do great work.

Allen

I would add to that, I don't know if anyone's getting it right in the major dominant academy, but I think lots of people are trying, and I think we should acknowledge that, that many of our institutions, particularly in the last decade, have really made strides to center more Indigenous knowledges, Indigenous pedagogies, and to think about how to care for Native students, whether they're traditional-age students, whether they're transfer students, whether they come back to school after having other careers or other lives. I think that's really important, and that individual faculty and groups of faculty, I think, are really trying very hard to think about this.

One of the things we've done at the University of Washington that I think has been very powerful for graduate education is we created a graduate certificate in American Indian and Indigenous Studies. It's like a graduate minor and it's open to any Ph.D. student in any discipline from across our university. We created it and anchored it in our Department of American Indian Studies. Even though our Department of American Indian Studies only has an undergraduate major and minor and doesn't have a graduate program, we were still able to anchor the graduate certificate there so that AIS faculty can control it. The way these graduate minors are set up at our university is through two required courses, an elective, and a capstone. We've created the required courses as an Indigenous methodologies course and an Indigenous theory course. We decided we're going to always team teach them, so it's always two faculty who have disciplinary expertise in two different disciplines working together. Students have to apply. They have to be doing the certificate to take the course, so we have quite a bit of control. Since we started it a few years ago, they fill every time we offer them.

There are so many students across disciplines who want access a) to Indigenous faculty members and b) to Indigenous methodologies and theories. I'm lucky I have colleagues like Dian Million, Charlotte Coté, Jean Dennison, and staff, who are teaching these courses. We have really amazing people teaching these courses and giving these students that experience. But the other part of it that's so important is that the students get to meet each other. Even if a particular Ph.D. student is isolated in their program, they're the only Native student, say, in their marine biology or something like that, they can find other Native students as well as Native faculty. We're finding that community-building is so key. This graduate certificate has really helped build community among graduate students, and helps them find faculty as well, and the faculty who get to teach these courses find it really helps them. People feel better about the academy when they get to work with these students in these situations.

We're kind of calling it now a whole ecosystem of support. We're realizing that you have to support undergrads and graduate students and faculty and staff and your community partners. If you only focus on one of those components, it doesn't work because it's not a complete ecosystem. Through our Center for American Indian and Indigenous Studies, and through our Department of American Indian Studies, we've been able to create a series of programs that support all of those different aspects of being part of the university.

It takes a lot of work, and it takes a lot of intentional thinking through what it looks like and how to support it. But I think lots of us are trying. I know I happen to be today, right before it got into this, we're hosting some faculty from the University of Victoria who are coming and from the University of Minnesota because they want to learn from us how to set up a center similar to ours. I think there's a lot of this conversation we're having right now where we're exchanging ideas and trying to help each other figure out how to support our students in different environments.

Mendoza-Mori

Maybe sometimes we want to answer the big question: which institution is doing it right? Maybe each of you is doing it or trying to do it right by building up projects, trying to listen, trying to exchange experiences, and then that might turn into long-term plans. I can think of here at Harvard, starting last year we have a Native and Indigenous commencement ceremony. That was a personal initiative, a particular initiative, that had an echo in the Harvard University Native American Program (HUNAP), which is a university Native American program, and now it's institutionalized. Sometimes many initiatives that Indigenous communities push as decolonizing institutions are embraced by the institution more as just diversity and inclusion. But each community will find a way to find the right compromise and then push for whatever at that particular moment could be a good shift. Sometimes we don't have to necessarily have everything right, but push as much as we can, and then things will keep improving. Hopefully. I want to be optimistic.

Spears

Here in our corner of the northeast – and this can be said, I think, across the country – there is an extractive relational dynamic between the universities here and the tribal nations on whose land these universities are built and where they're occupied. That extractive dynamic is really a hoarding of knowledge and capital. If we look at and take an approach that is an older and better approach to how knowledge is dispersed across communities, then we can see that these universities have an accountability and an obligation to disperse that knowledge, especially to the tribal nations that are within their own backyard.

There is an onus on all of our respective organizations and our universities to provide access to our universities for our tribal students, and that that addition or that influx of tribal students into the ecosystem will also, as Dr. Allen was saying, shape and transform the institution itself, which is really less of an extractive dynamic and more of one that is circular in nature. I see the work that we're doing at Brown as very intentional in dispersing the knowledge that's been hoarded there in that institution.

Joy James

What alliances or connections with African Americans and Afro-Indigenous people, given repression of historical texts about liberation and captivity?

Zientek

Certainly, a lot of work to be done in that area. Just one small thing that I'll share here from a tribal nation perspective, and actually I had to miss tonight's meeting for this presentation, but our tribal nation has partnered with our local Black community here in Shawnee to host a Juneteenth celebration each year. That was something that our tribal nation has committed resources to. It has a lot of aspects to it, but one that is extremely important to us is to acknowledge not just the history of Juneteenth, but also our local context, particularly with the five tribes, looking at Oklahoma and their history with the Freedman and how that liberation happens even after Juneteenth.

We're celebrating Juneteenth and yet their liberation from enslavement happens after that fact. It's a very small step, but it is something that we're hoping to acknowledge. We have some articles that we're sending out to the local schools for them to participate in an art contest, but it's explaining that history and it's making it local and it's including that intersectionality and that really fraught history between Afro-Indigenous, Black communities, Freedmen. Because it's still alive and well, unfortunately, here in Oklahoma.

Mendoza-Mori

Sometimes in academia, things can be very siloed. "I do this and therefore I don't know about that." The system doesn't punish us for actually not looking for a more holistic understanding. Even within the Indigeneity, many people are not aware or when they hear that word, they don't necessarily assume that there are Indigenous communities across the world in what we now know as Japan, South Africa, and Sweden. Therefore, that expansion also of Indigeneity has to come to solidarity with other groups, in this case, in the particular case of the US, with the African American community, but also, as Tesia was mentioning, the intersection. When we even think of the representation of US Native American communities, are we aware of Afro-Wampanoag here, for example, on Massachusetts land, where I am connecting from.

In Lenapehoking in the city of Philadelphia, there are many Afro-Lenape community members and leaders that don't necessarily come to our collective imaginary of Indigeneity and US Native American, let's say, community members. I would even start by that, just to engage more and listen more and, let's say, people who are in school or studying, to actively look for that. Because unfortunately not at least I would say right now it won't come naturally. We would need to intentionally go for and learn and engage, but that could be hopefully the right step to then care for the different aspects, reparations, and these positions from different communities. But again, we need Indigeneity to find the presence of Blackness within those boundaries as well.

Allen

I really agree with the idea that for all of us, depending on where we're situated, there are opportunities to think across multiple forms of Indigeneity and then also how, in particular, Indigenous populations have intersected with multiple others and not to always recenter whiteness. Which is the tendency of the academy, to center whiteness, and then everyone in relation to European history, white American history, dominant history, and instead to think about other forms of relationality. I know here at my campus, we've done some really interesting events inviting both a Native writer and an African American writer, not to speak separately, but to speak in conversation. We had Leanne Simpson and Pauline Gumbs here, for instance, and that was an amazing conversation because they spoke to each other as well as to the audience. The audience gets to watch them speak to each other, and having that conversation in a public forum was very powerful.

Seattle has a very long-standing and large Scandinavian settler population, but that also means there are Sámi people here who have been here for multiple generations, and Scandinavian Studies is a major department on my campus. We've helped Scandinavian Studies learn to do Sámi studies and to bring Sámi studies in conversation with American Indian Studies in the US and Canada but also, because we have a large Pacific Islander population on our campus, in conversation then with Oceanic Studies as well.

What does that look like when we talk about Sápmi, Oceania, and Native North America at the same time? We do a three-way conversation. We decenter whiteness. We decenter the dominant, but we think about Indigeneity in multiple forms and different histories that have intersections that might be productive, certainly productive for students to get out of, say, the typical binaries that have structured their education often K-12 and then when they come to college. I think a lot of us, one theme here is always localizing. What are your resources? Who are your communities? How could you bring them into conversation in ways that would really disrupt the business as usual at the dominant academy?

SOURCE NOTES

1. Gonzalez-Barrera, Ana. "'Mestizo' and 'Mulatto': Mixed-Race Identities among U.S. Hispanics." *Pew Research Center*, July 10, 2015. www.pewresearch.org/short-reads/2015/07/10/mestizo-and-mulatto-mixed-race-identities-unique-to-hispanics/
2. *Upstander Project*. Accessed July 12, 2023. https://upstanderproject.org/

3. "Resources – CPN Cultural Heritage Center." *Citizen Potawatomi Nation Cultural Heritage Center*. Accessed July 12, 2023. www.potawatomiheritage. com/resources/

4. Weiterman Barton, Sandra D. "Web Walkers: A Phenomenological Study of Adult Native American Distance Learning Experiences: Toward a Standard Model of Indigenous Learning." Carbondale, IL: Southern Illinois University at Carbondale, 2013.

5. "The Red Road is a phrase frequently used by Natives signifying a deep commitment to living life in the best way possible – with an intrinsic respect for others, oneself, and creation and a dedication to worshipping the Creator" ("Our History." *The Red Road*, March 26, 2019. https://theredroad.org/story/ history/).

9

Panther Pedagogy: Kim Holder

Interviewed by Joy James and seminar students, April 17, 2023

"Black Panther Party [Rank & File]: The Legacy Continues," photo collage by
Cyril "Bullwhip" Innis, Jr., n.d.

Kit Kim Holder

Let's begin by first talking about this picture titled "The Rank and File of the
Black Panther Party," taken in New York at the Harlem branch of the BPP. On
the top right is Jamal Joseph, presently Professor of Professional Practice at
Columbia University School of the Arts in the Film Department. He was the
youngest member of the "Panther 21." Those Panthers were framed by the

NYPD and FBI. They were arrested and imprisoned on fabricated charges of conspiracy to blow up subway stations or what have you. Basically, all would be acquitted in an enormous case, a maneuver to get rid of the Panther leadership in New York.[1]

To the left on that top, there is a photo of a woman in a white skirt, her name is Janet Searle. She passed. She was one of my best friends. She was a longtime Panther. Her daughter is a big-time activist in the Bay Area. Searle led the campaign to reduce the exorbitant phone costs when inmates call their families.

Then there is a photograph of Zayd Shakur, he's in the middle. He was with Assata Shakur when she was arrested. He was killed in that incident with NJ Troopers [in which a trooper was also killed, some say by "friendly fire"]. All the way to the right in that picture is a guy with the big Afro: Donald Cox, the National Field Marshall. To the left is the little guy with an Afro … that's me. That is the only picture of me in the Panthers.

I originally didn't plan on talking much about the Black Panther Party. I want to talk about my work and my perspective of academia and students.

I always call myself a "bus driver." In academia, that's my job. There is no such thing as a "revolutionary professor". There are revolutionaries and there are professors, but there is no such thing as a position of a professor being revolutionary. An academic institution is about maintaining the status quo.

I may do some very positive things; and other people may do some very positive things: influence people, provide resources. The reality is though that we're probably doing more to maintain the status quo than we're doing in terms of disrupting the status quo.

I always encourage students that when you're in these institutions, make sure you force your professors to give you the tools, or help you develop the tools, that will allow you to operate outside of the corporate structure. That's extremely important. I'm not saying anything about you being involved in the corporate structure. I'm saying give you the tools that allow you to operate outside of that.

I have to include the non-profit corporate structure. We were mobilizing to bring people down to New Orleans after Katrina in 2005 and a real grassroots effort to help the people rebuild New Orleans. I was bringing academics down there who had vocational tools like medicine or education, or other tools like philosophy. But many others were not equipped to be able to operate outside of the institutions.

Doctors weren't able to maneuver without their fully stocked exam room. Teachers were not able to have educational programs without the protocol and structure of school systems. Make sure that when you're getting these skills, information, that you're also being able to see how you apply them outside the corporate structure. Developing a business in the community is very different from how they're going to tell you in business school to develop a business. Center yourself outside of the corporate structure of academia. Make sure you get tools that allow you to do that.

Student struggles in school since the 1960s, in colleges, have always had a connection with the community. From the students in Greensboro, NC, in the 1960s with the sit-ins, to the Student Non-violent Coordinating Committee (SNCC) – that organized, mobilized and educated the people behind Martin Luther King's call to register to vote in the South – to the 1960s free speech movement on the predominantly white campus of UC Berkeley in California[2] to Columbia University's big uprising. They all had a connection to the community. Then, it was the working-class African American community which was an essential part of their struggle.

Students became/become aware that we/they could become a conduit between the community. The community, by the way, is how you define it. I define the community as the working-class people whose power is not recognized by the institutions in this society. I'm always imploring students, to make sure that we are channeling resources from our institutions into the community.

I teach at a New Jersey state college where there are a lot of lower-middle-class and working-class students. So, food pantries are a big thing. I'm consistently imploring students: "If you're developing food pantries for the students, why don't you partner that with the community and provide food pantries within the community for the people who are there?"

I wanted to mention also that I think that Dr. James and her work have been a really good example of how we start to center ourselves and provide a voice for the masses. When I first met Dr. James, she was one of the first people, and definitely one of the first feminists, advocating for the Central Park Five [now the "Exonerated Five"].[3] She has continued to be on the cutting edge of advocating and giving voice to people we consider voiceless, from working with mothers of children who are slain by the state, to doing work around Erica Garner [who advocated for her father Eric Garner who was wrongly attacked and killed by the NYPD in 2014]. Professor James touched a lot of people that I know with her work around providing a structure for the voices of imprisoned intellectuals and political prisoners to be out in the street. That work has gotten a lot of respect.

I was in New Orleans and talking to organizers who did good work, and were the precursors to Jackson Rising, a grass-roots organization in Jackson, Mississippi. They had been working with members of the Republic of New Africa (RNA). They were the major people working in New Orleans to rebuild the lower ninths, the really poor Black community. As soon as I mentioned Dr. James's name, they said, "You mean the one that wrote *Imprisoned Intellectuals?*"[4] Right away, they wanted to provide any kind of assistance they could.

I joined the Black Panther Party in the spring of 1969, during the downturn of the Panthers. We didn't know it at the time. The Panthers started in 1966. In 1969, we got a lot of support, because of the government/police attacks on the Panthers.

I joined the Black Panther Party a month after the Panther 21 case, where 21 Panthers of New York were arrested on fabricated charges tied to COINTELPRO.[5] I thought at the time: "I'm going to miss the revolution." I joined as a 12-and-a-half-year-old kid thinking: "I'd better hurry up, because it's going to be gone." Most of us as youths joined because we were angry. We were the second generation of northern African American urbanites. We rejected the old-school Civil Rights era mode of operation. We wanted a new style. We were followers of Malcolm X.

One of the first things that I became aware of was that the Black Panther Party was about serving the people. We were not just agents of change, but also agents of love for the masses of people. As Jamal Joseph said, "We had an undying love for the people."[6] It goes a little deeper than that. The one thing that makes the Black Panther Party unique, and it makes it a historical thing, was its advocacy for total and complete revolution. There had to be a total transformation of this society in order for people to truly be free. Anything that I say from now on is still within that context.

Early on, I learned a lot about how my relationship with the people in the community was historical, intellectual and revolutionary. I don't want to mystify it, but this is the deal. Through our relationship with the people, and working with the people, we came to understand what the major problems, what we called the major contradictions, in this society were. And through the programs that we developed, including the armed patrols, we were doing two things. One, we were learning about how to fight a revolution; and two, we were giving examples to the people of ways to control and develop their own lives.

I woke up every morning at 5 o'clock in the morning and went down to a church in central Harlem. We had the keys to the building. We prepared the meals. While we were feeding the kids, we were talking to the kids. We were giving them "history" lessons but most of what we were doing was teaching them from the Panther newspaper news articles with the interpretation and analysis of the Panthers. (In fact, that was how I first got interested in teaching.)

This work involved recruiting kids to come to the Free Breakfast Program[7] and then procuring the materials needed. You read Safiyah Bukhari's memoir, *The War Before*?[8] Safiyah Bukhari and I, in the fall of 1969, would go to the supermarket and identify ourselves as Black Panthers. I don't know what happened in terms of the relationship between the supermarket and the Black Panther Party, but by the fall of 1969, all they had to do was to certify that we were truly Panthers and they would just give us three shopping carts and we could get whatever we wanted for the breakfast program.

Working with the people, feeding and serving the people really got me to understand the politics of what I was doing in the community. Movies, documentaries, readings on the Panthers always talk about how many programs we had and how many breakfast programs we ran. To me, that's not an accurate gauge of what we were doing, because the whole idea was for us to create programs for the people to take them over and run them themselves. The whole idea was we were trying to show the people how they can develop institutions to take care of themselves, that the state was not taking care of them, and that they in fact had the ability to take care of themselves.

A lot of times I see some programs nowadays where people are giving away food. The Panthers started doing that too in the later part of the 1970s. The big cases such as the SLA (Symbionese Liberation Army) kidnapping of Patty Hearst, included the demands of the kidnappers for the Panthers to distribute food and stuff.[9] I'm against food distribution. The Panthers weren't a welfare program. Give a person a fish, they eat for a day; teach them how to fish, and they eat forever. Our thing wasn't to give people stuff, but to teach them and show them how they could provide for themselves and develop their own institutions.

Community gardens – "hood gardens" today – are a modern-day version of the old Black Panther Party breakfast programs. I've done a lot of work in Philadelphia as well as South Jersey in communities developing hood gardens. It's a good tool to use on so many different levels.

Joy James

What influences you and your work and life trajectory, as an activist, organizer, and intellectual grandparent? Is one influence, Paulo Freire? The

Brazilian educator wrote about pedagogy and worked in low-income communities. He fled the authoritarian Brazilian state, backed by the US, which sought to kill him and ended up with UNESCO in Europe. Later Freire's educational work took him to Africa. You also have noted the impact and contributions of Amílcar Cabral.

Holder

Cabral to me is like the next level from Marxism. It's the theory, the African moving or people of color, what we called the Third World, advancing that theory to the next stage of the second half of the twentieth century and into the twenty-first century. Freire did actually work with Cabral in Guinea-Bissau, and it's basically the definition of what revolution is. Leninists and Marxists, the workers, the proletariat will be in charge didn't mean much to the people in Africa and South America.

The concept is that people are taking control and becoming active participants in their lives and development; they can truly define what a people's state is. We could add the Zapatistas (Army of National Liberation) to that also. They're the twenty-first-century version of that concept. Cabral's concept, the way I interpret it, is that you utilize people's culture and help them to take control over their lives and to develop the institutions necessary for running their lives. That is the concept and the demand for freedom.

James

Revolutionary culture is international culture. Did the Panthers understand it as such ... considering their study and engagement with Africa, the Caribbean, Latin America, and Asia (China, Vietnam)?

Holder

From my perspective, I still define myself, as I did back then, as a revolutionary nationalist ... Within that concept, I am African American. I get a lot of my strength, energy, and spirit from my ancestors and the position of the runaway slaves. I believe that there is a concept of revolutionary culture. Our society is so interconnected, our world is so interconnected today, but I believe people still have their cultures. The strength of people's culture is that they're functioning outside of the confines and direction of the state, and institutions.

James

In your bio, you list your daughter and your grandsons. The seminar students viewed Lee Lew-Lee's documentary *All Power to the People!: The Black Panther Party and Beyond*. Decades ago, [after I invited you to the Colorado abolition conference] you told me to invite [New York Panthers] Lee Lew-Lee, Gabe Torres and Safiyah Bukhari to attend the 1998 "Unfinished Liberation" conference at the University of Colorado Boulder.[10] Both you and your brother appear in that documentary, and your brother is identified as a Panther, but also a member of the underground Black Liberation Army. I believe he did eight years in prison and was also tortured there. There is a link to other key personas: Jonathan Jackson and George Jackson [the older brother].

Holder

The Black Panther Party, at least from what I experienced, was terrible when it came to family. We were young, we were very against family. We really neglected family, and we're seeing the consequences of that today. The first community you have as humans is your family. If you can't take care of your family, you can't get energy and spirit from your family, how are you going to go out and work and build community and then society? It has to start with family, both historical and future.

My father was a member of the Communist Party. His father was a member of the Garveyites, so there's a historical connection, even though I learned about my father through my mother. My brother was a political prisoner, he was a member of the Black Liberation Army; he was hunted. There was an attempted murder on him, and then he was hunted for a couple of years before he was arrested and put in jail [prison] for seven years. When he was underground and when he was in jail, I viewed my primary job as being of assistance to him. I saw that as my service, and I was in that position to do that.

Thinking about doing this talk [with your seminar], I realized – and this is outside of the family – that my relationship with prisoners has been an ongoing one in terms of me as a student. For example, I'm dyslexic. I didn't learn how to read until I was in fifth grade. When I joined the Panthers in eighth grade, that was very instrumental in my learning how to read. Some of the first people that I wrote to were political prisoners. In fact, Jamal Joseph was the first person I wrote to, and it was some of the first coherent writing that I could do. So that was a big thing.

I remember going on the prison buses for hours and hours. New York City is in the southeastern part of New York. In Buffalo, Attica is in the northwestern part. I would have to take a bus, a nine or ten-hour bus, to go visit my brother. Nobody else in my family was doing that. And I was still young. I was 14 or 15 at that time. I was very dedicated to him. In college, undergrad, not only did I bring my classmates to go visit my brother, I used to go visit other prisoners too. In fact, my conversations with other prisoners kept me in college.

I think family is important. If we're not taking care of family and we're doing organizing and we're doing things for a change, I think we're only doing part of what is required. One of the things learned, I learned because I stayed alive, is that you survive longer than the movement you're working in. And there's only one other thing that survives as long as that: your family.

One of my first lessons that I got from one of the first books I read about revolution was, "A revolutionary, by 40, is either dead or sleeping on a park bench." As Panthers and as dedicated revolutionaries, what we didn't plan for was surviving. If we didn't plan to survive, we really didn't plan for our kids and our families to survive and thrive.

I remember sitting in the office and people talking about, "I'll do whatever it takes. I'll take out my family if it's for the revolution." I was sitting there thinking: "What the heck are these people talking about?" Family is one of the first units that we socialize in, and it's extremely important. It'll become even more important as society is less able to meet the needs of people, as we're starting to see. During the pandemic, family was crucial. I don't live in an urban area. You could tell when there's a crisis here because there are more and more cars in the driveway. So family is extremely important.

Student 1

As an academic, how do you reconcile working within an institution, with what I imagine to be forces that attempt to coerce you into accepting more reformist politics?

Holder

I perceive myself as a bus driver. You wouldn't ask a bus driver that. They go home, and to their political meetings, and organize. I've never taught a course on the Black Panther Party. I've done a lot of work on it, and I've educated a lot of people, but I've never personally taught a BPP course at my university. I separate my politics from my job.

That's not always the case, many things intertwine, especially when I'm dealing with grad students. I teach my grad students that "there is no reforming of these institutions, but we can create pockets of humanistic interaction, and that needs to be our job."

So, it's a job, and it has a lot of resources. I tell a lot of doctoral students that it's a hell of shield. For example, after Katrina, during nighttime, I'm in New Orleans in a parking lot outside of a famous church. I'm with a whole bunch of people from New Orleans, and the police surround us. That is when it's good that I, as a college professor, am talking to the police. It's a lot better than being a former Black Panther. So, it's a shield in that sense.

It also gives you a justification for being in places. And it provides some resources. I'm still an Assistant Professor and I've been in my institution for 30 years. When my dean asks "Don't you want to be promoted?" I told her, "No. I won't do that. I'll go teach another class for additional income."

The key aspect is to center yourself outside of academia.

The key role that prisoners have played in me centering myself outside. As an undergrad, I saw the parallels between academia and prison. One is institutionalized with privilege, and the other one's institutionalized without privilege, but they're very similar. When I was doing my doctorate, I taught in prison. Doing all that personal, Eurocentric, "intellectual" thing, out in the woods of UMass Amherst by yourself, what is that?[11]

You have to do that to get your doctorate. Every two days, twice a week, though I was going into prison, dealing with the folks there. So, I try to do that. Family has been extremely important. I teach in academia, and in a small working-class college town in New Jersey. Although I don't live in Philly, or Camden … academia's got a lot to offer in terms of resources that can be useful.

Student 2

Given what you've said about the neglect of the family within the Panther Party, what is your take on what survival might look like, if it is to resist anti-revolutionary complacency?

Holder

Huey Newton, the co-founder of the Black Panther Party for Self-Defense, came up with "survival pending revolution." It didn't give us any kind of clue on what we were supposed to do with it, but at least he was trying to address it.[12]

The state always helps us out with survival to some degree, because they don't like you to be independent, and so they always are challenging when you develop these independent institutions, and so it keeps you from being complacent. I don't really know the answer to that, but I do know that they really get uncomfortable when you start to become independent. I saw that a lot when I was in New Orleans. People were just trying to rebuild their lives and police were sabotaging them left and right, before they even were rescued, they were doing that.

As intellectuals, our seeking a new way of living and a new concept of what life is and independence becomes very exciting too. There are a lot of resources out here for us to utilize – and you guys have a lot more options than we had.

We challenged everything in society. You guys have to redefine what community is, communications. America's quickly becoming unable or unwilling to produce the rewards that it used to be able to produce for its citizens. And when America gets a cold, Black folks get pneumonia.

But I don't know how you maintain revolutionary zeal. Look at all the countries that have so-called one-state power. They don't seem to be too progressive unless they're being attacked.

Student 3

Do you see liberal institutions, specifically liberal academic institutions, as being a detractor to revolutionary struggle?

Holder

Well, my mother always said that the most anti-revolutionary person was President Franklin Delano Roosevelt. He was liberal, supposedly he was the most anti-socialist person. I don't know. Liberal institutions, as I mentioned before, the fact that they allow us to be there, they allow certain things if they help to justify the system.

But on the other hand, if we look back at history, how many revolutionaries have been able to go to those places and develop and flourish based on that? If we don't believe that they're truly about change, I think we could still use them in the defense of the people. For example, UMass Amherst just bought 15,000 abortion pills; and that was a key aspect of fighting the battle against criminalizing the abortion pill (mifepristone).[13]

You can't be liberal all the time. Eventually, you are going to have to take a stand. America doesn't want to be fascist, or exhibit fascist behavior.

Liberals have kidnapped our radical vocabulary. Media has kidnapped a lot of our vocabulary, but this is not the first time that that's happened. Academic vocabulary is not revolutionary. It is not resistance. Liberalism is neither of those two things.

Student 4

How would you define revolution and revolutionary nationalism?

Holder

The revolutionary is dedicated to the total transformation of society. Now, that cannot happen without some level of armed struggle. Are we at that stage now? Obviously not. As an African American in the concept of liberation, I don't have to think about any of that kind of stuff, because the reality is not my use of violence or my attitude toward violence. If I am striving for liberation, it is my behavior or response to state violence inflicted upon me or anybody else that I'm dealing with. I don't have to come up with a philosophy on nonviolence or violence, because all I have to do is to say how I'm going to respond to the state violence that is there. Always been there, is here now, and will be there for the near future. As Stokely Carmichael said when they were talking to SNCC organizers:

> Listen, it's up to you what's your struggle, what is your position on our struggle. But when you're down in Mississippi or Alabama in the woods and you're a guest at a sharecropper's house, and the clan comes up on them and they break out their shotguns in their house, what are you going to do?[14]

Now in terms of revolution, I believe that we need to organize people and win them over to understanding that the less that they rely on state institutions for survival and development and inspiration, and the more they develop their own institutions to define those things in their own way – that's moving toward revolution. I can't really tell you what revolution will look like, because I'm not going to be there. I'm here to do my historical role toward that.

I hear people say that the Panthers "didn't win because of X, Y, Z." I don't know what they're talking about. I never thought it was about winning or losing. One of the first things they did when I joined the Panthers was that they sent me to go watch *The Battle of Algiers*, a 1966 Italian-Algerian film/

documentary on the Algerian War against the French colonial government.[15] In *The Battle of Algiers*, all the revolutionaries died, and then a year later the masses rose up and took over the state.

I never had any kind of expectation that I was going to see victory. I remember telling my mother: "My friends want to be lawyers and doctors, they're going to be there. I want to be a revolutionary. I'm not going to see that." But you see change and you see progress.

I'm dedicated to African American liberation; but within that, I have my own radical politics within that concept. My job is to win African Americans over toward a radical idea of liberation. I also believe that's the only way we're going to be truly liberated, is if everybody's liberated.

I get my strength, I get my spirit, I get my energy from the history and examples of African Americans. I place myself like Assata Shakur – I'm a runaway slave, or I'm a maroon. Probably not historically correct, but I view myself in this society as such. And I believe that African Americans are placed within this society and within the system as some of the key vanguard elements in a change in society, period. I had a stronger answer 30 years ago.

Student 5

You said that you've never actually taught a class on the Black Panther Party, but I was wondering if your association with and your involvement in the Black Panther Party has helped you in your career?

Holder

Absolutely.

First, I was 12-and-a-half, and so that's the "wonder years." My principles and a lot of the foundation for who I became stem from my experience in the Black Panther Party. Absolutely. What I believe is right in terms of what institutions should do, and what I'm willing to do within an institution, is definitely influenced by my politics from the Panthers.

I'm always an advocate for the masses of people. I'm always an advocate for students. I am always getting in trouble because I will always stick up for students over administration. I'm bold at that level, and fearless, as Panthers …. So, there are things that I don't quite understand, but I understand the principle that any oppression has to be eliminated, and so that allowed me to further my understanding and to accept things before I even had a total understanding of them.

It might not be true, but I credit almost everything of who I am to the Panthers. The fact that I've been in this institution for 30 years, the fact that I'm an effing good teacher, I'm a dedicated parent and grandparent, all that I credit to the Party, the Panthers.

Student 6

Do you think it's possible for an organization dedicated to total and complete revolution, like the Panthers, to emerge in the near future?

Holder

I can't tell you how. You would have to tell me how.

Let's be clear, half the things that the Panthers are credited with, we ain't done that. Other people did that, or everybody did it. Half the stuff that we're credited with, SNCC did. There are organizations some of you may even never even heard of, like RAM (Revolutionary Action Movement). The myth of the Panther is much bigger than the Panthers itself.

That being said, I see there is more of a movement than there would be an organization. I think people are more decentralized, people believe in anarchy, unstructured stuff, more than they believe in [disciplined community]… That was one of our downfalls. I also think that a patchwork of issues are going to come together on united fronts. This pending "civil war" is scary, and not going away. I don't think the left addresses that enough, unless you're in the South, and then you got to figure out what you're going to do. I hear left people talk about that, but the right is closer to fighting than we are.

That mobilizes people. I mean, just look at Tennessee State expulsion of Representatives Justin Pearson and Justin Jones. [https://www.npr.org/2023/08/04/1192068281/the-2-expelled-members-of-the-tennessee-3-win-back-their-state-house-seats] That mobilizes people. You probably know more than I do about technology for communications and security. All I can offer are principles that we used that you then interpret for today.

Snapchat is a hell of a tool for mobilizing the development and the expansion of the educated poor. As society is unable to provide material goods and stuff, I think you're going to find more people being communal and sharing resources, and that's a good thing.

Student 7

Could you talk a little bit about your experience of the transition from the mentality of being in the Panthers to a survival stage, post-Panthers?

Holder

You mean the year of depression? Most of my friends had post-traumatic stress. And then, a lot of us put it into our careers until it didn't mean anything. I was lucky that I could make or find meaning and carve out certain things for myself. Family became really important to me. Addressing that meant taking care of the people who needed care. I get strength out of the masses of people too. You work with people and you have tiny victories and you have bigger victories.

I spent a lot of time explaining and articulating and analyzing. As you get older, you start remembering connectors. Trump was like Nixon. The difference then was that radicals were louder than conservatives now conservatives are louder than the radicals. I've seen and lived through history in which the left gets big and the electoral politics become more conservative. Look at the 1968 presidential race where Richard Nixon defeats Hubert Humphry. Look at Trump who defeated Hillary Clinton in 2016. What was true then is also true today.

I have a lot more resources at 66 than I had when I was 16 because African Americans are in a different position in 2023 with more resources and mobility than they had in the 1920s–1960s.

SOURCE NOTES

1. Holder, Kit Kim. "The History of the Black Panther Party, 1966–1971: A Curriculum Tool for Afrikan-American Studies." *University of Massachusetts Amherst*, 1990.
2. "Visual History: Free Speech Movement, 1964." *Berkeley FSM*. Accessed July 12, 2023. https://fsm.berkeley.edu/free-speech-movement-timeline/
3. James, Joy. *Resisting State Violence: Radicalism, Gender, and Race in U.S. Culture.* Minneapolis: University of Minnesota Press, 1996.
4. James, Joy. *Imprisoned Intellectuals: America's Political Prisoners Write on Life, Liberation, and Rebellion.* Lanham: Rowman & Littlefield Publishers, 2004.
5. COINTELPRO – counterintelligence intelligence program – was a covert operation conducted by the FBI between 1956–1971 to survey, intervene, and disrupt dissenting domestic organizations. The program targeted groups like the Black Panther Party, the Southern Christian Leadership Conference, and the American Indian movement. See Churchill, Ward, and Vander Wall, Jim. *The COINTELPRO Papers: Documents from the FBI's Secret Wars Against Domestic Dissent.* Boston, MA: South End Press, 1990.

6. Jamal Joseph was 16 years old when he was rounded up as one of the Panther 21. See also Taylor, Flint. "The Black Panther Party and the 'Undying Love for the People.'" *In These Times*, October 29, 2015. https://inthesetimes.com/article/the-black-panther-party-and-the-undying-love-for-the-people

7. "Independent Lens | The Black Panthers: Free Breakfast Program." *PBS*, February 16, 2016. www.pbs.org/video/independent-lens-free-breakfast-program/

8. Bukhari, Safiya. *The War Before: The True Life Story of Becoming a Black Panther, Keeping the Faith in Prison & Fighting for Those Left Behind*. New York: Feminist Press at the City University of New York, 2010.

9. "The Rise and Fall of the Symbionese Liberation Army." *PBS*. Accessed August 11, 2023. www.pbs.org/wgbh/americanexperience/features/guerrilla-rise-and-fall-symbionese-liberation-army

10. Lew-Lee, Lee. "All Power to the People – The Black Panther Party & Beyond," June 8, 2016. www.youtube.com/watch?v=pKvE6_sojyo

11. "I lived alone, in the woods, a mile from any neighbor, in a house which I had built myself, on the shore of Walden Pond, in Concord, Massachusetts, and earned my living by the labor of my hands only. I lived there for two years and two months. At present I am a sojourner in civilized life again" (Thoreau, Henry David. "Economy." Walden, 1854).

12. *The Black Panther* was the official newsletter of the Black Panther Party. Founded by Huey P. Newton and Bobby Seale, it was published from 1967–1980 and amassed an international readership. Archives, Freedom. Freedom Archives Search Engine. Accessed July 12, 2023. https://search.freedomarchives.org/search.php?view_collection=90. Choi, Rebecca. "The Avery Review: Survival Pending Revolution: The Black Panther Party on View." *The Avery Review*. Accessed July 12, 2023. https://averyreview.com/issues/22/survival-pending-revolution.

13. Medsger, Matthew. "Why Did UMass Buy 15,000 Abortion Pills?" *Boston Herald*, April 11, 2023. www.bostonherald.com/2023/04/11/why-did-umass-buy-15000-abortion-pills/

14. Carmichael, Stokely, and Ekwueme Michael Thelwell. *Ready for Revolution: The Life and Struggles of Stokely Carmichael (Kwame Ture)*. New York: Scribner, 2005.

15. www.youtube.com/watch?v=vRE3j8pDMds

10

Black Liberation: Rosemari Mealy

Interviewed by seminar students, May 1, 2023

Rosemari Mealy

I committed my adult life to being involved in some very, very unpopular causes. Therefore, I'm always trying to strike a balance between my own sanity, my family struggling, and enjoying my life as a Black radical feminist in the United States of America.

I'm constantly reinventing myself. But let's set the stage. Looking at my life from the frames of my humbled origins as a Black girl growing up in the state of Virginia during the era of segregation, desegregation, white vigilantes, violence, cross burnings, and where your parents would tell you when they were sending you to school or shopping or even venturing outside of your neighborhood, that they would always instruct you on how to act. How to act in front of white folks. And this was a safety precaution. So where even a small act of defiance could literally cost your life, young Black girls as well as young Black boys. I was always keenly aware of the disparities that existed between Black folk and white folk.

Economic disparities define the barriers of separating the lines of segregation and what was known as Jim Crow. And those, as you have studied, segregation and Jim Crow laws were validated by institutionalized as well as personal racism. So therefore, growing up in those environments, even at a very early age, I start rebelling. I start rebelling against that system. And you know how I would rebel? In real simplistic ways. I would go into the white toilets, because they were colored and white. I would go along with my cousins and other young darings, we would go into the white toilets, where the colored ones would be on the other side. And of course, we would do this out of the sight of white folks. And also, I refused to call them Miss or Mister.

When I was called "nigger," I fought back as a child. And you know how I fought back? I would use language that surely would've been a cause for my parents to lash me. On the other hand, I do have to say that it was my father who inspired me to be a fighter. My father was also a rebel and a risk-taker – being a risk-taker as a member of the National Association for the Advancement of Colored People (NAACP), an organization about which a lot of folks have criticisms. We lived in this backwoods country town, but I used to remember him discussing the importance of Black folks fighting back. And particularly, he always focused on the right to vote.

He would drive people to the polling places. He challenged the segregated and unequal education system. Because in my schools, when we would get our books, they would be used and frayed, because they were hand-down books that came from the white kids. I can remember my father meeting with some of the Black teachers and people in the town demanding that we had our rights to new books. All of my family viewed education, as most Black folks did, and do now, as the pathway to freedom. Both of them did everything that they could to ensure that we completed our formal schooling. Since I attended segregated schools, I had all Black teachers who inspired me to excel. We were taught at that time Black history.

Then it was called Negro History, and we celebrated Negro History Week. However, it was celebrated for only one week in February. We even had Black History clubs. They were called Negro History Clubs, they were the foundation for teaching Black pride. I'm not talking about a hundred years ago, guys. I'm talking about, you said, "Way back then." I'm talking about 50 or 60 years ago, the age of some of your grandparents and even some of your parents. So, I'm not talking about the 1920s or 1930s. I'm talking about a time that I can remember vividly. Oftentimes, I would be singled out for my writing and creative abilities. I love to write and I love to create poems, and I love to create stories and plays. And I love public speaking.

I was encouraged to run for leadership posts in clubs and sports activities, and I always beat out my male counterparts. When we finally got music classes, I also insisted on playing the trombone in the school band. I wasn't going to play the clarinet. Those gender-derived instruments that only girls were supposed to play, well, I wanted to play the trombone, because I had an aunt from New York who used to talk about this wonderful Black female trombonist whose name was Melba Liston.[1] One time I saw a picture of her, I think it may have been in *Ebony Magazine*, and I wanted to play the trombone like Melba Liston.

At that time, I was also interested in studying law or medicine. I wanted to become either a doctor or a lawyer because I wanted to serve my community. However, when I applied to the University of Virginia in Charlottesville,

I received a crushing letter denying my admission, because I was referred to at the time as, quote, "a Negro." Ironically, Professor Reginald Butler, my first cousin, would become the director of the Carter G. Woodson Center for African American Studies at the University of Virginia.

When I received this crushing letter, I had been granted a United Negro Fund Scholarship to an HBCU (Historically Black Colleges and Universities) in North Carolina, but because of my parents' financial situation, I had to forfeit the scholarship. But I was still encouraged by my family and my teachers and other relatives. I ended up migrating North to live with aunts who had professional careers. I got a job working for the Bell Telephone Company. In the 1960s, this was considered a good job for a Black woman. However, we were relegated to the worst hours, the racism of white supervisors who gave you poor evaluations, and rarely did you get a promotion. I definitely was not content with that kind of a situation, because I was still determined that I was going to get a college education.

After a year, I heard about a Catholic college in Wisconsin that was accepting Black girls to integrate into the all-white institution. I was accepted there. Initially I had some reluctance about going to Wisconsin. I mean, it's cold, I'm from the South. It's far away from my parents, but I went there, anyway. And let me tell you, it was one of the most alienating and devastating experiences that I had in my life. I left after the first year. I ended up joining the Civil Rights struggle. For a while, I went to live in Alabama and then New York. And along the way, I became a single parent. It would take me eight years to complete my undergraduate degree. Then about ten more years for the M.A., another eight or so for the J.D., and finally another eight for the Ph.D. I started getting my degrees in these determined spurts.

All of the time that I was acquiring each of the degrees, I was working as a full-time poor single parent, adult learner. I do not regret it at all, it transformed me. It really made me into a stronger and a more dedicated person. And now that I'm a single parent, I've got to look out for this young boy child. Young people have asked, "Well, what kept you motivated?" I just attribute this part of my journey to this persistence and motivation. But first and foremost, it was always important for me to claim my own motivation. I wanted to be the one to write my "why narrative" in order to realize my goals.

In the wake of the Black Power Movement in 1963, there emerged, as you've been studying within the political climate of the time, various creative forms such as music, art, and later the Black theater movement, which used various forms to dramatize the message of the Black freedom struggle. The conversations in those venues focused on the political climate of the time while using the various creative aspects of poetry, literature, music, dance within the theater. And all of that inspired a new revolutionary consciousness which did not espouse "Art for art's sake." I was definitely drawn to the movement as a performance poet and an actress, and I became a member of a theater in Philadelphia called The Freedom Theatre, where I began to act in plays. I wrote scripts and I taught theater to young people. This was the organizational context of how the Black theater for me espoused Black Power while combining the Black aesthetic.

It became the vehicle for me to embrace ideologies and perspectives of performance art that centered on Black culture and life. Through the Black Arts Movement, my worldview expanded to the point where I sought to be more active in grassroots politics. At this point I was introduced to the study of Marxism-Leninism. Black women activists such as myself were influenced by the words and actions of Malcolm X, El-Hajj Malik El-Shabazz. As a matter of fact, my son was born three days after Malcolm was assassinated in 1965. I really made a commitment to my son, and I would look at him and say: "I'm going to teach you as Malcolm taught me." I wrote that in a poem, and my son has lived up to that as well.

At this time, activists and organizations began to have these expansive ideological frames like Pan-Africanism and Black nationalism. There was also increased contact with African, Asian and Latin American liberation struggles and leaders, and that was coupled with this pervasive problem of racism and Black oppression at home. That would naturally drive me toward being influenced by individuals and groups whose practice reflected a blending of study with practice, resulting in the development of one's personal political ideology and your worldview that could be constructed to understand the material basis of race, gender, and class oppression.

With an ideological perspective or understanding of those things, it also allowed you to understand the interrelationship of racism, capitalism, imperialism, and global constructs. As I evolved, I was tied to the theory of intersectionality. We didn't call it that at the time. We called it "triple oppression." Fran Beal co-founded the Third World Women's Alliance,[2] which I joined. We talked about "triple jeopardy." In 1969, my politics led me to become one of the few female members in leadership in the Philadelphia chapter of the Black Economic Development Conference (BEDC). This organization was at the forefront of the Reparations movement. I became the editor of the organization's newsletter, *The Black Manifesto*.

The Black Manifesto was issued in July 1969, when hundreds of Black activists assembled in Detroit to advance an agenda that was predicated on Black people being forced to come to racist white America and exploited for our labor. This is all in the manifesto. The Black Economic Development Conference, following the perspective of *The Black Manifesto*, demanded reparations from white Christian churches, because they had been a part and parcel of the system of capitalism. The manifesto demanded $500,000 from churches and Jewish synagogues. As, I wrote those articles, a broadside, I developed my journalistic skills.

Now my next discovery of self was to affirm my political identity as a Black Marxist-Leninist. This was a natural flow from my experiences as a community leader, organizing sit-ins at dangerous bus stops. I was working by this time in a Black community-centered Young Women's Christian Association (YWCA). This job heightened my experiences as a community leader, organizing sit-ins at dangerous bus stops and advocating for childcare (since I was a single parent). Other community-based employment led me to work in community healthcare as a family therapist.

It has been affirmed that throughout history, Black women have always been on the front lines of liberation, even if opponents have tried to revise the history. It is just impossible to revise the history to say that Black people have not been an integral part of these fights and struggles for liberation.

When Fred Hampton was assassinated in his bed [Panther Mark Clark was also shot and killed as he sat by the entry door] on December 4, 1969, when the Chicago police entered his home at 4:30 in the morning, and fired more than 42 shots where he and his wife [Deborah Johnson, mother of Fred Hampton, Jr.], who was eight months pregnant, laid sleeping, this event became yet another turning point in my life. Chicago PD and FBI had infiltrated the Chicago Panthers with William O'Neill who rose in the ranks as the Panthers security chief. I was living in Philadelphia in a political commune. It was very interesting to be living in a commune with primarily all-white radicals. That was another experience which helped me to see another side of this struggle against imperialism, by living with progressive white folk. There was also a built-in daycare, which was great for me and other women who lived in the commune. The local chapter of the Black Panther Party was a few blocks from where we lived. We had a printing press in the basement, and we used to print flyers for them.

I would collect food for the breakfast program. A member of the party, Mumia Abu-Jamal, who had just turned 14 or 15, approached us after Fred had been assassinated. He asked our commune if we would provide a car to drive out to Chicago to show solidarity and to pay our condolences to Fred's family and members of the Chicago chapter of the Black Panther Party. Of course, we did. A small group of us arrived in Chicago and joined the massive outcry against the criminal behavior of the Chicago Police. I was so devastated at going into that little house and seeing the bloodstained mattress. I can still see it now.

There were all these bullet holes in the walls of the bedroom. And when I returned to Philadelphia to our house, I never went back to my job as a therapist at the hospital. I went straight to the Black Panther Party headquarters, and that's how I joined and became a member of the Black Panther Party. I did agree with the Ten-Point Program and Platform. I'm coming out of a strict Marxist-Leninist bag. However, I was able to work within the confines of that structure because I believed in what the party was doing. My ascension to leadership was quick. I immediately thrust myself into Party work 24/7 utilizing my skills and the resources as a seasoned and mature organizer. When you came into the party, your skills were respected where you could utilize your skills, you could give to the party. As I said, because I had written for the *Black Manifesto* newspaper which published the demands of the National Black Economic Development Conference. I came into the party with writing and editing skills. I also wrote articles about local matters for the Party's national newspaper, *The Black Panther*.

I sold newspapers. I got up just like everyone else before dawn to work in the free breakfast programs. I accompanied community people to court, and people who were being evicted from their homes. I organized lead paint campaigns against landlords whose dwellings were often unfit for habitation. Being in an organization that was doing something was so fulfilling. I also organized transportation for families visiting their incarcerated loved ones.

In the spring of 1970, not too long after I joined the party, I was transferred to New Haven, Connecticut, where I was assigned to work on the infamous trial of Bobby Seale, Ericka Huggins, and other Panthers, mostly women, who were on trial for their life in New Haven. They had been accused of the murder of a Panther who was suspected of being an agent. So, the trial of Seale and Huggins had made the city a magnet for Black Panther mobilization, and some say that had pushed New Haven to the brink of anarchy during May Day 1970. My role as a courier to the prison where Bobby was incarcerated allowed him to communicate and maintain leadership within the Party. I was responsible for conveying his messages to other party leaders.

We organized a free health clinic, which was one of the best-equipped health clinics in New Haven and staffed by the Party on the East Coast.

I taught at liberation schools, where I created puppet shows for the children that explained the political nuances of what was going on at that time. And my other responsibility included being the liaison to various support committees that the party had, especially among white radical women. I helped to organize fundraising events among the white liberal community. But what's important for me to acknowledge at this stage, even over the years, is that I always have to reflect on the mental toll and how it impacted our daily lives, where the office was always under constant surveillance by the New Haven Police. We would get death threats, telephone monitoring, and we always have to defend ourselves against the military style raids that were constantly being carried out by the local police and the FBI.

Did I have fear about being in an organization which was constantly under surveillance? An organization that the United States government labeled a terrorist group? While the FBI and the local police and law enforcement were infiltrating the organization, they were sowing dissent, and they were even destroying lives of individuals. Yet, I was not afraid. I believed in what I was doing. As an anti-state and anti-capitalist organization, the Panther Party drew the ire of Richard Nixon who would be elected president in 1968. In 1967, the state and federal law enforcement officials escalated their attacks on the party. There was the infamous [FBI] counterintelligence program designed to disrupt, misdirect, and discredit. But the party was my home, and my comrades, both men and women, were my family. We lived collectively, often sharing apartments, and in some cities, our living quarters were actually in the party.

In the party, we used our revolutionary ideals, as it's been written often by many others who were not in the party. But we used our revolutionary ideals to galvanize our community. Through our practice, we demonstrated to the community that we believed in them, that we were there to serve them. And at the same time, we would assert our determination, our radical political vision. And that's reflected in the Ten-Point Program and Platform.

The other thing I want to mention here is that as the reputation of the party soared, so did its female membership. The women made up between 60 to 65 percent of the party's leadership and the organization of the party. And I was a part of that historical phenomenon of women in the Black Panther Party. In an effort to align our activism, political theory, and our emancipatory goals, the Panther Women, we theorized a gender-specific version of the Panthers' political identity. That gender-specific version of the party's vision was the "Black Revolutionary Woman," an ideal that's person-ified gendered formulations of the party's political ideology.

I was eventually expelled from the party, as were so many others, during the highest levels of infiltration in the party, during the time when the morale of the cadre had sunk to new levels as a result of the split that was taking place between Huey Newton and Eldridge Cleaver who was in Algiers, and I was forced into exile. Now this is where I had fear. I was forced into exile because I feared for my life. Because if you were expelled from the party, you were identified in the paper – based in Oakland led by Newton – as an enemy of the people, and nobody wanted to have that tag. So, I remained quiet for about a year.

Then the beauty of my re-emerging, it was because of sisters who embraced me in the organization known as the National Alliance of Third World Women. This organization was led by Black and other women of color, feminist activists. They were African American sisters, Native American sisters, from the Middle East, Indigenous women, Latinx women, and women who identified themselves as LGBTQ women. It was just an amazing organization at that time, because one was thrust into recogniz-ing the centrality of gender exploitation and oppression. While at the same time we recognized, and we respected each other for our cultural differ-ences. When we meshed all of that together, it strengthened our unity as women. We participated in anti-war demonstrations, we challenged the police, violence in the community. We led protests against forced steriliza-tion of Puerto Rican women, and we actively engaged in the massive support of Palestinians. Of course, we met with women from the Middle East. As an organizer, our understanding of that struggle became more real.

For me, it naturally aligned who I was as a woman with all women in the struggle. During these times I was able to embrace a worldview that broad-ened my ability to self-identify as an internationalist. Because the world is a global, we are just a part of this global struggle. I became active in leadership in Venceremos Brigade,[3] formed some 50 years ago to demonstrate solidar-ity with the Cuban Revolution. In the latter part of the 1980s, I was asked to come to live and work in Cuba, and also had an opportunity to visit Burkina Faso, in West Africa, with a film crew.

I met President Thomas Sankara in Burkina Faso;[4] that country was on the verge of possibly becoming one of Africa's first real socialist states. When I returned from Cuba to the United States, it was very difficult to find full-time employment. The sum total of my political activism if I look at it now, it's probably more, but it was documented in more than 2000 pages of FBI files. Imagine that.

For more than 28 years, I've been working as an adjunct professor. I did get one full-time job, working for a trade union. These experiences are one of the reasons why I ended up going to law school. I wanted to be a part of a movement of progressive legal educators. I wasn't necessarily interested in litigating, but I wanted to teach and work in the community on behalf of political prisoners.

I wrote or contributed to several books.[5] I've been able to parlay my educational experiences, my trade union organizing, my commitment to worker education with public service employees. I've been recognized for my activism, being a human rights advocate. A few years ago, I received a United States House of Representative Proclamation from Congresswoman Yvette Clarke because of our work around Cuba. I still have a lot of work to do.

Intergenerational themes, for me, are transitional herstories, and they bind us together. I teach in courses such as "Race, Gender, and the Law," "Immigrant Rights and the Law." All of that links to the Black Lives Matter movement.

Student 1

What are some of the reasons ... that another party like the BPP [has not emerged with] the same militancy, community engagement, anti-police self-defense, and social programs that the party represented and followed?

Mealy

The social and political reality of what's going on in this country at this moment require that there be new strategies and new tactics for dealing with what's happening in the US. At the height of the Black Panther Party, the state, as we know the state now, the role of imperialism as we know it now, the social realities that exist now and the political realities that exist now were not the realities that we had to confront and deal with 40 years ago. So, you're not going to see a replica. Organizations that truly want to challenge the system must analyze your reality now. You may borrow from what existed then, but you're not going to try to replicate it, because it's a different reality.

Let's just take the Black Lives Matter movement, a critique of the Black Lives Matter movement. We heard the slogan "Black Power" back in the

1960s. The Black Lives Matter movement, their slogan was like a Black Power slogan because it became a galvanizing tool, which awakened the youth, especially in this country, with a direct alert to the fact that the systemic killing of Black youth, especially Black male youth, required direct action. Because Black lives mattered, right? Black lives mattered to us, but Black lives mattered less in the society of those law enforcement personnel and their response. It was necessary for militant street action to take place, in order to bring that reality or to bring that understanding that had been crushed, in a sense. Our movement had been crushed. It had been destroyed. It had been infiltrated. So, the Black Lives Matter movement captured the spotlight, once again propelled by the practices and age-old criticism of how the criminal justice system has continuously failed Black people.

The Black Liberation Movement was destroyed. Hundreds of Blacks, primarily men, were incarcerated until the ages 70, 80, and 90 years old, because they were a part of that movement. Because the masses of Black folk don't even know that there are Black political prisoners who fought back then. I don't think you're going to see a replica of the Black Panther Party. What is really positive today, is that we're seeing an amalgamation of organizations and groups that are addressing all of the issues, plus more issues than the Black Panther Party addressed.

Youth are leading those movements, the environmental justice movement, the movement around militarization. There's no one political party, that progressive political party with a full ideological perspective, that is guiding that movement. That's one of the issues that we have now, also, because everybody is struggling on all fronts, but we haven't unified ourselves to deal with those issues that are far more pronounced today than they were during the era 40 years ago during the time of the Black Panther Party. I do have a lot of hope in what I see. And the other dimension to your question is that it's not just movements domestically that are struggling against these issues that are in front of us.

We're dealing with the question in this country of whether this country is going to survive or if it is going fascist or not. That's a reality. How do you strike up a balance in taking up a struggle in your community when the nation is politically going fascist, and people are struggling to live on far less than minimum wage, especially during the advent of COVID-19? We're dealing with different political structures. We're dealing with different political times. We're dealing with global capitalism and the rise of fascism globally.

I don't know if we can expect the emergence of a Black Panther Party. We need more than a Black Panther Party. We need a more united party that recognizes the central role of Black folk in this country, but also recognizing the fact that right now, the United States of America is a country of Brown immigrants. It's going to be left up to young people such as yourself who become the scholar-activists who can determine and define the theory, and that's going to direct these actions out of the mire that we're in now. Especially, we're in a situation now where we're on the cuff of fascism. And I think that that's how serious the situation is.

Student 2

Could you talk more about acting as a liaison between Marxist radical white spaces and the Black Panthers?

Mealy

Any organization that you are part of, you need to study. You need to engage in reading and understanding history, different ideological viewpoints and perspectives. One of the problems that I think that has happened now with the present formations is that they're more responsive and they're acted on, but not built within those structures is the opportunity for people to develop ideologically.

I just don't want to ride the wave without understanding it. I think that everybody needs to be taught. Even in community groups, that's what we did. We had political education with the people coming for classes. It was like liberation school, where you took complex ideas and you broke them down so that people could understand. Then people go back in the community, and they work in their local housing organizations, and they're able to explain how landlords operate, profit loss and the economic frameworks. Those are important. I think that that's what's missing right now. We act without really understanding this thing that we're dealing with.

Then, of course, we have the media and we have social media. And we have the opportunity to use these forms to teach people, but we don't. Organizations have that responsibility. And I think that a lot don't do that. That's one thing that the party did. We may go out and sell newspapers and we start breakfast programs and what have you. But when we talked to parents, we explained the basics of how this system runs, how it operates. And like I said, we taught people basic economics to understand. And then once people begin to see that there's a correlation between their reality and the kind of system, that capitalism does not work. It doesn't work. We are taught that it does, that this is the only kind of system that works. We're not taught alternatives. We are so anticommunist. Our idea of socialism is that everybody has no freedom, and that people can't move around freely, when that's not true.

It's our responsibility as teachers and as students who are aware that in our structures, that we just explain that we cannot go to a demonstration and demonstrate against the fact that they're cutting down trees along my canal, without explaining what corporation has gotten a contract to do that. I think it's so basic. We have the information, knowledge, but sometimes we just think that we just need to act without teaching people what are we acting against.

Student 3

How do you stay hopeful and how do you keep people hopeful?

Mealy

Let me put it this way. It's the youth that have to be hopeful. You have to have hope. You have to know that there can be a different kind of world. You have to believe that. If you don't believe that there can be a different kind of world, then you lose hope. One of the things that I've been doing with young people such as yourself, there's a place 90 miles away from the United States of America where there is a socialist experiment going on, where youth are hopeful, while at the same time many youths are leaving because the economic reality of a 60-year-old embargo has created situations in their country that's just very difficult to live. And I'm talking about Cuba.

When we take young people to Cuba, and they return here, they don't try to replicate what they saw. But they say,

> 90 miles away from here, there's people who really believe that there can be a different kind of world. And it could even be a better world if there wasn't a blockade, an embargo against the nation that does not allow them to trade on the world market, that calls the country a member of a terrorist state. That they're on that list.

Talk to young people in other countries, in the streets in France today, even living with their parents, they're struggling; you shouldn't have to get so old to retire before you can live your life, after you've made a contribution and developed a state and made it what it is.

I think we have to instill in those of us who know and understand that there's a different kind of world. We become the advocates for saying,

> Oh, no, we have to change this kind of system that we are living in. We have to join people around the world, especially young people who are raising these questions. Because they do believe that it can be a better world. And I know it can be a better world myself.

And you have to believe yourself. If you don't believe that things can change, then you're doomed. So that's why it's so important to have people that will inspire you. Go to other parts of the world, talking to those young people who are fleeing countries around the world, who want to come to the United States, thinking that this is going to be a great place. Then once they get here, they're confronted with racism, and they're confronted with all the issues that we live with every day. Talk to them and ask, "Well, why did you come here? Now that you're here, what do you think?" We have to be almost like ambassadors with our neighbors; we have a responsibility to instill hope and to change the world. Otherwise, given all of the struggles that have taken place, we would have forsaken all of the hope and sacrifices planted by our fore-parents and ancestors. We stand on their shoulders.

Talk to your grandparents, and your parents, and others who have participated in changing the society. Your question gives me a lot of hope, because you are asking, "Should I continue to have hope?" Do you believe that there can be another kind of world? I do.

Student 4

Could you speak to your experiences as a professor, and how you think that educational systems may or may not play into or support revolutionary struggle, as opposed to reform?

Mealy

Well, I smile a lot when I have students who write to me after they've been out of school for maybe three or four years, and they refer back to something that they learned, and they tell me that they're involved now. So, I never think that we're going to win over everybody. But I think when you give people the information, then they can take that information and recharge themselves, and redefine their initial viewpoints about things. I think those of us who still have some foot in the academy, we have a responsibility to continue to pass on this information. And we're not, they're saying here in Florida, I could never teach here again, because I taught critical race theory. Really, it's so absurd, because the truth is there's an attempt now to deny truth. The books are banned all over the country.

Students that I've had, they're making little dents. They're passing on the information and they're aware. Many of them have become activists. I believe that we have a responsibility to teach the truth and to challenge the fallacies. We're not trying to indoctrinate anybody with this information. Just there's another side to the story. And when there are other sides to the story, there's always an attempt to suppress that. There may be a grain of something that I've said today that is inspiring, and then just take that and build on it. Take that information out into the world wherever you go.

SOURCE NOTES

1. "Melba Liston." *National Endowment for the Arts*. Accessed July 12, 2023. www.arts.gov/honors/jazz/melba-liston
2. "Third World Women's Alliance, Women in the Struggle (1971)," 2000. www.marxists.org/history/erol/ncm-6/women-in-struggle.pdf
3. "About the Venceremos Brigade." *Venceremos Brigade*, March 3, 2023. https://vb4cuba.com/about-the-venceremos-brigade/
4. Murrey, Amber, ed. *A Certain Amount of Madness: The Life, Politics, and Legacies of Thomas Sankara*. London: Pluto Press, 2018.
5. Mealy, Rosemari. "Sitting Down to Stand up: Black Student Suspensions/ Expulsions at Historically Black Colleges and Universities (HBCUs), 1960– 1962: A Phenomenological Study." *ProQuest Dissertations Publishing*, 2009; Mealy, Rosemari. *Fidel and Malcolm: Memories of a Meeting*. Baltimore, MD: Black Classic Press, 2013; Mealy, Rosemari, "An Incomprehensible Omission: Women and El-Hajj Malik El-Shabazz." In Jared Ball and Todd Steven Burroughs, eds., *A Lie of Reinvention: Correcting Manning Marable's Malcolm X*. Baltimore, MD: Black Classic Press, 2013.

11

BIPOC Pedagogy:
Roberta Alexander and
Khalid Alexander

Interviewed by Joy James and seminar students, May 8, 2023

Roberta Alexander

My family told stories. Especially, my father told stories. At one point we even did an oral history of my dad's life. I think it's one of the things I am happiest to have done, to have heard those stories and to be telling those stories. It became just something that we do in the family.

In fact, it's in our DNA. My sister, Vicki Alexander, MD, MPH, works in public health. She is distraught that the statistics for the health of Black people have gone down. Black infants have 3.8 times higher infant mortality than that of white babies. The country of Costa Rica does better than the United States as a whole in terms of infant mortality. My sister talks to me about what she wants to do with the organization that she put together called "Healthy Black Families."[1]

Healthy Black Families is located in Berkeley, California. My sister says, "We have to make our organization not just a support organization for women, which of course is very important and children in our communities, but we need to be revolutionary to really make a change." I'm going to interpret that a little bit ... I think what she's saying is we have to change this structure of capitalism that we're living in, and that's being a little bit revolutionary.

From my father's oral history, which I did in 1975 when he was 62, I learned in a formal way because we were recording his stories. He described growing up on an Indian reservation and his family living between Nebraska and Sioux City, Iowa. His mother was Scott Irish, but she always told the kids, and there were ten of them, that the word at that time was probably you are colored. Don't anybody tell you you're white. He had that consciousness right from the beginning of his life. One of his earliest memories was going to work the harvest, I think it was in Wisconsin or Minnesota (Red Lake Falls), in the summer. He rode the rails, of course, even though he was 12 or 13. He got off I think in Minnesota. He found a farmer who was looking for someone to work for him.

The farmer said, "I'll pay you 50 cents a day." My father thought that was great. He accepted and he walked out to the farm, which was about 5 miles out, he said, and he was helping the farmer with the chores. Then he goes to the bunk house and there's a bunch of white guys there, and these guys asked him, one of them in particular asked him, "So what are you doing here?" And he says, "I'm here to work the harvest." Because my father was not only Black, but he was also just a kid. And the white guy says, "How much you getting paid?" My dad said, "50 cents a day." And the guy says, "50 cents a day, we don't get paid 50 cents a day, we get paid a dollar a day. What's that?" And the man tells the other guys, this little coon is talking about 50 cents a day.

My dad thought, "That's kind of strange. He's calling me these names." But anyway, then he let the gentleman tell this story, and the guy said, look, if this guy's going to do 50 cents a day, he's got to understand that he can't be doing chores, that he's going to work with us, and we make a dollar a day. My dad said, wow, that's something. So, the next morning at breakfast, this same guy, Scandinavian guy gets up and tells the boss, we understand you got this little kid here working for 50 cents a day, and that's not going to work. We work for a dollar a day, so either you pay him a dollar a day or we go on strike. You can imagine if you are a little 12-year-old kid in this situation, that these guys are supporting you. They're using funny names to talk about you … insulting names to talk about you … but they're talking about going on strike [for you to] get a dollar a day.

The farmer gave my dad a dollar a day. This is a formative experience from which my dad I think largely became the person who became a union organizer who believed that people should stick together. We have a better chance if those of us who are oppressed or marginalized or doing the dirty work of the society, if we stick together, we have a better chance of winning. So, this is a story that he told me that I thought Wow. Those guys were in the Industrial Workers of the World (IWW) in the 1920s.[2] They would have serious strikes.

Speaking about strikes, when the family went to Iowa, my grandmother worked in the packing house and she somehow got targeted, clearly because she had ten Black kids. There was a strike of the packing house workers and their house was among others that got targeted.

The windows got broken; my dad knew what racism was. He knew what the racism of the Midwest could be. The workers were from all over. They were from Mexico, Syria, Scandinavian countries, Eastern European countries, all kinds, Jewish people. He talked about how they all struggled together when they were in the same situation. This is something that we see in packing house workers today. Some children are working in the packing houses. I believe in North Carolina or South Carolina, they're in the packing houses doing the dirtiest work, just like my father was doing in the packing houses 85 to 90 years ago.

His formal schooling went to about third grade, fourth grade. They had a substitute teacher. She's walking around with the kids and hitting them over their fingers with the ruler. And she hit my dad once. After she did that, my dad thought, she's not going to do this to me again. She did hit him again, he took her ruler, broke it in half and threw it out the window. And this teacher was all scared, saying "What are you doing? You are in trouble! Everything like that. But when his mother heard what happened to her son, she walked to the school with my dad, and she confronted the teacher saying, "Who do you think you are to be treating our children in this way, in this disrespect-ful way?" And my dad, once again was reinforced to who he was and who he believed he was and what the family would not put up with. The family is simply not going to be rolled over in that way.

This was his last day of going to school. He never went back to school. He only got as far as the fourth grade. He wasn't allowed to attend school because he didn't have shoes and shoes were required. He didn't have shoes in Nebraska. [It might have been] in the wintertime. He never went back to that school. He became actually an autodidact. He taught himself a lot of stuff. He was always reading. Many years later, when I was in junior high school, somebody during fourth period stole somebody's watch or some kid had lost his watch. The principal took four of us into her office and said, "Nobody's going home till one of you confesses that you stole this watch."

I went home, I told my dad about it, he said, "What kind of nonsense is that?" Next day he went straight to the principal and said, "Who do you think you are? Those are fascist tactics. Those are the tactics that the Nazis use in Germany. What are you thinking of to have four kids in this office?" I'll never forget, she was just saying, "Oh, Mr. Alexander, I'm so sorry. You're right. I got you. Yeah, Mr. Alexander, I understand it." I went Whoa! Look at my dad. I was so proud that he stood up for me. My parents did it on other occasions as well. This is to the formal school system of the 1950s. My brother went to Manual Arts High School in Los Angeles. He was told he couldn't take algebra. My parents went to school and fought that out, and he got his algebra class. And 25 years after that, he was the chief medical officer of the Kaiser Permanente Medical System for southern California.

We need to go back and talk to these people so that they realize that who they're trying to shut up and who they're trying to hold back. The first time I remember my father talking to me seriously and sitting me down and having a conversation was when Emmett Till was killed in 1955. He took me to the back of our shoe store because at that time we had a shoe store and the whole family worked there. He took me to the back. He sat me down. He says, "We need to talk about this. This is stuff that you don't know about because some of it's not as obvious when you live in California and when you live where we are. But you have to know that this happens in our country." And he showed me the photograph of Emmett Till's body [in an open casket in a funeral home] in Chicago published in the *Jet Magazine*. I think this is an experience that almost every Black person my age will talk about during our childhood actually.

Those experiences created the person who I am today, certainly the person who I was in the 1960s and the 1970s. My father was that he was taken off to Indian school with his friends from the reservation. There's an example of education being used to try to control a population. The residential school didn't let the kids speak their Native languages. They didn't let them have their hair traditional. By the time they returned home, the kids were really barely members of their family because they didn't fit into the culture. However, they figured out that my dad was not a Native American officially, and they sent him back home. But he did experience this part of American history where Indian children were just rounded up. Nobody told the parents nothing. They just rounded up their children and had them taken a few states away to these Indian schools to be deculturized.[3]

My experiences with education have been very different. I think I've been fortunate enough to be in some classes like this seminar. I'm sure you have a liberation pedagogy. And I was fortunate enough to study with a few people like Sylvia Wynter[4] and Carlos Blanco Aguinaga,[5] who helped me put together many of my personal experiences and helped me frame and see a bit more analysis of my experiences. That takes me to the Black Panther Party. When I joined the Black Panther Party in 1969, one of the things that I did was work on the newspaper and I gave political education classes.

The Black Panthers were seriously trying to expose everybody in the party to reading certain materials: we read Mao's *Little Red Book* and other important documents available to us.

I learned from experience in the Black Panther Party distrust. By 1969, some 29 people had been killed, largely by police and the FBI. We had many more in jail in different stages of prosecution. Fred Hampton would be murdered within a couple of months [December 4, 1969]. A new person showed up at the party headquarters in Richmond, California, North Richmond, where I was staying at that time. He said he wanted to join, and that he had just gotten out of prison, he was an ex-con, and the party was welcoming those folks.

But I started to think, and everybody else did too, if this person was on the up and up, or was some kind of stool pigeon or provocateur who was going to mess with us and get us in trouble? This particular guy said to me, "I want to put some stuff in your trunk. Knives." (I think he said knives.) I said, "No, you can't put anything in my [car] trunk." Next morning, I am driving to the party headquarters to Berkeley, and there's an area of North Richmond at that time with no houses or businesses, nothing. It was just roads to get onto the freeway. I hear a siren, and then police stopped me. Within just a couple of minutes, there were six or seven police cars that had come screeching into where I was.

They said, well, we want to take a look at your trunk. Having forgotten my rights totally under the circumstances, I said, "Okay, you can." There was nothing in my trunk. I am convinced that there would've been something in my trunk if I had to let that guy put something into it. There was an attempt to set me up. Lessons learned. You don't want to get paranoid because that is dangerous if you're paranoid about everybody. I realized that we were infiltrated in the sense that we had provocateurs inside of the organization. The police had plans for the Panthers who they considered public enemy number one.

I left the Panthers. I went to participate in a very exciting project, the Lumumba-Zapata College[6] [Lumumba-Zapata College was also known as Third College], which was going to be a college within UC San Diego. Because UC San Diego was a new university at that time, and they decided it would be better to have smaller colleges so it would be more personal than being in these big lecture halls at UCLA or UC Berkeley. The previous year, there had been a number of activists in the Black Student Union and also in the Chicano organization who got together [and made a statement]:

Well, why don't we get this next college that's coming through to be a progressive college and to teach the histories of Black and Brown people and poor folks so that we can get a truer history or get another history from the standard Western history that we are used to having and have had over and over and over again?

They mobilized. They demanded a college. It was granted to them. It was wonderful. The students were hiring professors. They were hiring deans. Everybody was working together.

However, students did not want to have a particular counselor but the provost gave that individual a position anyway. That individual, who the provost had been pressured to give a position to, on the very first day started talking shit about Chicanos. He was African American, and he started talking about, "What is the point of everybody being together? What are you guys doing here? We got different interests." He created, with other people participating, a split between the Black students and the Chicano students and the white students. I was in the middle of that and I was charged with being on one side: "You like Mexican people better than you like Black people" – or something ridiculous like that. Unfortunately, that kind of divisive stuff led to destroying the project. And it was frightening. I [had gotten] the job of Resident Dean. I was about 23-years-old at that time. I lived in a house which was surrounded by bigger dorms, so students had access to see me. It was kind of like a fishbowl. One night, a group of Black students came to my door. They were armed and they threatened me. I actually left my home and I went and stayed with Carlos Blanco.

This example of Third College, to my knowledge, has not been thoroughly evaluated or written about except in one chapter in a book about Chicanos that only talks about the Chicano experience in Third College. It doesn't discuss the entirety of that experience. But it went to show how dangerous they thought that simply having courses that taught authors like Frantz Fanon was just to be reading about those things. [The repression] was hidden. It wasn't like, "These books are banned." In essence, it really did destroy a project that would have been a good example of liberation pedagogy.

Khalid Alexander

My mom is downplaying the latter part of her life and how influential she was in San Diego. I continuously have people coming up to me and telling me how appreciative they are of her and the work that she's done in San Diego. Through the work that she did on campus at UCSD, but also the continued work of allyship and fighting for all oppressed people who are looked over in San Diego, and throughout California.

My name is Khalid. Actually, Paul Alexander is what my mom named me. I found out later that the "Paul" was after Paul Robeson. I grew up listening to the same stories that my mom was talking about now, but never really had any points in time where I can remember any type of intentional pedagogy being taught to me. Like: "I'm a former Panther and these are the ideologies that we should believe in. These are things that we fight for." But just through hearing those stories, I think subconsciously I ended up embracing a lot of those same worldviews, whether it be the importance of solidarity with other oppressed minorities or fighting for what we see as justice regardless of the circumstances. I was not a standout student in my K-12 education experience. I barely passed my senior year. I became Muslim in 1995, which was my senior year of high school. I had the opportunity to travel. I wasn't really interested in higher education. After coming back to the States, I kind of realized that being poor wasn't what I thought it was cracked out to be. So I enrolled in a community college where I eventually transferred to San Diego State University where I got my MA in comparative literature. Around the same time, I was also a volunteer imam in the local jail.

But my kind of consciousness, my awareness of liberation, and liberatory pedagogy, actually came through studying West Asian studies or Middle Eastern studies and reading about Edward Said, and eventually Frantz Fanon. Edward Said enabled me to see the struggle of Black Americans and my own struggles and the struggle of the communities that I was a part of from an outside perspective that I did not naturally have, at least from a pedagogical standpoint when it came to our situations in the community. I had the opportunity to study the Crusades while living in Syria. Part of what that study brought to me was this idea that Salahuddin Ayyubi who reconquered Palestine and the Holy Lands is always held up as this central figure. I began to grapple with the idea that by holding up a central figure as somebody who led to the reconquest of the holy land, we were actually dismissing hundreds of thousands, millions of people in the Middle East that were a part of that. What does it mean when we hold up leaders at the expense of the kind of rank and file, for lack of a better word, or the everyday people who are already feeling pressured by the injustices that they were seeing?

Long story short, I ended up coming back to the United States after studying there off and on for three years and was looking into Ph.D. programs while teaching as a part-time instructor in the community college district. Three things happened around the same time. One, a student of mine who was formerly incarcerated, getting As, one of those students who really participated in class discussions and helped others, ended up being arrested for a violation of his parole two weeks before finals. The reason why he was arrested is because his parole officer did a standard check of the house and found a blue shirt crumpled up on the floor of his closet. And because he was a documented gang member, they used that as a violation of parole and sent him to prison. They essentially ruined his higher education career.

Around the same time, I moved to Southeast San Diego and was pulled over by the police about three times in two weeks. Two questions asked by the police stood out to me that I didn't remember being asked before. One: "Are you a fourth waiver?"[7] In California, fourth waiver is tied to the people who have spent time in prison, upon release they are forced to waive their Fourth Amendment rights. Essentially what that means is they don't have the same right to privacy as you and I supposedly do. So, they can be pulled over, they can be stopped, they can be searched, their houses can be searched, they can be detained for as long as law enforcement feels like it.

The second question was, "Are you a gang member?" Until recently, I had forgotten how often that I had been pulled over or stopped by the police because I was walking. Police used to always ask us this question when we were ages 12, 13, and 14. What I didn't know is that they were creating a gang database at the time where they were doing stops of random young people in neighborhoods, like the one I grew up in, but also in neighborhoods such as Los Angeles, South Central, and beyond.[8] If people said they were a gang member or if police felt they were talking to a gang member, they were adding them to a database. I started recognizing that a lot of the obstacles that were getting in the way of my students inside of the classroom were actually coming from outside of the classroom. I realized that our ability as instructors, as professors, to actually help address the larger issues that get in the way of the success of our students, we had to look beyond the campus.

The third thing that happened is a number of the brothers who I had met while being a voluntary imam in jail were getting out. In addition to all of the obstacles that people who have been incarcerated face on re-entry, they were also dealing with cultural issues. For example: going home and their mother or grandmother telling them that there wasn't enough room in their house for them and Jesus. Or, because they were Muslim, not being welcomed in any space. Initially, we started the organization Pillars of the Community in order to address some of those needs and bring support that

I was lucky enough to have with my mom to help people not only be successful in higher education, getting into community college, but also helping them find work and living spaces.

What I quickly realized is that no matter how many jobs you find people, no matter how many places to live you find them, if you're not addressing the structural cracks that led to their incarceration in the first place, essentially, it's like filling a bucket full of water that has holes in the bottom of it. No matter how much water you put into it, it'll continuously spill out. So, we changed relatively quickly from a service organization to an advocacy organization.

I also used to have a speech that I would give to anybody who was trying to get me to vote or sign a petition, that I didn't believe in the American system of democracy. But I realized that those structures and those cracks that I talked about are actually directly related to some of the systemic issues that are implemented essentially from voting and a number of other influences also. The first awareness of that came with a proposition called Proposition 47,[9] which happened in San Diego. It took what used to be "wobblers," meaning a district attorney can choose to charge somebody with a felony or a misdemeanor however they want. So, Tyrone and LaShonda in Southeast San Diego were getting hit with felony charges, while Todd and Jennifer at San Diego State University were being hit with misdemeanors. What Prop 47 did is it took wobblers and it made it so that they all became misdemeanors. That was the first time when I realized that there was actually something I could vote for that would make a difference in the lives of the people who I lived with, who I taught, and who I worked with in the community. It was the first time that I voted.

The only thing on the entire ballot that I voted for was actually Prop 47. That ended up passing. A friend of mine who was locked up at the time said, "We went from living in jail cells where there weren't enough bunks, so people literally had to roll out their bedding onto the floor and sleep on the floor, to being essentially emptied overnight because it was retroactive." So, I saw that my little speech or understanding of the power or disempowerment of the ballot, depending on how you wanted to look at it, wasn't the full story. Voting, particularly on policies, can actually impact the real lives of people.

The second thing that happened in the progression of Pillars of the Community[10] is that 33 African American men were rounded up and charged with 50 years to life under an obscure penal code 182.5 by then-District Attorney Bonnie Dumanis. District attorneys, as you all probably know, but I didn't know at the time, are also elected officials. So, this person who was elected had found an obscure penal code that was voted into law in 2000. This happened around 2013, 2014, by the way, when these 33 Black men were locked up. She had found an obscure penal code that was a part of Proposition 21, which passed in 2000, which essentially said that anybody who is allegedly from an alleged gang can be charged with any crimes that that alleged gang has committed.

Inside of court, most of the young men took plea deals. Two of them ended up fighting their case. In court, Bonnie Dumanis said, "We don't think that they committed a crime. We don't even think that they knew about the crime. But under penal code 182.5, we can charge them with 50 years to life." They were able to get a number of grassroots-kind of community support. But again, a majority of them took plea deals. One of the people is doing 25 years in prison on a plea deal just because he was worried about spending the rest of his life in prison. His only charge was 182.5. District attorneys are elected. While I was living in my isolated, self-righteous stance when it comes to voting, I was against voting, a proposition had passed that I didn't vote for or against, [but led to] the mass incarceration of 33 people. That's just one example of many different laws that pass every day that end up impacting us.

Over the years, Pillars of the Community has developed an approach to advocating for people who are negatively impacted by law enforcement by doing two things. One is our policy work and the other is our community-building. The idea between the policy work is no matter how strong a community you have, if you're not aware of the policies that are being passed, whether you vote for them or not, if you're not aware of them, they're going to be impacting your life. But similarly, if we pass all the policies in the world but don't have a community to stand up and fight for their implementation, that we're also kind of wasting time. A lot of our policy work is actually what I've begun to think of as survival work in trying to limit the carceral system and the pain that the punishment bureaucracy impacts on our community.

The community-building work is where most of the hope, for lack of a better word, of the future lies. Our policy work focuses on gang documentation, incarceration, racial profiling, and a number of different laws that appear nearly every other day. The community work is more the heart and soul of the work that we do at Pillars, it is focused on anything in everyday life, e.g., from eating together, to cooking food. I got an understanding from my mom's experience in the Panthers when she talks about how Bobby Seale would come in and be cooking food for people while they were typing on the computer, bringing people together and building community. We also need political education. If we eat together, understand one another, have good relationships with one another, but do not understand the forces that surround us and impact our everyday lives, that's not sufficient.

We try to include political education in most of the policy work that we do. Rather than telling people to vote, we say, "We don't necessarily expect you to vote. We don't want you to play the game. We want you not to get played." And so, understand what's happening and decide, make a conscious decision of when you are going to vote and when you're not going to vote. Voting certainly isn't the only tool that's out there for liberation, but it is arguably one of the most important tools. And again, as a technique for survival, as we begin to build communities, that can replace the systems that we're living in now.

In the last few days, and few years, I've become increasingly concerned about technology and how technologies are coming to replace a lot of the carceral systems and the punishment bureaucracy. A few years ago, they announced that San Diego was going to be the largest smart city in the world. They were basing that off the 5000 smart streetlights they put up. That in addition to having video recordings, they also had the capacity for audio, but also tracked metadata. The impacts that this surveillance can have in the communities that we're a part of and what type of negative consequences could come along with that. Again, tied into gang documentation, which I didn't talk too much about. Does it make sense for me to talk a little bit about that, mom? You need to correct me over here. I don't always have the opportunity to have my mom check me in the middle of a talk.

RA

I wanted to add the *Reclaiming Our Stories* book and project to bring it back to not just education.[11] It's kind of like formation and how important that was for so many people who are close to or in the periphery of Pillars of the Community. When you mentioned eating together, it reminded me of my one regret in the Black Panther Party. We were working all the time, like twelve-hour days, sleeping in the same place, often not even having a chance to go home. I regret not having a space for the women in the Party to become closer and to become supportive of one another. Or maybe at some points during the history of the party that did happen. I can only talk to 1969. In some ways, it's a criticism of myself. I can't tell you what to do.

KA

In regards to the Reclaiming Our Stories Collective, and if you all have questions about gang documentation and enhancements, I can always answer that. Essentially, what we realized while doing the work in Southeast San Diego is while we're teaching books in the classroom and autobiographies of Malcolm X, Assata Shakur, and others is that the lives of the, quote-unquote, everyday people around me were actually just as fascinating and impactful once you had the ability to sit down and listen to it.

Initially, we started the Reclaiming Our Stories Collective by just having regular old community members come together and say, "Hey, write a chapter out of your life," without any real prompts or anything like that. And almost universally, they would all end up going straight to some of the most traumatic and painful experiences. But this is a group where we would have men and women, African Americans and Latinos. And I think by telling these painful stories in front of one another, they began to realize that they weren't alone, that they were a part of a community, and that they had all of these shared experiences. And more important than the pain that they talk about in the stories, or the traumatic experiences that they talked about in their stories was the fact that they had survived all of those things.

In addition to creating a kind of community there, again, I think they also created a sense of agency, and that you actually have the ability to change the world that we're a part of. Now, we're on our third volume. Most of the authors, if not all of them, continued to be involved in social justice and liberation movements, which again kind of goes back to that insight that I was mentioning when we talked about Selah Houdin. Unless we believe in a collective movement of everyday people who are politically aware of the powers and structures that shape our lives, we are never going to be able to actually push back against it.

Rather than looking for leaders or trying to be leaders ... [we are] focusing on liberatory pedagogy that reaches all people. Most important are those people who don't have an opportunity to go to a community college ... to a four-year university or do graduate studies. [We must] figure out ways to really work with and learn from the stories of the people who are directly impacted; and then [offer] support and try to bring the tools and the pedagogical understanding ... to get them on this liberatory path. We're not going to be able to make [gains] unless we do it with one another.

Joy James

This notion of knowledge production not always being tied to the conventional academy (which is often an expression of the state) offers a lot to digest. Was the District Attorney defeated at the polls?

KA

Bonnie Demanis did not get defeated at the polls. She finished her term but ran for the board of supervisors. We thrashed her there. She lost by an unbelievably large number. [We] ended her political career.

Student 1

Is policy work sufficient, or are there other pieces that need to be pursued in what you're calling "survival work"?

KA

There's a tension between reform and abolition. Looking at reform and just dismissing it purely as reform and something that gets in the way of abolition – this isn't to dismiss people who say that, so take the words that I'm saying – it's a little bit self-righteous. You have people who are living under an oppressive carceral system right now. If you talk to the majority of folks inside the carceral system, whether they consider themselves abolitionists or not, they're involved in reform every time they write up a CO (correctional officer). They're involved in reform every time they write a complaint, or every time they're looking to change a law.

I agree with the perspective that reform actually gets in the way of us changing the system. The problem with that philosophy is that it ignores the actual pain that people are going through now ... I consider myself an abolitionist. But I think are much closer to abolitionists in the sense of Harriet Beecher Stowe and not Harriet Tubman. If we really believe in abolition, we need to be asking ourselves: How can we be out there actually changing the systems?

At the same time, there are some reformists who actually believe that the system itself is a valuable system, and that if we make enough tweaks to the system that everything will be okay. Anybody who has been at the brunt of systemic oppression knows that that's absolutely not true, and that we absolutely have to be working to demolish not only the carceral system, but abolish the police and all of these other things that are part of a larger kind of punishment bureaucracy. That shouldn't happen at the expense of the people who are dealing with it right now. I think strategically. It's a flawed strategy to just sit back and wait until things are absolutely so horrible that all of a sudden there's going to be a revolution.

Those people who are involved in reform, I think if there ever is a revolution, are going to be important in helping us shape policies and systems as we move forward. We struggle with this all the time as a non-profit organization. What it comes down to is the way we balance the tendency of reform and policies to take up all of our time and energy is to constantly check in with ourselves on how much effort we're putting toward policies and how much effort we're putting toward community-building.

You could pass all the policies you want, but if you don't have a community to implement them, it doesn't really do anything. You can have a really strong community, but if you're not aware of the policies that are happening, that community can be destroyed in seconds. As I think we've seen with the Black Panther Party, as I think we've seen with most mass movements in the United States and smaller movements, once they begin to actually challenge the structures, they're dismantled fairly quickly. Figuring out a balance between the two is really, really important.

[What we need is not] a type of political education that preaches a particular ideology, but a political education that helps people understand that shit is complex; that is probably the most important approach to beginning to create a community that can envision a better alternative. I believe in reform on the path to abolition. If we're embracing reform as some type of a saving grace for all of us, I think we're in a lot of trouble because the system itself is rotten.

James

What can be said about the violence of the police, or the proxy to the police, e.g., the white Marine Corp. Sergeant Daniel Penny who choked out the Black performer Jordan Neely in a NYC subway car. Neely never touched anyone but was screaming that he didn't have food, was unhoused, and was willing to go to prison. NYPD let Penny go home [the man-slaughter trial is set for 2024]. Protests keep happening because the killings keep happening … the counterrevolutionary is easy for me to identify, because of the police apparatus. The anti-revolutionary, it feels much more complicated because there are calls or demands to "behave as a good citizen." I find the conflation of revolution with abolition to get really gnarly. I'll give an example since you brought in the ancestors. The CIA commercial claims that Harriet Tubman is one of their spies; the agency head stands beside a statue of Harriet Tubman in the CIA quad.[12] Given the credible allegations and facts that the CIA assassinated African liberation leaders such as Cabral, Lumumba (Malcolm X's daughters are suing the CIA, NYPD, and FBI for his murder). How do we liberate our histories, our ancestors, from being swept up as props for the state? How do we remind ourselves to vote and seek reforms, but acknowledge that's not the same as a revolutionary struggle?

KA

I think political education and liberatory education require figuring out how we counter-propaganda. Look at the Fred Hampton movie, the agent provocateur was kind of the focus of the story, in the Hollywood film *Judas and the Black Messiah*.

I mean, we grow up, and our kids grow up watching PAW Patrol. Almost every gangster rapper who said "Fuck the police!" is now playing the police in film. What does that do to our psyche? I think political education really is the only way to get people to think outside of the narrative that we're being fed. Paulo Freire in *Pedagogy of the Oppressed*, every time I read the book, I get more from it.[13]

I might be getting too far off-topic, but I'll try to bring it back around. Another one of the topping points that we see in people who might consider themselves social justice advocates – I won't say revolutionary – is this idea that people who are closest to the pain need to be leading the movement. And so, then their task becomes: "Well, let's just get somebody who is closest to the pain, put them at the front. Regardless of what their pedagogy or their ideology or the philosophy is, we'll just kind of follow behind them."

That's why I think there is an importance for academia or for an intellectual political education movement. Because a lot of times you'll talk to people who are formally incarcerated, and the first thing they'll start talking about is: "I was a monster. I was horrible. Prison saved my life." If that's a narrative that helps them do better and stay out of prison, I think that that's great. What's interesting for me is what kind of system convinced this person that when they were a child, that they were actually a monster? And unless we begin to figure out ways to counter that, I think we're going to be in trouble.

I think political education in the sense of not just reading books and memorizing points, but actually sitting down and having deep conversations and recognizing the contradictions and having those discussions is difficult. And then, not just having the discussions, but then being able to take that and apply it to our lives. Again, Freire talks about *conscientização*, which is this idea that critical consciousness isn't just a word, but it requires inquiry. So, asking questions, looking at the system and identifying, can lead you to root problems, then identifying those problems, and most importantly, actually moving to change them. I hope that came close to answering the question.

James

How is this self-hatred or this projection of one's self shaped by the state? Part of the state narrative is: "Look, we helped them out by putting them in prison."

KA

When you talk to these people, some of them believe that narrative because they went before a parole board, until they really believed that they were monsters. You can't go before a parole board and start talking about systemic justice and carcerality and all those things. It doesn't work.

Given those people's experience, they do need to be at the forefront. Yet [we are also] figuring out ways to understand the complexity of the situation and not allow ourselves to fall into the narrative of "Our ancestors died for the vote." That's not totally true. [Our ancestors] died to be *liberated*. If the vote isn't liberating us, well, that's not what the purpose is. It is important to not allow ourselves to fall into a didactic understanding of abolition versus reform, and just continue to work to create a better system. That can't happen without deep political education. When I say deep, I don't mean reading difficult books. I mean, deep discussion and understanding, and not talking points.

RA

I think also constant vigilance and mobilization. You can elect somebody who seems kind of progressive. You can have progress, and then you find ten years later, seven years later, even three years later, that the problem is still there, or they're not representing us in the way that they said they would. We have to also combine what you're talking about with that constant vigilance about how to stop the progress that we have made from going backward.

KA

We have a police accountability program that's loosely based on what the Panthers did. And actually, before the Panthers. But I used to think that in order to hold police accountable, that we had to change the narrative and get elected officials to understand the pain and the problems of police and their interactions with people.

While some people look at the police as armed forces that bring safety, others look at the police as people who molested them when they were 14 years old claiming to look for drugs or 13 years old or 12 years old. If elected officials just understood that and if they understood how much money was being wasted on the police and if they understood that that money could be better invested in other places, they would then hold police accountable for the crimes that they commit on a daily basis. We have a few people who ran in San Diego on policies that are clearly not pro-police. This is kind of scary, but to my mom's point of constantly learning from our actions, so as we're moving to create a better situation for all of us, we think that if we let this person in, they're going to change it. And then things don't change.

As we do our police accountability work and we write up police and we get people to tell their stories, I'm no longer convinced that elected officials actually have the power to hold police accountable. And this part is actually scarier. Some of our elected officials now, both in the county and arguably our mayor, I don't believe that they have any love for the police. Our mayor is the first non-white mayor, the first openly gay elected official. And the police hate him. And the police have social media files and stuff like that. The things they say about him are absolutely horrible. And when he ran, he wasn't the person who was embracing the police. He talked about accountability and all of these things, but to use COVID-19 as an example, when COVID-19 hit, all of a sudden, they said that police need to get vaccinated. The police said No. They said that police had to wear masks and the police said No. These are policies, these are laws that were made that the police just decided they're not going to follow. Elected officials didn't have a response for that. Rather than being able to hold police accountable, I think elected officials are actually afraid, thinking if we ever need somebody to protect us physically, maybe the police won't show up. Maybe they'll show up and do harm. They're afraid of them politically, which is what I thought. I used to think it was only politically because of the police unions and pro-law enforcement folks and lobbyists and policies that fight tooth and nail to support the police.

I think the biggest fear is almost like banks failing; police are "too big to fail." So, if you do try to rein them in, what do you do when they just say No? At that stage, it forces us as people who are on the ground to ask, well, if elected officials can't hold police accountable, who can? I think those are the questions that come about from political education, that come about from action. Our actions don't have to all end in liberation, but they should all end in us learning. And so again, as we're doing political education, as we're involved in reform, as we're involved in abolition, in whatever ways we see it, we have to also be able to sit back and see what's working, what's not, and create new approaches to ending police terror in the carceral state.

James

This is the same reality that they figured out when Roberta was at the Black Panther Party. Everybody's afraid of the police and nobody controls them. That's a weird democracy.

Student 2

Professor Roberta Alexander, you said that you learned distrust in the party. Could you could talk more about the training you got there to detect what was invasive to the party?

RA

I was teaching political education classes in like my third week after starting to participate in the Breakfast for School Children program. I'm sure they must have had classes on what the laws are and that you don't have to succumb to a search unless they have a search warrant. But I wasn't privy to that information. Not that I wasn't invited, they just didn't happen while I was around. The distrust came because 1969 was a pivotal year in many ways in that the party started talking more about the lumpenproletariat, which is fine. That would be your pimps and your gang members and stuff like that. We started to grow too fast. The party, the number of offices across the country, maybe tripled. I don't remember the number, but it was quite large.

I don't think that there was a lot of cohesiveness in the party in terms of what we believed, even sharing what we believed. Sometimes the leadership that I knew, I mean not Huey Newton, but I knew Bobby Seale very well, Ray Hewitt very well, and other people who were in the national office. And at least among a few of them – not Ray Hewitt, I think he was an exception – the ideology seemed to flop around. It's hard to say. It's like we would talk about our white supporters and unity with white people, but then there would be a lot of pretty nasty jokes about white folks. I'm not sure exactly how to explain it. It's something that we'd just do sometimes, but it was done on a pretty serious level. Basically, the distrust was not knowing if this person who just came in yesterday is reliable and should be privy to everything that the party's doing or not.

I'm going to be honest, there was fear. Before I left the party, a newspaper article came out talking about how the Berkeley Police were going to "vamp" on the Panther office. They were going to go in with sub-machine guns and shoot the upstairs part of the office where I would be sitting typing and it would all be in a flame in a couple of minutes. People would be running out of this particular set of stairs. That was a document that somebody managed to get out of the Berkeley Police headquarters. We had seen those kinds of things. So that's not talking particularly about distrust; but in the party there were those who were provocateurs that got other people in the party to do things that we shouldn't have been doing and were not the policy of the party, if you follow what I mean.

I was there when the dispute between Maulana Karenga and the US Organization and the Black Panther Party took place and people were killed [on the UCLA campus in 1969]. People were killed in San Diego around the COINTELPRO [FBI violence that] sent vicious letters pretending to be Karenga, vicious letters to the leaders of the party and vice versa like, "We're going to kill you motherfuckers." That kind of stuff actually led to violence within the party. And that's the kind of stuff that they started to do at Third College too. Except in Third College, I was more directly attacked. Third College for me was much more difficult, actually quite a bit more difficult than having been in the party. It's very dangerous not to trust people or to start talking about, "I don't trust that person." That's dangerous because you can get to a level of paranoia that really goes south. Although, I did not witness any of that personally.

KA

I think Safiya Bukhari's autobiography [*War Before*][14] is one of the books that you all read. In there, she talks about the importance of security. Most of us, when we talk about security, it's like how are we going to physically stop somebody? I think intelligence is probably the best way to discuss security and understand where people are from. For example, now with Pillars we deal with the lumpen. That's who I believe are the people who instinctually already understand that the system is not for them and is a flawed system.

Inside of prison, they have entire structures where you do backgrounds on people. So, when we have somebody that just shows up within a day or two, we can know whether or not this is somebody that's dependable, that you can trust or not. Those connections and figuring out systems can give insight into how much you can trust somebody or not. The biggest thing is to avoid trying to become the Panthers that we see in the documentaries, at least in having talking points, dressing a certain way and spreading really quickly and focusing more on making sure that we have relationships that are built off of trust. When you have relationships that are built off of trust, you can do a lot and it lasts a lot longer. It's a lot more difficult to actually mobilize lots of people at one time and have any amount of trust toward one another because of that.

I want to make sure also that I point out, especially since this is being recorded, I don't think I or my mom feel like we actually have the answers and that anybody should listen to what we're saying. I think the questions that these conversations bring up are actually what's important in really thinking through these questions and moving forward for change is really what the most important thing is. If any of you come up with the answer, please email it to me because I definitely need it.

Student 4

What motivated you to leave the Black Panther Party, Professor Roberta Alexander?

RA

Well, a lot of it is personal. I'll share even though this is going to get published. One part was that I was pregnant and another part was that that relationship wasn't going to work out. Then this article about how they're going to kill us all [as Panthers] came out. I had growing alienation. Alienation is the wrong word. I was distancing from the party because I didn't feel safe there. Because both individual actors as well as the state were coming down on us. I decided at some point ... [that] I didn't want to die. So, I left ... Yeah, that's why.

Student 5

What role do you think militancy or armed resistance plays today in political struggles? Do you think, maybe, it doesn't necessarily have a role ... in the present day, in the US specifically?

RA

I'm not too optimistic about armed resistance being successful here or maybe anywhere from what little I understand about AI, about weapons with drones, and about the information they surely have of us, about us. I don't even know how much I really believed [in resistance] back then when I was in the party. But it was a hope. I don't know that I believe that we could actually copy Cuba [as a template for our society]. We were much more complicated than that. One thing that we did do that was really good [were] the community programs. At the same time ... the community needed to do the community programs, not the Panthers simply doing them a service.

I read recently that "The purpose of the community programs was to get the community to do that [labor]." While I was in Oakland and Berkeley, I didn't recognize that purpose. I think Erica Huggins did say one good thing in a documentary [*The Black Panthers: Vanguard of the Revolution*] about the Black Panthers, and she said, "The party was different in different places." That that is actually a real smart thing to say because I can just talk to what I saw.

KA

It is hard for me to see that any real meaningful change is going to happen without considering violence as a possible tool, especially when we start to look at the police brutality that we're seeing, which has always been bad, but this kind of open violence that we see happening on subway stations where a man [Daniel Penny, who is white] can literally choke and kill somebody [Jordan Neely, who is Black] ... there was a Black man ... that was actually holding [Neely's] hands as the [Neely] was being choked out. I think we have to go back to Frantz Fanon ... there's a reason we've been taught that violence is always okay [only] for the master. I'm not saying use violence. I'm saying we definitely need to consider violence, as, again, if not a tool of revolution, at the very least as a tool of protection.

If the mayor, city council members, chief of police can't control their own folks, what do you think is going to happen? The majority of police are pro-Trump ... allow for the veneer of the rule of law to pass. We have a real risk of going back to some of the most in-your-face violence. If we're not ready to protect ourselves, if we're not ready to dismantle that system ... [and] consider ... tool[s] of revolution in creating another world, I think we're going to be in trouble.

RA

It should probably be remembered that the beginning of the party, at least the first couple of years, the name was the Black Panther Party *for Self-De-*

fense. That was different. That was self-defense. I [also] know the party was at different times involved in violent activities.

KA

It's important not to romanticize violence too. Living in Syria, meeting people who are coming from Iraq, meeting Palestinians … violence is a whole other story when you meet somebody whose mother, father, brother, son, neighbor, best friend died in it. Dying is sometimes [for some] the best [option] as opposed to being wounded for the rest of their life. It's important not to romanticize it, but we have to also look around and say, "Hey, you know what? We have people who are brothers, sisters, fathers dying … the state kind of criminalizes them and claims it has been able to create an idea that they don't really count in the same way that maybe I do." That's a contradiction and it's something that you can read about … Frantz Fanon does a really good job of breaking those things down.[15]

James

On this level of defense, we're talking about war resistance. We didn't start the wars that come to our doorsteps. You have to make decisions. There'll be pain either way. My former [Union] seminary classmates opened NYC non-profits around domestic family violence to confront violence [and assist] battered women, children, men, nonbinary. The women organizing these formations stated that self-defense was *not* violence or an act of aggression. The women who were seminarians maintained that it is an act of love.

SOURCE NOTES

1. "About." *Healthy Black Families.* Accessed July 12, 2023. https://healthy blackfam.org/about
2. "IWW Yearbook: 1920." *IWW History Project.* Accessed July 12, 2023. https://depts.washington.edu/iww/yearbook1920.shtml
3. Bear, Charla. "American Indian Boarding Schools Haunt Many." *NPR,* May 12, 2008. www.npr.org/2008/05/12/16516865/american-indian-boarding-schools-haunt-many
4. McKittrick, Katherine. *Sylvia Wynter: On Being Human as Praxis.* Durham: Duke University Press, 2015.
5. "Carlos Blanco Aguinaga, One of Founders of UC San Diego Literature Department, Dies20." *UC San Diego Today,* September 26, 2013. https://today.ucsd.edu/story/carlos_blanco_aguinaga_1926_2013

6. "Lumumba-Zapata College: B.S.C.-M.A.Y.A. Demands for the Third College, U.C.S.D." *UC San Diego Library, Digital Collections.* Accessed July 12, 2023. https://library.ucsd.edu/dc/object/bb2392060k
7. "Fourth Waiver Searches." *Office of Justice Programs.* Accessed July 12, 2023. www.ojp.gov/ncjrs/virtual-library/abstracts/fourth-waiver-searches
8. Munoz, Lorenza. "Gang Database Raises Civil Rights Concerns," July 14, 1997. www.latimes.com/archives/la-xpm-1997-jul-14-me-12650-story.html
9. See also Proposition 47 FAQ. Accessed August 11, 2023. www.sandiego county.gov/content/sdc/public_defender/prop_47_faq.html#1
10. "About." *Pillars of the Community.* Accessed July 12, 2023. www.potcsd.org/about
11. Alexander, Paul Khalid, Darius Spearman, Roberta Alexander, and Manuel Paul López. *Reclaiming Our Stories: In the Time of COVID and Uprising.* San Diego, CA: San Diego City Works Press, 2021.
12. "Honoring Harriet Tubman: A Symbol of Freedom and an Intelligence Pioneer," September 7, 2022. www.cia.gov/stories/story/honoring-pioneer-harriet-tubman/
13. Freire, Paulo. *Pedagogy of the Oppressed.* Translated by Myra Bergman Ramos. New York: Bloomsbury Academic, 2020.
14. Bukhari, Safiya. *The War Before: The True Life Story of Becoming a Black Panther, Keeping the Faith in Prison & Fighting for Those Left Behind.* New York: Feminist Press at the City University of New York, 2010.
15. Drabinski, John. "Frantz Fanon." *Stanford Encyclopedia of Philosophy,* March 14, 2019. https://plato.stanford.edu/entries/frantz-fanon/

Conclusion
Reflections on social action, critical archiving, and education

The dialogues gathered here came together primarily because Joy James and her circles of collaborators are committed to decolonial and anti-racist ethics, and substantive forms of greater accountability to African American, Afro-Indigenous, and Indigenous communities. Many people and institutions profess such priorities these days. Fewer take up the long-term efforts to nurture or wrest into being the conditions required for those transformations. This multi-year endeavor involved many frustrations and limitations, as Joy James's introduction acutely observes. Arising from these challenging paths is a multivocal collection that reflects a specific moment of the early twenty-first century. It emerged amid intertwined exigencies. These include an ongoing pandemic; myriad dispossessions, violences, and forms of unfreedom; and human-driven climate catastrophe fueled by racial capitalism and colonialism. The volume also expresses longer arcs of critical intellectual, educational, and social justice work. For all who devoted time and knowledge to enter these conversations, thank you.

Reflecting on what has developed through this initiative, a significant through-line is self-determination. In one respect this involves narrative or discursive autonomy. Indigenous, Afro-Indigenous, and African American individuals and collectives maintain the power and right to describe their own experiences, on their own terms.[1] In this spirit, participants from the northeast and other hemispheric and global locations shared accounts grounded in their own lived experiences and ways of knowing. They spoke frankly about the profound harms of stolen children, disappeared and murdered kin, and forcibly curtailed reproductive futures. They described the existential threats of rising seas inundating cherished homelands and neighborhoods; and of waters, the life-bloods of communities, poisoned by corporate interests and governmental inaction. They diagnosed pervasive undermining of community and tribal nation sovereignties and self-determination by state and private entities. They detailed the severe repression of non-Eurocentric knowledge systems that for thousands of years have supported human and more-than-human thriving. Equally important, they articulated visions and tactics for pursuing restitution, community continuance, and opposition to genocidal destruction.

Participants did more than tell their own stories. They engaged relationally by listening and speaking with each other, and collectively taking up matters of converging importance. Their communities grapple, in different ways, with experiences of being plundered – having lands, waters, kin, resources, knowledge, belongings, politics seized and appropriated. We hear in these conversations how the colonizer state and US imperialism attempts to render community members vulnerable or precarious. There's no smoothed-out singular narrative or attempt to conflate distinct experiences. Instead, these dialogues bring to view the contingent or more durable connections and alliances that communities have made. They also recognize important specificities or divergences of respective goals, struggles, and political commitments.

Self-determined stories matter. They help ensure that the fuller truths of what most powerfully impacts present existences and future well-being is not forgotten or censored into oblivion. Gathered into both digital and anthology forms, these narratives present an alternative to domineering and authoritarian structures of knowledge production. This is all too timely. National and local developments in the headlines just this week raise alarms about the escalation of information manipulation in the United States. These systems of silencing are nothing new. Understood in a longer historical perspective, the communities to which many participants belong have been contending for generations with white supremacist and colonizer bids to suppress, distort, or deny representations of truth, whether through state control of media and school curricula, corporate messaging, or other forces. In recollecting and bearing witness to reality, these dialogues are resistant memory acts.

Archiving has been a continuous thread in this endeavor. We have sought to document this work forthrightly, registering what we have learned and been pushed on through these many engagements, and the opportunities and sometimes intractable constraints attendant to them. The voices brought together in the present anthology have prompted me to see in a new light the continuously evolving quality of archives ... *when* people intentionally push them to take on new commitments. How might this anthology speak to the archival collections presently held at Williams College Libraries, to take just one example of an institutional site of knowledge production? That repository counts among its tally of "rare books" a 1493 printing of Christopher Columbus's letter after his earliest voyage to the Americas. That action set in motion more than half a millennium of genocidal and colonizer impacts upon Indigenous and African peoples. This same archive also encompasses documents of protest, protection, and self-determination that communities have authored and strategically leveraged. This archive includes, too, oral histories and activist records generated by students and campus colleagues taking up justice efforts in their own places of significance.[2] Now *ENGAGE* presents a new archive (or counter-archive), 530 years into the wake of Columbus, available for those who wish to take it up.[3]

As vital as self-determined storytelling is, it cannot be the endpoint. This is not an endeavor about simply adding to or shifting narratives. The dialogue participants speak clearly to the translation of rhetoric into action, and the material conditions required for securing greater justice and framing its possibilities. "[W]e must use varied tools to spark transformations," Joy James writes. If we indexed the implements that those featured here bring to bear on social transformation, it would be an extensive list. Some use legal research and lobbying. Others devote their energies to youth education, whistleblowing, liberatory farming, anti-carceral activism, environmental science. Still others focus on humanistic critique of the very conditions of being to expose the deep structures and assumptions that underpin struggle. And much more. Participants surface the dissonances, obstructions, betrayals, and fraught compromises that occur in their work, and describe how they nonetheless keep moving and building.

When this initiative was initially formulated in 2020, its close focus was on the historical. For our group, its shape has evolved into a sharper accounting of the *now and tomorrow*. The communities represented in this volume maintain clear understandings of how all that has come before shapes the current movements. They refuse to relegate these issues to a historicized past or frame these injustices as artifacts of a prior time, now transcended. The function of history here can be as critical genealogy: recognition of what prior generations of organizers, truth-tellers, and resistors have done as a wellspring of knowledge for today and tomorrow.[4]

I'll conclude with a few words on education, partly because this initiative received funding through the Mellon Foundation's "Higher Learning" stream. The dialogues explore learning theories and practices that occur in places well apart from formal classrooms, or even in opposition to them. Communities undertake life-sustaining intergenerational learning out on the land and rivers and seas, at kitchen tables, in city halls and public libraries and carceral sites, in courtrooms and street protests. Justice movements originate from and are propelled by communities, often at high cost to well-being, rather than arising from elitist degree-granting academic institutions. Communities (in all their complexity) develop the priorities, the resource needs, the necessary protocols and pathways forward.[5] These vantages on the broad world in which "education" has always operated put into appropriate perspective the types of education that colleges and universities tend to authorize and value.[6] Are there roles for colleges and universities in these efforts?[7] Perhaps institutions can help support, amplify, or provide space for people to gather in furtherance of these goals, and re-direct resources. But it must be done without co-opting, undercutting, or replicating existing structures of power. Classrooms can cultivate spaces of co-learning, offering breathing room for students with their own agency and strength. Students themselves are oftentimes leading the pushes for learning where everyone is thinking and *doing* together, with genuinely mutual and relational ethics.

ENGAGE: the title of this work is at once an invitation and an imperative to continue these efforts. We hope these contributions will resonate.

– Christine DeLucia, July 2023

SOURCE NOTES

1. Theorists and practitioners of "knowledge sovereignty," in Indigenous and other contexts, have articulated related issues; see Whyte, Kyle. "What Do Indigenous Knowledges Do for Indigenous People?" In Melissa K. Nelson and Dan Shilling, eds., *Keepers of the Green World: Traditional Ecological Knowledge and Sustainability,* 2017.

2. See the growing field of community archiving; e.g., Zavala, Jimmy, et al., "'A Process Where We're All at the Table': Community Archives Challenging Dominant Modes of Archival Practice." *Archives and Manuscripts* 45, no. 3 (2017): 202–215; Association of Tribal Archives, Libraries, and Museums, "Sustaining Indigenous Culture: The Structure, Activities, and Needs of Tribal Archives, Libraries, and Museums," 2012. www.atalm.org/sites/default/files/sustaining_indigenous_culture.pdf

3. On "wake work," see Sharpe, Christina, *In the Wake: On Blackness and Being.* Durham: Duke University Press, 2016, and Terrefe, Selamawit. "What Exceeds the Hold?: An Interview with Christina Sharpe." *Rhizomes: Cultural Studies in Emerging Knowledge* 29 (2016), www.rhizomes.net/issue29/terrefe. html. For one accounting of campus efforts and calls for substantive next

steps, see The Committee on Diversity and Community of Williams College, "Report for 2020–2021: Recommendations for Reckoning with Our Institutional Histories," June 4, 2021., https://diversity.williams.edu/files/2021/06/CDC-2020-2021-Final-Report.pdf

4. Nick Estes writes, "There is no separation between past and present, meaning that an alternative future is also determined by our understanding of the past" (*Our History Is The Future: Standing Rock versus the Dakota Access Pipeline, and the Long Tradition of Indigenous Resistance*. New York: Verso, 2019, p. 14).

5. I wish to cite here the powerful work led by the Stockbridge-Munsee Community, whose homelands Williams College occupies (www.mohican.com). Their commitments have opened pathways for many others to learn and act. A student-developed resource is Jogwe, Jayden, Hikaru Hayakawa, and Gwyn Chilcoat, "Mohican Homelands," https://linktr.ee/MohicanHomelands, created in the fall of 2021 in the independent study Mohican Nation in Williamstown.

6. Simpson, Leanne Betasamosake. "Land as Pedagogy." In *As We Have Always Done: Indigenous Freedom through Radical Resistance*. Minneapolis: University of Minnesota Press, 2017, pp. 147–173.

7. La paperson/Yang, K. Wayne. *A Third University Is Possible*. Minneapolis: University of Minnesota Press, 2017; Peña Lorgia, García, *Community as Rebellion: A Syllabus for Surviving Academia as a Woman of Color*. Haymarket Books, 2022; Harney, Stefano and Fred Moten, "The University and the Undercommons," in *The Undercommons: Fugitive Planning and Black Study*. New York: Minor Compositions, 2013, pp. 22–43.

Contributor Bios

Khalid Paul Alexander, Ph.D.
Khalid Paul Alexander is the president and founder of Pillars of the Community, a non-profit organization for systemic change. He initiated the Reclaiming Our Stories Collective and published *In the Time of COVID and Uprising* in 2020, and is currently focused on challenging racist gain laws in California.

Roberta Alexander, Ph.D.
Roberta Alexander has previously served as a member of the Black Panther Party and as a professor emerita from San Diego City College. She now collaborates with San Diego Pillars of the Community on the Reclaiming Our Stories initiative. Alexander is currently writing her autobiography.

Chadwick Allen, Ph.D.
Chadwick Allen is a Professor of English and Adjunct Professor of American Indian Studies at the University of Washington. He has authored books such as *Blood Narrative, Trans-Indigenous,* and *Earthworks Rising,* and played roles including former editor for Studies in American Indian Literatures, past president of NAISA, and founding co-director of UW's Center for American Indian and Indigenous Studies.

Akeia de Barros Gomes, Ph.D.
Akeia de Barros Gomes is the Senior Curator of Maritime Social Histories at Mystic Seaport Museum and Director of the Frank C. Munson Institute of American Maritime Studies and is a Visiting Scholar at Brown University's Center for the Study of Slavery and Justice. Her prior roles include Curator of Social History at the New Bedford Whaling Museum and professor at Wheelock College.

Sandra Barton, Ph.D.
Sandra (Sandee) Barton, an enrolled member of the Stockbridge-Munsee Band of Mohican Indians, authored the *Standard Model of Indigenous Learning* (SMIL) and now serves as the Training and Improvement Coordinator for

the Stockbridge-Munsee Community. Her current article (forthcoming) is titled "A Reflective Revisit of the Standard Model of Indigenous Learning (SMIL): Turning a Theoretical Model into Application."

Whitney Battle-Baptiste, Ph.D.
Whitney Battle-Baptiste, a Professor of Anthropology at University of Massachusetts, Amherst, currently directs the W.E.B. Du Bois Center, promoting scholarship on global race, labor, and social injustice. Her publications include: *Black Feminist Archaeology* (2011), and *W. E. B. Du Bois's Data Portraits: Visualizing Black America*, co-edited with Britt Russert (2019).

Anthony Bogues, Ph.D.
Anthony Bogues is the Director of the Center for the Study of Slavery and Justice and Professor of Africana Studies and of Humanities and Critical Theory at Brown University. He is the author of *Caliban's Freedom: The Early Political Thought of C.L.R. James* (1997), *Black Heretics and Black Prophets: Radical Political Intellectuals* (2003), and *Empire of Liberty: Power, Freedom and Desire* (2010).

José Constantine, Ph.D.
José Constantine, associate professor of Geosciences at Williams College, researches the evolution and construction of riverscapes and water resource management, striving for environmental justice and actionable solutions.

Christine DeLucia, Ph.D.
Christine DeLucia is Associate Professor of History at Williams College. She is the author of *Memory Lands: King Philip's War and the Place of Violence in the Northeast* (2018), and has also written for *The Journal of American History*, *William and Mary Quarterly*, *Early American Studies*, and *Los Angeles Review of Books*. She recently held a fellowship at the Newberry Library in Chicago to work on her second book, a study of Native American, African American, and colonial relationships in the northeast in the era before, during, and after the American Revolution.

Katy Robinson Hall, J.D. (1984, Williams-Mystic)
Katy Robinson Hall, an environmental attorney and Associate Professor at Williams-Mystic, empowers students to solve coastal issues through cross-disciplinary research and policy strategies. Professor Hall is an

appointed member of Rhode Island's Coastal Resource Management Council.

Leah Hopkins

Leah Hopkins, a citizen of the Narragansett Indian tribe, manages Museum Education and Programs, promoting Indigenous perspectives and histories in New England. Leah has previously served as Community Engagement Specialist and worked with the Mashantucket Pequot Museum and Research Center, the Wampanoag Tribe of Gay Head (Aquinnah), and more.

Joy James, Ph.D.

Joy James is Ebenezer Fitch Professor of Humanities at Williams College. She is the author of *Resisting State Violence*; *Shadowboxing: Representations of Black Feminist Politics*; *Transcending the Talented Tenth* and *Seeking the Beloved Community*. James is editor of *The New Abolitionists: (Neo)Slave Narratives and Contemporary Prison Writings*; *Imprisoned Intellectuals*; *Warfare in the American Homeland*; *The Angela Y. Davis Reader*; and co-editor of the *Black Feminist Reader*. James's most recent books include: *In Pursuit of Revolutionary Love*; *New Bones Abolition: Captive Maternal Agency and the (After)Life of Erica Garner*; *Contextualizing Angela Davis: The Agency and Identity of an Icon*; and *Beyond Cop Cities: Dismantling State and Corporate-Funded Armies and Prisons*.

Barbara Krauthamer, Ph.D.

Dean of the College of Arts and Sciences and professor of history at Emory University, Barbara Krauthamer is the former professor of history and Dean of the College of Humanities and Fine Arts at UMass Amherst. She is the author of *Black Slaves, Indian Masters: Slavery, Emancipation, and Citizenship in the Native American South* (2013) and a coauthor, with Deborah Willis, of *Envisioning Emancipation: Black Americans and the End of Slavery* (2012).

Margaux L. Kristjansson, Ph.D.

Margaux L. Kristjansson is currently a Mellon Postdoctoral Fellow in Native American and Indigenous Studies in the Rethinking Place: Bard-on-Mahicantuck Initiative at Bard College. Her book project, *Waging Care: Indigenous Economies of Care against the Carceral Child Protection System*, argues that Canada securitizes its colonial occupation Indigenous lands through the confinement of Indigenous children in the child protection system.

Brad Lopes
Brad Lopes, Aquinnah Wampanoag, is the program director of the Aquinnah Cultural Center located in the territory of the Wampanoag nation. A public school social studies teacher in the Wabanaki territory (Maine), Brad participates with the Brown–Mystic Seaport partnership.

Stephanie Lumsden, Ph.D.
Stephanie Lumsden (Hupa) is a scholar and teacher. Stephanie is currently a University of California President's Postdoctoral Fellow in the History department at UC Santa Cruz.

Taija Mars-McDougall, Ph.D.
McDougall's research positions the question of time in relation to both finance capitalism and Blackness. Her work has appeared in *liquid blackness, Anthurium,* and *Décalages.*

Kyle T. Mays, Ph.D.
Kyle T. Mays (Black/Saginaw Anishinaabe) is an Indigenous and Afro-Indigenous scholar with expertise in urban history and Indigenous popular culture and a professor at UCLA in African American Studies and American Indigenous Studies. His books include: *An Afro-Indigenous History of the United States; Hip Hop Beats, Indigenous Rhymes: Modernity and Hip Hop in Indigenous North America."*

Joyce McMillan
Joyce McMillan is an advocate and educator dedicated to dismantling systemic barriers in communities of color. She completed a restorative certificate program at the New School and strives to foster conversations about systemic oppression and healing, with the aim of abolishing harmful systems and creating community resources.

Mary McNeil, Ph.D.
Mary McNeil (Black, Mashpee Wampanoag) is a Mellon Assistant Professor in the Department of Studies in Race, Colonialism, and Diaspora at Tufts University. Her research and teaching interests sit at the intersections of Black Studies, Native American and Indigenous Studies, social history, and geography, with particular attention to Black and Indigenous histories of the northeast.

Rosemari Mealy, J.D., Ph.D.

Rosemari Mealy has taught as an adjunct at several CUNY Schools since 1989. Publications include: *Fidel and Malcolm X-Memories of A Meeting*; *Activism and Disciplinary Suspensions/Expulsions at Historically Black Colleges and Universities (HBCUs): A Phenomenological Study of the Black Student Sit-In Movement, 1960–1962*; and *Lift These Shadows From Our Eyes.*

Brittany Meché, Ph.D.

Brittany Meché is Assistant Professor of Environmental Studies and Affiliated Faculty of Science and Technology Studies at Williams College. Her work has appeared in *Antipode, Acme, Society and Space*, and in the anthology *A Research Agenda for Military Geographies*, and Meché is completing her book manuscript, "Sustainable Empire," about transnational security regimes, environmental knowledge, and the afterlives of empire in the West African Sahel.

Américo Mendoza-Mori, Ph.D.

Dr. Américo Mendoza-Mori is a Lecturer in Latinx Studies and Faculty Director of the Latinx Studies Working Group at Harvard, co-founder of the Quechua Alliance, and a prominent researcher in Latin American, US Latinx, and Indigenous communities. His work spans academic journals, United Nations presentations, and media features.

Dian Million, Ph.D.

Dian Million, Tanana Athabascan, is an Associate Professor at the University of Washington, Seattle, affiliated with American Indian Studies, Canadian Studies, Comparative History of Ideas, and the English Department. She authored "Therapeutic Nations: Healing in an Age of Indigenous Human Rights," and has contributed articles and chapters such as "Felt Theory: An Indigenous Feminist Approach to Affect and History," "Intense Dreaming: Theories, Narratives and Our Search for Home," and "A River Runs Through Me: Theory from Life."

Ngonidzashe Munemo, Ph.D.

As the Vice President for academic affairs and dean of faculty, Ngonidzashe Munemo at Hamilton College. He is the author of *Domestic Politics and Drought Relief in Africa: Explaining Choices.*

Samaria Rice
As a mother, political advocate, and the founder and CEO of the Tamir Rice Foundation, Ms. Samaria Rice proudly serves as an advocate for juvenile rights. Since the murder of her 12-year-old son Tamir by Cleveland Police in 2014, Ms. Rice has committed her life to being on the frontlines for change and has used her voice in the service of her son's legacy.

Ernest Tollerson
Ernest Tollerson served as a journalist for nearly 25 years, serving as a reporter or editor for *Philadelphia Inquirer, Times, Mirror, New York Newsday, New York Times*, and *Metro Desk*, as well as a member of the *Times* Editorial Board. Notably, he directed the Environmental Sustainability and Compliance at the Metropolitan Transportation Authority (MTA), leading initiatives like the Blue-Ribbon Commission on Sustainability and serving on multiple environmental NGO and museum boards.

Tom Van Winkle, Ph.D.
Tom, the Executive Director of Williams-Mystic, brings 25 years of experience in public schools and non-profit education organizations. He has previously served as a teacher, middle school principal, school designer, director of professional development, managing director of school services, and chief operating officer.

Amanda Wallace
Amanda Wallace, a former child abuse investigator, founded Operation Stop CPS in 2021 to challenge the oppressive Child Protection System in North Carolina, where she had worked for a decade as a child abuse investigator. Her mission is to combat the growing power of CPS and protect families' rights.

Rebecca A. Wilcox
Rebecca A. Wilcox, Ph.D. student at Princeton Theological Seminary, concentrates on religion and society. Her research engages Black religion, Hauntology, and critical Black Studies to explore anti-Black antagonisms in underground economies.

Frank B. Wilderson, Ph.D.
Frank B. Wilderson, III is an award-winning writer, poet, scholar, activist and emerging filmmaker. Wilderson previously served as an elected official

in the African National Congress during the country's transition from apartheid and was a member of the ANC's armed wing uMkhonto we Sizwe. He has extensive engagement with education and theater in South Africa.

Dawn Wooten, L.P.N.

Dawn Wooten, worked as a nurse at the Irwin County Detention Center (ICDC), an Immigration and Customs Enforcement (ICE) immigration detention center in Ocilla, Georgia. Concerned about failures at ICDC to comply with CDC guidelines, Ms. Wooten secured pro-bono legal counsel to assist her in filing whistleblower complaints with the Department of Homeland Security (DHS) Office of Inspector General (OIG) and with Congress.

Tesia Zientek

Tesia Zientek, a Potawatomi Nation tribal citizen, established her tribe's first Department of Education, where she continues to serve as director. She serves as President of the National Indian Education Association, President of the Oklahoma Council for Indian Education, Vice President of the Tribal Education Department's National Assembly, and Potawatomi Leadership Program Adviser.

Bibliography

"(1951) We Charge Genocide." *BlackPast*, August 30, 2019. www.blackpast. org/global-african-history/primary-documents-global-african-history/ we-charge-genocide-historic-petition-united-nations-relief-crime-united-states-government-against/

"7-Year-Old Girl Accidentally Shot by Swat Team." American Civil Liberties Union, March 5, 2013. www.aclu.org/documents/7-year-old-girl-accidentally-shot-swat-team

"About the Venceremos Brigade." Venceremos Brigade, March 3, 2023. https:// vb4cuba.com/about-the-venceremos-brigade/. Ray, Carina. "Thomas Sankara."

"About." Healthy Black Families. Accessed July 12, 2023. https://healthyblackfam. org/about

"About." Pillars of the Community. Accessed July 12, 2023. www.potcsd.org/about

"Ali Sets Example." *Chicago Defender (Big Weekend Edition)*, March 15, 1975.

"Angela Davis To Speak At CU-Boulder March 15." *CU-Boulder Today*. www. colorado.edu/today/1998/03/01/angela-davis-speak-cu-boulder-march-15

"Assembly Bill 3099 (Ramos, 2020) – Tribal Assistance Program." State of California – Department of Justice – Office of the Attorney General, July 5, 2023. https://oag. ca.gov/nativeamerican/ab3099

"Biography." Paul Cuffe, September 6, 2022. https://paulcuffe.org/biography/

"Black Manifesto." Omeka RSS. Accessed July 12, 2023. https://episcopalarchives. org/church-awakens/exhibits/show/specialgc/item/202

"California Climate Investments to Benefit Disadvantaged Communities." CalEPA. Accessed July 11, 2023. https://calepa.ca.gov/envjustice/ghginvest/

"Campaign." FREE MADDESYN GEORGE. Accessed July 11, 2023. www. freemaddesyn.com/campaign

"Carlos Blanco Aguinaga, One of Founders of UC San Diego Literature Department, Dies20." *UC San Diego Today*, September 26, 2013. https://today.ucsd.edu/story/ carlos_blanco_aguinaga_1926_2013

"Charleston Church Shooter: 'I Would like to Make It Crystal Clear, I Do Not Regret What I Did.'" *The Washington Post*, May 24, 2023. www.washingtonpost.com/ world/national-security/charleston-church-shooter-i-would-like-to-make-it-crystal-clear-i-do-not-regret-what-i-did/2017/01/04/05b0061e-d1da-11e6-a783-cd3fa950f2fd_story.html

"Code Section." California Legislative Information. Accessed July 12, 2023. https:// leginfo.legislature.ca.gov/faces/codes_displaySection.xhtml?sectionNum=182&la

"CWA 50th Anniversary Landing Page." Potomac Riverkeeper Network, March 24, 2023. www.potomacriverkeepernetwork.org/clean-water-act-50th-anniversary/

"Edward W. Said – Scholars and Historians (1935–2003)." Palquest. Accessed July 12, 2023. www.palquest.org/en/biography/16018/edward-w-said

"Elbert 'Big Man' Howard Oral History Interview Conducted by David P. Cline in Santa Rosa, California, 2016 June 30." The Library of Congress. Accessed July 12, 2023. www.loc.gov/item/2016655436/

"Enslaving Colonial North America." National Museum of African American History & Culture. Accessed July 11, 2023. www.searchablemuseum.com/enslaving-colonial-north-america.

"Fourth Waiver Searches." Office of Justice Programs. Accessed July 12, 2023. www.ojp.gov/ncjrs/virtual-library/abstracts/fourth-waiver-searches

"Home: Jericho Movement." Home | Jericho Movement. Accessed July 11, 2023. www.thejerichomovement.com/

"Home: Missourians for Alternatives to the Death Penalty." MADP, December 29, 1969. www.madpmo.org/

"Home." Black Mothers March. Accessed July 11, 2023. www.blackmothersmarch.com/

"Hydro-Quebec and Native People." Cultural Survival. Accessed July 11, 2023. www.culturalsurvival.org/publications/cultural-survival-quarterly/hydro-quebec-and-native-people

"Independent Lens | The Black Panthers: Free Breakfast Program." PBS, February 16, 2016. www.pbs.org/video/independent-lens-free-breakfast-program/

"Introduction." Semtribe. Accessed July 12, 2023. www.semtribe.com/stof/history/introduction.

"IWW Yearbook: 1920." IWW History Project. Accessed July 12, 2023. https://depts.washington.edu/iww/yearbook1920.shtml

"Lumumba-Zapata College: B.S.C.-M.A.Y.A. Demands for the Third College, U.C.S.D." UC San Diego Library | Digital Collections. Accessed July 12, 2023. https://library.ucsd.edu/dc/object/bb2392060k

"Maddesyn's Story." FREE MADDESYN GEORGE. Accessed July 11, 2023. www.freemaddesyn.com/maddesyns-story

"Melba Liston." National Endowment for the Arts. Accessed July 12, 2023. www.arts.gov/honors/jazz/melba-liston

"Mission, Vision & Values." Wabanaki REACH. Accessed July 11, 2023. www.wabanakireach.org/mission

"Native American Policies." Office of Tribal Justice, June 15, 2022. www.justice.gov/otj/native-american-policies

"New York Proposal 2, Environmental Rights Amendment (2021)." Ballotpedia, November 2, 2021. https://ballotpedia.org/New_York_Proposal_2,_Environmental_Rights_Amendment_(2021)

"NJ Environmental Justice Law and Rules." State of New Jersey, n.d. https://dep.nj.gov/ej/policy/

"Obama to Announce Africom Joint Force Command HQ in Liberia." US Department of Defense. Accessed July 11, 2023. www.defense.gov/News/News-Stories/Article/Article/603259/obama-to-announce-africom-joint-force-command-hq-in-liberia/

"Oh Freedom!" African American Spiritual.

"On Black Aesthetics: The Black Arts Movement." The New York Public Library. Accessed July 12, 2023. www.nypl.org/blog/2016/07/15/black-aesthetics-bam

"Operation Bring Zephaniah." Operation Stop CPS. Accessed July 11, 2023. www.operationstopcps.com/Operation-Bring-Zephaniah.

"Our History." The Red Road, March 26, 2019. https://theredroad.org/story/history/

"Proclamation on Missing and Murdered Indigenous Persons Awareness Day, 2021." The White House, May 4, 2021. www.whitehouse.gov/briefing-room/presidential-actions/2021/05/04/a-proclamation-on-missing-and-murdered-indigenous-persons-awareness-day-2021/

"Resources – CPN Cultural Heritage Center." Citizen Potawatomi Nation Cultural Heritage Center. Accessed July 12, 2023. www.potawatomiheritage.com/resources/

"Ryan's Daughter." IMDb, December 10, 1970. www.imdb.com/title/tt0066319/

"Sonderkommandos." Holocaust Encyclopedia. Accessed July 11, 2023. https://encyclopedia.ushmm.org/content/en/article/sonderkommandos

"Staff." Native Women's Collective. Accessed July 11, 2023. www.nativewomens collective.org/staff.html

"Tamir Rice Shooting: Justice Department Investigation Ends without Charges." *The Guardian*, December 30, 2020. www.theguardian.com/us-news/2020/dec/30/tamir-rice-shooting-justice-department-investigation-ends-without-charges

"Technology Refresh – Smart Streetlights." San Diego Police Department. Accessed July 12, 2023.

"The Climate Leadership and Community Protection Act of 2019 (CLCPA) commits to 100% zero-emission electricity by 2040, and a reduction of at least 85% below 1990-level GHG emissions by 2050," from Climate Leadership and Community Protection Act (CLCPA), n.d. https://climate.ny.gov/

"The Uhuru Movement." The African People's Socialist Party. Accessed July 11, 2023. https://apspuhuru.org/about/the-uhuru-movement/

"The Rise and Fall of the Symbionese Liberation Army." PBS. Accessed August 11, 2023. www.pbs.org/wgbh/americanexperience/features/guerrilla-rise-and-fall-symbionese-liberation-army/

"Third World Women's Alliance, Women in the Struggle (1971)," 2000. www.marxists.org/history/erol/ncm-6/women-in-struggle.pdf

"Tribes – Native Voices." US National Library of Medicine. Accessed July 11, 2023. www.nlm.nih.gov/nativevoices/timeline/271.html#:~:text=In%20Johnson%20v.,no%20title%20to%20the%20land

"UN Permanent Forum on Indigenous Issues Calls for an Expert Group Meeting on Missing and Murdered Indigenous Women." Indian Law Resource Center, 2019. https://indianlaw.org/swsn/unpfii-calls-expert-meeting-mmiw

"Visual History: Free Speech Movement, 1964." Berkeley FSM. Accessed July 12, 2023. https://fsm.berkeley.edu/free-speech-movement-timeline/

Abu-Jamal, Mumia, and John Edgar Wideman. *Live from Death Row*. New York: Perennial, 2002.

Alexander, Michelle. *The New Jim Crow Mass Incarceration in the Age of Colorblindness*. New York: The New Press, 2020.

Alexander, Paul Khalid, Darius Spearman, Roberta Alexander, and Manuel Paul López. *Reclaiming Our Stories: In the Time of COVID and Uprising*. San Diego, CA: SD CWP, San Diego City Works Press, 2021.

American Indian Religious Freedom Act of 1978 (AIRFA) (42 U.S.C. § 1996). Accessed July 11, 2023. www.law.cornell.edu/uscode/text/42/1996

Archives, Freedom. Freedom Archives Search Engine. Accessed July 12, 2023. https://search.freedomarchives.org/search.php?view_collection=90

Baggins, Brian. "The Black Panther Newspaper." *Black Panther Party Newspaper*. Accessed July 12, 2023. www.marxists.org/history/usa/pubs/black-panther/index.htm

Bates, Karen Grigsby. "Bobby Hutton: The killing that catapulted The Black Panthers to fame." *NPR*, April 6, 2018. www.npr.org/2018/04/06/600055767/bobby-hutton-the-killing-that-catapulted-the-black-panthers-to-fame

Battle-Baptiste, Whitney. *Black Feminist Archaeology*. London: Routledge, 2017.

Bear, Charla. "American Indian Boarding Schools Haunt Many." *NPR*, May 12, 2008. www.npr.org/2008/05/12/16516865/american-indian-boarding-schools-haunt-many

Benard, Akeia A. "Narratives of Transfer, Dependence, and Resistance: Rastafarian Perspectives on Colonialism in the Virgin Islands." *Anthropology of Consciousness* 30, no. 2 (2019): 117–131. https://doi.org/10.1111/anoc.12114

Biden, Joseph R. "Violence against Women: The Congressional Response." *American Psychologist* 48, no. 10 (1993): 1059–1061. https://doi.org/10.1037/0003-066X.48.10.1059

Bloesch, Sarah J., Meredith Minister, and Charles H Long. "Perspectives for a Study of Afro-American Religion in the United States." Essay. In *The Bloomsbury Reader in Cultural Approaches to the Study of Religion*, 126–134. London: Bloomsbury Academic, 2018.

Bowers, Dana, Logan Cornell, Darcie Dreher, Jake Harder, and Jennifer Minnis. *Dred Scott v. Sanford*, 60 U.S. 393 1857. Accessed July 12, 2023. www.americanhistoryk12.com/wp-content/uploads/Court%20Trial%20Documents/dred_scott.pdf

Bremen, SchädelMädel. "Zangbeto Voodoo Benin." YouTube, January 27, 2019. www.youtube.com/watch?v=p4B2ku08uso&feature=youtu.be

Buchanan, Kelly. "Indigenous Rights in New Zealand: Legislation, Litigation, and Protest: In Custodia Legis." The Library of Congress, November 18, 2016. https://blogs.loc.gov/law/2016/11/indigenous-rights-in-new-zealand-legislation-litigation-and-protest/

Bukhari, Safiya. *The War Before: The True Life Story of Becoming a Black Panther, Keeping the Faith in Prison & Fighting for Those Left Behind*. New York: Feminist Press at the City University of New York, 2010.

Burney, Shehla. "CHAPTER TWO: Edward Said and Postcolonial Theory: Disjunctured Identities and the Subaltern Voice." *Counterpoints* 417 (2012): 41–60.

Cabral, Amílcar. *Return to the Source: Selected Speeches of Amilcar Cabral*. New York: Monthly Review Press, 1973.

Carmichael, Stokely, and Ekwueme Michael Thelwell. *Ready for Revolution: The Life and Struggles of Stokely Carmichael (Kwame Ture)*. New York: Scribner, 2005.

Carmichael, Stokely. *The Red and the Black*, 1975.

Changa, Kalonji, and Joy James. "Kevin Johnson Speaks from Death Row About His Impending Execution This Month." *Truthout*, December 14, 2022. https://truthout.org/articles/kevin-johnson-speaks-from-death-row-about-his-impending-execution-this-month/

Choi, Rebecca. "The Avery Review: Survival Pending Revolution: The Black Panther Party on View." *The Avery Review.* Accessed July 12, 2023. https://averyreview.com/issues/22/survival-pending-revolution

Churchill, Ward, and Jim Vander Wall. *The COINTELPRO Papers: Documents from the FBI's Secret Wars Against Domestic Dissent.* Boston, MA: South End Press, 1990.

Clifton, Lucille, Kevin Young, and Michael S. Glaser. "New Bones." Essay. In *The Collected Poems of Lucille Clifton 1965–2010.* Rochester, NY: BOA Editions, 2012.

Colonial Pathways Policy. San Diego Museum of Man, June 2018. https://museum.bc.ca/wp-content/uploads/2023/02/Museum-of-Us-Colonial-Pathways-Policy-Public-Janauary-2020.pdf

Deloria, Vine. *Behind the Trail of Broken Treaties an Indian Declaration of Independence.* Austin: University of Texas Press, 2000.

Dionne, Brittany. "One Year Later, Marissa Alexander Speaks out on Her Release, Corrine Brown." *The Florida Times-Union*, January 27, 2018. www.jacksonville.com/story/news/2018/01/27/one-year-later-marissa-alexander-speaks-out-her-release-corrine-brown/15332075007/

Drabinski, John. "Frantz Fanon." *Stanford Encyclopedia of Philosophy*, March 14, 2019. https://plato.stanford.edu/entries/frantz-fanon/

Elks, Sonia. "Haiti Government Demands Justice for Women and Girls Abused by U.N. Peacekeepers." *Reuters*, December 19, 2019. www.reuters.com/article/us-haiti-women-peacekeepers-idUSKBN1YN2HH

Fanon, Frantz. *Black Skin, White Masks.* London: Paladin, 1970.

Five Civilized Tribes: Dawes Records. Accessed July 11, 2023. www.archives.gov/research/native-americans/dawes/background.html#:~:text=Cherokee,%20Chickasaw,%20Choctaw,%20Creek,%20and%20Seminole%20Tribes%20in%20Oklahoma

Forman, James. "Black Manifesto." *Black Economic Development Conference*, presented at the Black Economic Development Conference, July 1969.

Freire, Paulo. *Pedagogy of the Oppressed.* Translated by Myra Bergman Ramos. New York, NY: Bloomsbury Academic, 2020.

Gagosian. Alice Smith: I Put a Spell on You | Sessions | Gagosian Premieres, December 9, 2021. www.youtube.com/watch?v=kz506sFHeJY

Gilson, Christopher. "Congress Strikes $1 Trillion Budget Deal, Democrats Clear the Field for Hillary Clinton and Will Puerto Rico Default? – US National Blog Round up for 11–17 January." *LSE American Politics and Policy*, 2014.

Glissant, Édouard. *Poetics of Relation.* East Lansing, MI: University of Michigan Press, 1997.

Gonzalez-Barrera, Ana. "'Mestizo' and 'Mulatto': Mixed-Race Identities among U.S. Hispanics." *Pew Research Center*, July 10, 2015. www.pewresearch.org/short-reads/2015/07/10/mestizo-and-mulatto-mixed-race-identities-unique-to-hispanics/

Goodman, Amy, and Omali Yeshitela. "'Bogus Charge': FBI Raids African People's Socialist Party; Group Dismisses Russian Influence Claims." *Democracy Now!*, August 10, 2022. www.democracynow.org/2022/8/10/black_socialist_chairman_fbi_raid_response

Gunn, John. "Medical Powers in Prisons, the Prison Medical Service in England 1774–1989." *Criminal Behaviour and Mental Health* 3, no. 2 (1993): 119. https://doi.org/10.1002/cbm.1993.3.2.119

H.R.5237 – Native American Graves Protection and Repatriation Act. Accessed July 11, 2023. www.congress.gov/bill/101st-congress/house-bill/5237/text

H.R.7919 – Maine Indian Claims Settlement Act of 1980. Accessed July 11, 2023. www.congress.gov/bill/96th-congress/house-bill/7919

Hartman, Saidiya V., Keeanga-Yamahtta Taylor, Marisa J. Fuentes, Sarah Haley, and Cameron Rowland. *Scenes of Subjection: Terror, Slavery, and Self-making in Nineteenth-Century America*. New York: W. W. Norton & Company, 2022.

Hartman, Saidiya. *Lose Your Mother: A journey along the Atlantic Slave Route*. S.l.: Macmillan, 2008.

Hearne, Joanna. *Smoke Signals: Native cinema rising*. Lincoln: University of Nebraska Press, 2012.

Hirschfield, Martha. "The Alaska Native Claims Settlement Act: Tribal Sovereignty and the Corporate Form." *The Yale Law Journal* 101, no. 6 (1992): 1331. https://doi.org/10.2307/796926

Holder, Kit Kim. "The History of the Black Panther Party, 1966–1971: A Curriculum Tool for Afrikan-American Studies." *University of Massachusetts Amherst*, 1990.

Honoring Harriet Tubman: A Symbol of Freedom and an Intelligence Pioneer, September 7, 2022. www.cia.gov/stories/story/honoring-pioneer-harriet-tubman/.

Hotel Rwanda. United Artists, 2004.

Indian Law Enforcement History. Accessed July 12, 2023. www.tribal-institute.org/download/Indian%20Law%20Enforcement%20History.pdf

James, Joy. "Academia, Activism, and Imprisoned Intellectuals." *Social Justice* 92, 30, no. 2 (2003): 3–7.

James, Joy. "Airbrushing Revolution for the Sake of Abolition." AAIHS, August 12, 2020. www.aaihs.org/airbrushing-revolution-for-the-sake-of-abolition/

James, Joy. "Antiracist (Pro) Feminisms and Coalition Politics: 'No Justice, No Peace.'" Essay. In *Men Doing Feminism*, 238. Routledge, 2013.

James, Joy. "Dishonored Citizenry: Black Women, Civic Virtue, and Electoral Powers." *Community as the Material Basis of Citizenship*, 2017, 49–60. https://doi.org/10.4324/9781315113159-5

James, Joy. "The Captive Maternal and Abolitionism." *TOPIA: Canadian Journal of Cultural Studies* 43 (2021): 9–23. https://doi.org/10.3138/topia-43-002

James, Joy. "The Womb of Western Theory: Trauma, Time Theft, and the Captive Maternal." *Carceral Notebooks* 12, no. 1 (2016): 253–296.

James, Joy. *Imprisoned Intellectuals America's Political Prisoners Write on Life, Liberation, and Rebellion*. Lanham: Rowman & Littlefield Publishers, 2004.

James, Joy. *In Pursuit of Revolutionary Love*. S.l.: Divide Publishing, 2022.

James, Joy. "Maternal (in)coherence." *Parapraxis*, November 21, 2022. www.parapraxismagazine.com/articles/maternal-incoherence#:~:text=When%20

Feminism%20Meets%20Fascism&text=Whether%20they%20are%20
biological%20females,of%20maternal%20lives%20and%20bodies

James, Joy. *Resisting State Violence: Radicalism, Gender, and Race in U.S. Culture.*
Minneapolis: University of Minnesota Press, 1996.

James, Joy. *Warfare in the American Homeland: Policing and Prison in a Penal Democracy.* Durham: Duke University Press, 2007.

Julien, Sydney, and Laura Rabinow. New York's Environmental Bond Acts. *Rockinist,*
April 28, 2022. https://rockinst.org/blog/new-yorks-environmental-bond-acts/

Kim, Cristina. "Advocates Urge San Diego City Council to Delay Vote on Surveillance Technology Contract." *KPBS Public Media,* July 26, 2021. www.kpbs.org/
news/public-safety/2021/07/26/san-diego-city-council-delay-vote-surveillance

Krauthamer, Barbara. *Black Slaves, Indian Masters: Slavery, Emancipation, and Citizenship in the Native American South.*

Lacan, Jacques. "Intervention on Transference." Translated by Juliet Mitchell
and Jacqueline Rose. *Feminine Sexuality* (1982): 61–73. https://doi.
org/10.1007/978-1-349-16861-3_4

Lew-Lee, Lee. All Power to the People – The Black Panther Party & Beyond, June 8,
2016. www.youtube.com/watch?v=pKvE6_sojyo

Long, Charles H. "The West African High God: History and Religious Experience."
History of Religions (1964): 328–342. https://doi.org/10.1086/462641

Lorde, Audre, and Adrienne Rich. "An Interview with Audre Lorde." *Signs:
Journal of Women in Culture and Society* 6, no. 4 (1981): 713–736. https://doi.
org/10.1086/493842

Lorde, Audre. "Coal." In *The Collected Poems of Audre Lorde.* New York: W.W. Norton
& Company, 1997.

Lorde, Audre. "Learning from the 60s," 1982.

Malcolm X., Warner Bros, 1992.

Mays, Kyle T. *Indigenous Detroit: Indigeneity, Modernity, and Racial and Gender
Formation in a Modern American City, 1871–2000.* Urbana-Champaign, IL: University of Illinois at Urbana-Champaign, 2015.

McDougall, Taijia. "Left out: Notes on Absence, Nothingness and the Black Prisoner
Theorist." *Anthurium A Caribbean Studies Journal* 15, no. 2 (2019). https://doi.
org/10.33596/anth.391

McKittrick, Katherine. *Sylvia Wynter: On Being Human as Praxis.* Durham: Duke
University Press, 2015.

McTell, Blind Willie. "I Got to Cross the River Jordan." The Library of Congress.
Accessed July 11, 2023. www.loc.gov/item/afc9999005.12065

Mealy, Rosemari, Jared Ball, and Todd Steven Burroughs. "An Incomprehensible
Omission: Women and El-Hajj Malik El-Shabazz." In *A Lie of Reinvention: Correcting Manning Marable's Malcolm X.* Baltimore, MD: Black Classic Press, 2013.

Mealy, Rosemari. "Sitting Down to Stand Up: Black Student Suspensions/Expulsions
at Historically Black Colleges and Universities (HBCUs), 1960–1962: A Phenomenological Study." *ProQuest Dissertations Publishing,* 2009. Mealy, Rosemari. *Fidel
and Malcolm: Memories of a Meeting.* S.l.: BLACK CLASSIC Press, 2013.

Medsger, Matthew. "Why Did UMass Buy 15,000 Abortion Pills?" *Boston Herald*, April 11, 2023. www.bostonherald.com/2023/04/11/why-did-umass-buy-15000-abortion-pills/

Moten, Fred, and Stefano Harney. "The University and the Undercommons." *Social Text* 22, no. 2 (2004): 101–101. https://doi.org/10.1215/01642472-22-2_79-101

Munoz, Lorenza. Gang Database Raises Civil Rights Concerns, July 14, 1997. www.latimes.com/archives/la-xpm-1997-jul-14-me-12650-story.html. Native-Land.ca: Our Home on Native Land, October 8, 2021. https://native-land.ca/

Murrey, Amber, ed. *A Certain Amount of Madness: The Life, Politics, and Legacies of Thomas Sankara*. London: Pluto Press, 2018.

Nmaahc. "Enslaving Colonial North America." National Museum of African American History & Culture. Accessed July 11, 2023. www.searchablemuseum.com/enslaving-colonial-north-america

Odinga, Sekou, Dhoruba Bin Wahad, and Jamal Joseph. *Look For Me in the Whirlwind: From the panther 21 to 21st-century revolutions*. Oakland, CA: PM Press, 2017.

Ojewale, Oluwole. "Is Cameroon Becoming Central Africa's Baby Trading Hub?" *ENACT Africa*, July 14, 2021. https://enactafrica.org/enact-observer/is-cameroon-becoming-central-africas-baby-trading-hub

Packtor, Chrissy. "Racial Gaps in Children's Lead Levels." Public Health Post, July 13, 2019. www.publichealthpost.org/databyte/racial-gaps-in-childrens-lead-levels/

Pelton, Tom. "Clean Water Act's Promises Half Kept at Half Century Anniversary." Environmental Integrity Project, March 17, 2022. https://environmentalintegrity.org/news/clean-water-acts-promises-half-kept-at-half-century-anniversary/#:~:text=The%20U.S.%20Congress%20passed%20the,into%20navigable%20waters%20by%201985

Qiu, Linda. "Fact-Checking Kamala Harris on the Campaign Trail." *The New York Times*, June 8, 2019. www.nytimes.com/2019/06/08/us/politics/fact-check-kamala-harris.html.

Riley, Angela R. "The History of Native American Lands and the Supreme Court." *Journal of Supreme Court History* 38, no. 3 (2013): 369–385. https://doi.org/10.1111/j.1540-5818.2013.12024.x

Rios, Edwin. "Families of Tyre Nichols and George Floyd to Attend State of the Union." *The Guardian*, February 7, 2023. www.theguardian.com/us-news/2023/feb/07/families-black-people-killed-by-police-state-of-the-union

S.1214 – Indian Child Welfare Act 95th Congress (1977–1978). Accessed July 12, 2023. www.congress.gov/bill/95th-congress/senate-bill/1214/text

S.3623 – 117th Congress (2021–2022): Violence against Women Act Reauthorization Act of 2022. Accessed July 12, 2023. www.congress.gov/bill/117th-congress/senate-bill/3623

Santana, Sandy. "UN Calls for US Action to Address Racial Injustice in Child Welfare System." Children's Rights, March 3, 2023. www.childrensrights.org/news-voices/un-calls-for-us-action-to-address-racial-injustice-in-child-welfare-system

Satz, Martha. "Dawnland by Adam Mazo and Ben Pender-Cudlip." *Adoption & Culture* 8, no. 1 (2020): 119–121. https://doi.org/10.1353/ado.2020.0015

Schneider-Mayerson, Matthew, and Brent Ryan Bellamy. *An Ecotopian Lexicon*. Minneapolis: University of Minnesota Press, 2019.

Schwegler, Marc. "Frank B. Wilderson III: Afropessimism." Various Artists, July 17, 2021. https://various-artists.com/afropessimism/

Shakur, Afeni, and Jasmine Guy. *Afeni Shakur: Evolution of a revolutionary*. New York: Simon and Schuster, 2010.

Shakur, Assata. *Assata: An Autobiography*. Chicago: Chicago Review Press, 1999.

Shames, Stephen, and Ericka Huggins. *Comrade Sisters Women of the Black Panther Party*. Melton: ACC Art Books, 2022.

Sharpe, Christina Elizabeth. *In the Wake. On Blackness and Being*. Durham: Duke University Press, 2017.

Smith, Christen Anne. "Towards a Black Feminist Model of Black Atlantic Liberation: Remembering Beatriz Nascimento." *Meridians* 14, no. 2 (2016): 71–87. https://doi.org/10.2979/meridians.14.2.06

Sullivan, Ronald. "Court Erupts as Judge Frees an Ex-Panther." *The New York Times*, March 23, 1990. www.nytimes.com/1990/03/23/nyregion/court-erupts-as-judge-frees-an-ex-panther.html

Taylor, Flint. "The Black Panther Party and the 'Undying Love for the People.'" *In These Times*, October 29, 2015. https://inthesetimes.com/article/the-black-panther-party-and-the-undying-love-for-the-people

Terrefe, Selamawit. "What Exceeds the Hold?: An Interview with Christina Sharpe." *Rhizomes: Cultural Studies in Emerging Knowledge*, no. 29 (2016): 1–1. https://doi.org/10.20415/rhiz/029.e06

The African People's Socialist Party. Accessed July 11, 2023. https://apspuhuru.org/

The Black Alliance for Peace. Accessed July 11, 2023. https://blackallianceforpeace.com/

The Black Panthers: Vanguard of the Revolution. PBS, 2016.

The Buffalo News, February 15, 2023. https://buffalonews.com/news/local/complete-coverage-10-killed-3-wounded-in-mass-shooting-at-buffalo-supermarket/collection_e8c7df32-d402-11ec-9ebc-e39ca6890844.html

Thoreau, Henry David. "Economy." Walden, 1854.

Upstander Project. Accessed July 12, 2023. https://upstanderproject.org/

Wahad, Dhoruba Bin, Mumia Abu-Jamal, Assata Shakur, Jim Fletcher, Tanaquil Jones, and Sylvère Lotringer. *Still Black, Still Strong: Survivors of the U.S. War Against Black Revolutionaries*. New York: Semiotext(e), 1993.

Walker, Jack. "Wampanoag Language Immersion School Navigates Linguistic, Cultural Education Remotely." The Brown Daily Herald, April 7, 2021. www.browndailyherald.com/article/2021/04/wampanoag-language-immersion-school-navigates-linguistic-cultural-education-remotely/

Weiterman Barton, Sandra D. "Web Walkers, A Phenomenological Study of Adult Native American Distance Learning Experiences: Toward a Standard Model of Indigenous Learning." *Southern Illinois University at Carbondale*, 2013.

Wilderson, Frank B. "The Black Liberation Army and the Paradox of Political Engagement." Bukhari, Safiya. *The War Before: The True Life Story of Becoming a Black Panther, Keeping the Faith in Prison & Fighting for Those Left Behind*. New York City: Feminist Press at the City University of New York, 2010.

Wilderson, Frank. "Gramsci's Black Marx: Whither the Slave in Civil Society?" *Social Identities* 9, no. 2 (2003): 225–240. https://doi.org/10.1080/1350463032000101579

Wilkie, Laurie A. *Unburied Lives: The historical archaeology of buffalo soldiers at Fort Davis, Texas, 1869–1875.* New Mexico: University of New Mexico Press, 2021.

Wisecup, Kelly, and Paula Peters. "Telling Our Story: An Interview with Paula Peters." *Early American Literature* 56, no. 1 (2021): 209–218.

Yancy, George. "Afropessimism Forces Us to Rethink Our Most Basic Assumptions about Society." *Truthout*, September 15, 2022. https://truthout.org/articles/afropessimism-forces-us-to-rethink-our-most-basic-assumptions-about-society/

Zakirzianova, Zhanna. "New York City Waterfront Development in the Post-Sandy Era: The East Side Coastal Resiliency Project and Community Response." *ETD Collection for Fordham University*, 2021.

Zug, James. "The Italicized Life of Frank Wilderson '78." *Dartmouth Alumni Magazine*, October 2010. https://dartmouthalumnimagazine.com/articles/italicized-life-frank-wilderson-%E2%80%9978

Acknowledgments

This book developed from the Mellon Just Futures project. AS, IB, and ST contributed to the editorial team. Philosopher Carol Wayne White shared her photographs of the Atlantic Ocean – the conduit for European enslavement and trafficking of Indigenous and African peoples – which appear on the book cover and frontispiece. Williams College Oakley Center and Office of Institutional Diversity, Equity and Inclusion (OIDEI) co-sponsored several Williams Just Futures roundtables. Staff and students assisted with transcriptions of roundtables (edited here for clarity). Vice President of OIDEI Leticia Haynes and Assistant Vice President of OIDEI Ivonne Garcia provided support to connect communities and intellectuals with students, staff, and faculty. Colleagues served as moderators for roundtables. Thank you, to all contributors to this project.

Index

The Pluto Press Newsletter

Hello friend of Pluto!

Want to stay on top of the best radical books we publish?

Then sign up to be the first to hear about our new books, as well as special events, podcasts and videos.

You'll also get 50% off your first order with us when you sign up.

Come and join us!

Go to bit.ly/PlutoNewsletter

Thanks to our Patreon subscriber:

Ciaran Kane

Who has shown generosity and
comradeship in support of our publishing.

Check out the other perks you get by subscribing
to our Patreon – visit patreon.com/plutopress.
Subscriptions start from £3 a month.